Augustus C. George

Short Sermons on Consecration and Kindred Themes

For the closet, the fireside, and the lecture-room

Augustus C. George

Short Sermons on Consecration and Kindred Themes
For the closet, the fireside, and the lecture-room

ISBN/EAN: 9783337255817

Printed in Europe, USA, Canada, Australia, Japan

Cover: Foto ©Lupo / pixelio.de

More available books at **www.hansebooks.com**

SHORT SERMONS

ON

CONSECRATION

AND KINDRED THEMES,

For the Closet, the Fireside, and the Lecture-Room:

By Rev. A. C. GEORGE, D. D.,

(Of the Central New York Conference.)

AUTHOR OF "COUNSELS TO CONVERTS," "THE SATISFACTORY PORTION," ETC.

NEW YORK:

NELSON & PHILLIPS,

CINCINNATI: HITCHCOCK & WALDEN.

1873.

CONTENTS.

SERMON		PAGE
I.	CONSECRATION: ITS NATURE AND OBLIGATION.......	7
II.	CONSECRATION MUST BE COMPLETE...................	19
III.	CONSECRATION A CONSTANT SERVICE..................	32
IV.	THE CONSECRATION OF SELF..........................	45
V.	THE SEPARATING POWER OF THE DIVINE PRESENCE...	54
VI.	FORMER FAITH CALLED TO MIND......................	63
VII.	GIVE THE CHOICEST THINGS TO JESUS................	76
VIII.	CONSECRATION OF MONEY AND INFLUENCE...........	81
IX.	RICHES IN POVERTY...................................	88
X.	THE INSPIRATION OF A GREAT PRESENCE.............	96
XI.	THE PERFECT MAN......................................	101
XII.	PURPOSE OF HEART....................................	108
XIII.	SALVATION THROUGH GOD'S FORBEARANCE...........	113
XIV.	THE PERFECTION OF BEAUTY...........................	118
XV.	WELLS WITHOUT WATER................................	123
XVI.	THE MOUNTAIN OF MYRRH.............................	130
XVII.	HELP ONLY IN GOD....................................	137
XVIII.	THE JOY OF OUR LORD................................	144
XIX.	THE LORD'S PECULIAR TREASURE.....................	150
XX.	THE HOLY HATRED OF GOD............................	157
XXI.	A DRIFT, OR A VOYAGE?..............................	163

SERMON		PAGE
XXII.	The Holy Spirit the Gift of God	169
XXIII.	The Glory of the Gospel Dispensation	174
XXIV	The Long Waiting for God	185
XXV.	The Privileges of the Sons of God	191
XXVI.	Christian Women, Gospel Helpers	196
XXVII.	The Child's Growth in Christian Character	207
XXVIII.	The Armed Suppliant	219
XXIX.	Life, Capital for Immortality	229
XXX.	"Strengthen the Things which Remain"	247
XXXI.	The Law of Christian Charity	263
XXXII.	The Sanctifying Truth	278
XXXIII.	The Eternity of Character	289
XXXIV	The Amaranthine Crown	296

SHORT SERMONS ON CONSECRATION.

I.

CONSECRATION: ITS NATURE AND OBLIGATION.

"And who then is willing to consecrate his service this day unto the Lord?"—1 CHRON. xxix, 5.

CONSECRATION, taken in a religious sense, is, according to Richard Watson, "A devoting or setting apart any thing to the worship or service of God." It is a demand, therefore, resting on the assumption that God has a right to our service, possessions, and love. And this demand we are expected to meet, however revolting it may be to our carnal natures, or however inconsistent with what appears to be our worldly interest. It is for this reason that consecration is described in the Scriptures as a *sacrifice*. Every injunction of self-denial, mortification of the flesh, and renunciation of the world, imposes the duty of consecration. And the work of faith, the experience of love, and the patience and perfection of hope, suppose that consecration has been performed, and is constantly and conscientiously maintained.

"And the Lord spake unto Moses, saying, Sanctify unto me all the first-born." The word rendered sanctify "signifies," according to Dr. A. Clarke, "to *consecrate, separate,* and *set apart* a thing or person from all secular purposes to some religious use, and exactly answers to the import of the Greek *hagiadzo,* from *a,* privative, and *ga, the earth,* because every thing offered or consecrated to God was *separated from all earthly uses.* Hence a holy person or saint is termed *hagios,* that is, a person separated from the earth; one who lives a holy life entirely devoted to the service of God." Accordingly, the father of the Israelitish household was required to explain these things to his children, and to say to them, "I sacrifice to the LORD," even all "the first-born of man." These, of course, were not sacrificed in the sense of being slain upon the altar, but they were *consecrated* to the LORD, and deemed as absolutely devoted to sacred uses as if their flesh had been consumed in the sacrificial flames. And in regard to the firstling of the flocks and herds, the command was, "Thou shalt set apart," or, as the margin reads, "*cause to pass over,*" "unto the LORD" all these for holy uses. And the reason assigned is, They are *Mine.* "Sanctify unto ME all the first-born." "MINE shall they be; I am the LORD." The original right of property which Jehovah has in all things, and in all souls, is made the ground of this obligation to consecrate unto him the firstling of the flock and the first-born male of the household, that is, the most cherished and endeared of our earthly possessions, in proof that we hold the whole in subjection to his will, and as stewards of his manifold gifts. "Then will I give him unto the Lord all the days of his life," is the form of consecration with which Hannah dedicated her child unto the

Almighty when "she was in bitterness of soul, and prayed unto the Lord and wept sore." In regard to temporal possessions, the Scripture affirmation is, "All the tithe of the land, whether of the seed of the land or of the fruit of the tree, *is the Lord's;* IT IS HOLY UNTO THE LORD." And this dedication of the tithe to religious uses is an acknowledgment of God's right to all. The consecration of property to God is the doctrine it teaches. The followers of Jesus, in their character as Christians, are consecrated persons. "Christians in general," says Richard Watson, "are consecrated to the Lord, and are a holy race, a chosen people." Or, as St. Peter has expressed it, "Ye are a chosen generation, a royal priesthood, a holy nation, a peculiar people, that ye should show forth the praises of Him who hath called you out of darkness into his marvelous light."

Consecration, then, is an acknowledgment of God's supremacy—that all right of property and moral government is in him, and that he is worthy of our best, purest, and noblest affections. It is a solemn devotement of ourselves, our possessions, our households, our affections, our honors, and whatever we most esteem on earth, to our Lord and King. It is loyalty to God, in heart and life, at any expense, sacrifice, peril, or loss, for time and for eternity. It is the honest choice of Christ as our portion, with his cross, the contempt of the world, and the malice of hell, for the sake of the communion of his love, and the partnership of his throne. It is self-denial in principle and in practice, under the inspiration of the loftiest sentiments of religion. It is the purpose to give up the right hand and pluck out the right eye, rather than to displease God. It is that disposition which leads us to account all things loss for the excellency of Christ—which heeds the command, "Likewise reckon ye also yourselves to be dead indeed unto sin, but alive unto God, through Jesus Christ our Lord." It is the solemn abjuration of all selfish objects and ends, that we may fulfill our course with joy, and reap an eternal reward. It is the divinely-begotten strength and heroism which enables us to endure tribulation and persecution for Christ's sake, cheerfully, with the conviction and assurance that because he hath overcome we also shall obtain grace to triumph, and glory to crown our immortal years. It is to come out from the world and be separate, and touch not the unclean thing. It is to "take pleasure in infirmities, in reproaches, in necessities, in persecutions, in distresses, for Christ's sake." It is to yield the heart always to the influence of the grace of God, to be crucified with Jesus, and to live the life which we now live in the flesh with constant reference to the will of God. It is to seek not our own, but the things which are Jesus Christ's. It is to press on incessantly, forgetting those things which are behind, for the prize of the high calling of God in Christ Jesus. It is to set our affection on things above, not on things on the earth. It is to endure hardness as good soldiers of our conquering Captain and Prince. It is to do all things in the name of the Lord Jesus, giving thanks to God and the Father by him. It is to walk worthy of God, who has called us unto his kingdom and glory.. It is to turn from all ungodliness and worldly lusts, and to live soberly, righteously, and godly in this present world. It is to labor constantly to enter into that rest which remaineth to the people of God. It is to follow peace with all men and holiness, without which following after peace and holiness no man shall see the Lord. It is to rejoice in fiery trials, if thereby we are made partakers of the sufferings of Christ. It is to resist the devil, with sobriety, vigilance, and steadfastness, and to fly the corruption which is in the world through lust, as the only means of apprehending the exceeding great and precious promises, and becoming a partaker of the Divine nature—the sum of all attainment. It is to give all diligence to obtain an abundant entrance into the everlasting kingdom. It is to account ourselves servants, stewards, and soldiers of Jesus Christ, and to act in the world as those who are his representatives—who have his work to do, his battles to fight, and his kingdom to maintain.

Such is the nature of consecration to God. There is in it martyr heroism and sublimity. There is in it that which dignifies and ennobles the humblest and commonest life. It lifts us to a higher grade of being. It inspires us with a worthy object of pursuit. It enriches our natures, and aggrandizes our whole career on earth. O, to feel that we live not for ourselves, not for mere secular ends and objects, not for temporary expedients and perishable results, but for God, for his kingdom and glory, for our fellow-men and their highest good, for the grand and glorious issues of our immortal state—that is genuine nobility, kingly privilege, and everlasting honor! Just because consecration overcomes selfishness, lifts us out of the glare of worldly splendors, and makes us strong in purpose to resist evil, and to consummate in our experience all possibilities of virtue, does it bring to us abundant satisfaction. Did it require less, it would accomplish less in our behalf. We let go of the creature; we devote ourselves to the Creator. It is a relief to be able to let go of self; it is a mercy to be permitted to devote the life and heart to God. O for grace to nail our carnal natures to the cross, till the last quivering motion of the flesh shall cease! O for power to devote body and soul, time, talents, friends, possessions, all things to Jesus, till he shall come and illumine our whole being with the light of his glorious presence!

Consecration, considered as a religious act, is an *obligation.* It is a duty which we owe to God and our fellow-men. It is not to be regarded as a matter of speculation or opinion, in respect to which men may innocently differ, both in theory and action, but as the essential demand of the irrepealable law of Jehovah. To withhold the sacrifice and offering which God requires at our hands is not merely a mistake, a source of personal wretchedness, and a deprivation and wrong toward others: IT IS A SIN. To the full measure of our capacity and resources, according to the best light we have or can obtain, we owe ourselves to do or to suffer, with all things appertaining to us, to our Lord and Master.

It is a plain demand of justice. As GOD is our Creator, Preserver, Redeemer, Friend, he has a right to our service and affection. And as none can equal him, or be to us what he has been, or sustain to us relations so high and holy as those which he sustains, or meet the necessities of our natures, with such infinite provisions of mercy and love; so none can ever rightfully come between our souls and the Lord of life and glory. Our noblest powers, our purest affections, our grandest possibilities, must be offered up to God. "For ye are bought with a price; therefore glorify God in your body, and in your spirit, which are God's."

> "He justly claims us for his own,
> Who bought us with a price;
> The Christian lives to Christ alone;
> To Christ alone he dies."

"I beseech you, therefore, brethren," importunes an apostle, "by the mercies of God, that ye present your bodies a living sacrifice, holy, acceptable unto God, which is your reasonable service." The language is sacrificial. As the bodies of beasts, slain for sin, were offered on an altar of sacrifice, so are we exhorted to present our bodies, that is, ourselves, the whole of us, the body including the soul, the complete victim, as an offering to God. "The body," says Bengel, "generally encumbers the soul; present the body to God, and the soul will not be wanting." How can the body become a sacrifice? Chrysostom answers: "Let the eye look on no evil, and it is a sacrifice. Let the tongue utter nothing base, and it is an offering. Let the hand work no sin, and it is a holocaust. But more, this suffices not; but, besides, we must actively exert ourselves for good; the hand giving alms, the mouth blessing them that curse us, the ear ever at leisure for listening to God." The mind must be employed in the service of Christ, all our objects in life must be conformed to the Divine will, and our hearts must be so transfused with heavenly grace as to throb constantly with desire for his presence and satisfaction in his love. Though we are dependent on the Holy Spirit for every good impulse, yet this work of consecration is emphatically a human achievement. God gives the grace; it is for man to perform the act. "He himself," as Dr. Merrick has expressed it, "must bring the sacrifice and lay it upon the altar. God will have a voluntary service or none. This may be a difficult work. It always is. The will bends reluctantly; self pleads persuasively; unbelief suggests a thousand fears; the great adversary, and all the influences which operate upon the soul in opposition to God, combine to prevent such a step. But it can be taken, and it *must* be taken. The will must yield, self must be denied, God must be trusted, the devil resisted, and the offering made."

To consecrate ourselves to God is an obligation of gratitude. We are moved thereto by a consideration of the mercies of God. He hath not dealt with us according to our sins. He hath followed us with goodness and grace all our days. Life and health and reason, and the use of our senses, and the members of our bodies, friends, home, country—all these are arguments for consecration. But beyond all these, and above all, is the love of God in redemption—his mercy in Jesus Christ. "Herein is love; not that we loved God, but that he loved us, and sent his Son to be the propitiation for our sins." And the joyful sound of Gospel grace has reached our ears, and stirred our hearts. Does no obligation of gratitude rest upon us to consider ourselves the servants and followers of Jesus Christ?

"Every drop of my blood thanks you," said a criminal to Dr. Doddridge, when he had been released from prison in consequence of the Doctor's kind interposition, "*every drop of my blood thanks you; for you have had mercy upon every drop of it. Wherever you go, I will be yours.*" Does not this apply to our case? May not we take up this strain, and chant our gratitude to Jesus? Have we not been brought forth, by the blood of the covenant, "out of the pit wherein is no water?" Have we not been permitted, as prisoners of hope, to turn to the stronghold for refuge, deliverance, and comfort? Have not our prison-doors been opened, and have not our enslaved souls found the liberty of the Gospel? If we are this side of perdition, we have occasion for gratitude to God; and a sense of benefits received always moves a soul, not utterly debased, to attempt some return of service and affection.

But how strong is the argument for consecration—constant and full—based upon the facts of Christian experience! If one has known any thing of God, through the apprehensions of his own faith, how plain does duty seem in regard to this matter! The consciousness of salvation, in any measure, shows the possibility and propriety of consecration to God. It is an incentive and an argument for the preservation of covenant relations with the Great Head of the Church. And many a man can tell his experience in the triumphant language of Charles Wesley:

> "Long my imprisoned spirit lay,
>   Fast bound in chains and nature's night;
> Thine eye diffused a quickening ray;
>   I woke—the dungeon flamed with light:
> My chains fell off, my heart was free;
> I rose, went forth, and followed Thee.

> "No condemnation now I dread;
>   Jesus, with all in him, is mine;
> Alive in him, my living Head,
>   And clothed in righteousness divine,
> Bold I approach the eternal throne,
> And claim the crown, through Christ, my own."

And he who has broken our chains, illumined our darkness, delivered us from condemnation, and given us the right of access to the eternal throne, has a claim upon us, founded in justice and gratitude, for the constant service of our lives, and the fullest homage of our hearts.

Consecration involves self-denial, and self-denial is the generic demand of the Gospel.

In a brilliant essay on "Covetousness," by Rev. John Harris, it is contended that selfishness is the generic sin, the antagonist of the Gospel, the frustration of the divine plan, "the disease of the world," and "the prevailing malady of the Church." I add that self-denial is the generic demand of the Gospel, that it is in harmony with the divine plan, that it overcomes and destroys selfishness, and that it acts as an antidote to the malady and misery of a self-seeking world and a formal Church. Nothing hinders consecration when the mind is enlightened in regard to duty and privilege, but selfishness, in some one or more of its Protean forms; and consecration, when consummated, involving as it does, self-denial, self-surrender, and complete self-devotement to God, counteracts selfishness, and leaves the mind open for the inflowing of the divine love in all its fullness, sweetness, and transforming power. Then the inquiry arises, "Lord, what wilt THOU have me do?" and God becomes the spring of all our activities, the fountain of all our inspirations, and the end of all our labors.

"The very core of all religion," some one has said, "is not to live to ourselves but to God; not to consider ourselves our own, but the property and servants of Jesus Christ; not to feel as though we are set up in the world to work for ourselves, to spend the most of our time in promoting what is termed our innocent gratifications, but to hold our time, powers, influence, and property as talents intrusted to our care, to be used for Christ, keeping our eye on his lips to learn his will, and aiming habitually to please and honor him."

"They that wait upon the Lord," saith the word of inspiration, "shall renew their strength; they shall mount up with wings as eagles; they shall run and not be weary; they shall walk and not faint." To "wait upon the Lord" is to stand as a servant in his master's presence, watching for the motion of his hand or the movement of his lips, which shall indicate his will, ready to run at his bidding, prepared for any errand or labor which he shall designate, willing also to see others sent on honorable messages, rendering distinguished service, while he lingers and suffers, knowing that

"They also serve, who only stand and wait".

Such truly consecrated souls shall never faint, nor fail or flag through weariness; but shall renew their strength day by day, till they can soar like the eagle, with his eye on the sun, above the clouds and storms and tempests of earth, into the pure cerulean of God.

"Who in the strength of Jesus trusts,
Is more than conqueror."

Faith and repentance are required in the Scriptures as conditions of acceptance and eternal life, but consecration must precede the former, and is an element of the latter; there is no salvation, therefore, without consecration.

The soul which truly repents turns to God, or, in other words, becomes consecrated to his service; this is the chief fact in repentance. That is genuine and sufficient penitence which leads a man to forsake his sins, abandon his selfish life, and devote himself to God; while that is superficial and delusive, notwithstanding tears, emotions and agitations, which does not lead to such results of consecration and covenant engagement with Christ. Faith is not possible while the soul is unconsecrated, while any gift is withheld from the altar, or while the heart shrinks from any sacrifice which the Gospel demands; so that the one grand condition of acceptance with God cannot be met without consecration.

II.

CONSECRATION MUST BE COMPLETE.

"Likewise reckon ye also yourselves to be dead indeed unto sin, but alive unto God, through Jesus Christ our Lord."—ROM. vi, 11.

THAT we should be wholly devoted to God is plainly a demand of justice. Our obligation hath this extent. All the service and affection of which we are capable belongs to our supreme Head. A partial offering, therefore, will not satisfy the claims of the divine law. If I owe my friend money, service, honor, influence, affection, will a part pay the whole? Could I say to my father, for instance, in discharging a pecuniary obligation which I might owe to him, "This meets all your demand upon me?" Might he not retort, "Nay, my son, you owe me your *life;* and the extent of your obligation can only be measured by your possibility of service, honor, and love?" And our heavenly Father has the completest claim upon our time, talents, affections, devotions, sacrifices, and upon whatever capacities we may have for doing or suffering what may be in accordance with his will and to the glory of his name. There is no pertinent reason why I should love or serve God at all, which is not equally conclusive to establish the position that I ought to love him with all my heart, and serve him with all my powers. Hence the justness and authority of the evangelical law: "Thou shalt love the Lord thy God with all thy heart, and with all thy soul, and with all thy mind." God cannot require less than this on the principle of justice and equity; nor can man render less without wronging his own nature, and dwarfing and distorting the powers of his own soul.

"I call heaven and earth to witness," says Whitefield, speaking of his ordination, "that when the bishop laid his hands upon me, I gave myself up *to be a martyr* for Him who hung upon the cross for me. I have thrown myself *blindfold*, and, I trust, without reserve, into his almighty hands." And is this any thing more than the Gospel requires of every Christian? Is not the martyr-spirit a vital spirit in our holy religion? Except a man come to Jesus, giving up all that he hath, how can he be his disciple? "In recompense for the love you may show your country," said Garibaldi, addressing the young men of Italy, "I offer you hunger, thirst, cold, war, and death; who accepts these terms let him follow me." And so Jesus saith: "Whosoever will be my disciple, let him deny himself, bear his cross, count all things loss for my sake, welcome privations and persecutions, defy the scorn and opposition of the world, turn from father, mother, wife, and children if they stand in the way of my service, lay down his life if need be, for my cause, and count it all joy if sacrifice, peril, and martyrdom bring him nearer the communion of my love; who accepts these terms let him follow me." Ay, let him follow! It is a pathway of fire, of fierce and terrible conflicts, of anguish and death; but it is also the pathway of victory, of unfailing consolations, and of immortal renown.

The will, the understanding, the affections, the whole being, must be dedicated to Christ. The world and the devil require as much as this in the service of sin—in the idolatry of fashion, honor, and ambition. Lady Fowell Buxton, in one of her charming letters, gives an account of a dinner at her husband's house, at which Baron Rothschild, the millionaire, was present. He sat at Lady Buxton's right hand, and his whole discourse was of money and money-making, and of the way in which he had trained his sons to preserve and expand his colossal fortune. Lady Buxton expressed the hope that he did not allow them to forget that never-ending life so soon to begin, for which, also, preparation must be made. "O," replied he, "I could not allow them to think of such a thing. It would divert their minds from business. It would be fatal to their success. To get and keep a great fortune is a very difficult thing, and requires *all one's time and thoughts.*"

Such is the demand which Mammon makes upon his worshipers! Is it marvelous that entire consecration should be the requirement of the Gospel? Men have made sacrifices scarcely less on the altars of patriotism for the unity and salvation of the republic. They have given of their fortune; they have sent their sons to the field of combat; they have endured discomforts, losses, and bereavements; they have sundered the most endearing of earthly relations, and they have been ready to sacrifice the last dollar and the last life for the national flag—for constitutional freedom. Indeed, every loyal heart in the land responded to the noble sentiment of Secretary Seward, written in March, 1863: "He that preferreth himself, his fame, his fortune, his friend, his father, his mother, his wife, his party, or his section, above his country, is not worthy to be a citizen of the best and noblest country that God has ever suffered to come into existence."

Hear now the words of Jesus: "He that loveth father or mother more than me is not worthy of me; and he that loveth son or daughter more than me is not worthy of me. And he that taketh not his cross, and followeth after me, is not worthy of me. He that findeth his life shall lose it; and he that loseth his life for my sake shall find it."

Could we regard the religion of Jesus as divine, if it did not require this utter self-surrender, and this complete sacrifice of every thing which we hold dear, in order to the enjoyment of the Saviour's presence and love?

How sublime a spectacle was that when Dr. Thomas Coke stood before the British Wesleyan Conference, pleading for a mission in India! He had seen more than threescore years; he had spent two large fortunes, preaching the Gospel; he had crossed the ocean eighteen times on his mission of mercy; he had been recognized as the first Bishop of the New World, but found not, as the historian of Methodism affirms, in a diocese co-extensive with a continent, room for his energies. Now his heart was turned toward India, and he pined, with a holy ambition, to preach the Gospel to the millions of Asia. Ceylon, "the threshold before the gate of the East," was open to missionary labor, and Coke was determined to go in spite of every obstacle. To a friend, who remonstrated with him on account of his age and the need of his services at home, he replied: "I am now dead to Europe and alive for India. God himself has said to me, Go to Ceylon! *I would rather be set naked on its coast, and without a friend, than not to go.*" He presented himself before the conference with his project for a mission in India. The conference was startled and astonished. "Many rose to oppose" it. Benson declared "with vehemence" that it would compromise the honor of the denomination and "ruin Methodism." Coke returned to his lodgings with the tears flowing down his face, passed the night in an agony of prayer, and came back the next day to the conference-room to offer himself and thirty thousand dollars in money upon the altar of this great sacrifice. The conference relented, and yielded to what was manifestly the voice of Providence. Coke did not live to reach his coveted field of missionary labor; but his holy enthusiasm and sublime consecration still live, an inspiration to the Church in every land.

This spirit of entire consecration will lead us to conform all our plans and purposes to the manifest designs and purposes of the almighty Providence. Dr. Bushnell has a sermon entitled, "Every Man's Life a Plan of God." The fully-consecrated soul recognizes this truth. It constantly inquires for the divine mind. It seeks to realize in its history the divine ideal. It makes life a discovery, an unfolding of the gracious purposes of Jesus in redemption, providence, and grace. In the Church and in the world, in business and in society, in devotions and in relaxations, in health and in sickness, at home and abroad, for time and eternity, the aspiration of such a soul is to be conformed in word and act, in doing and suffering, to the mind and heart of the blessed Jesus. To fulfill God's highest ideals for life and immortality is its ceaseless ambition. Nothing is coveted but the will of God and the fullness of his love. "I desired neither life nor death," said the Methodist hero, Staniforth, when going into the battle of Fontenoy, "but was entirely happy in God." Every such soul can say to the Almighty Father:

> "To do or not to do, to have
>   Or not to have, I leave with Thee;
> To be or not to be, I leave;
>   Thy only will be done in me:
> All my requests are lost in one,
> *Father, thy only will be done.*
>
> Welcome alike the crown, the cross;
>   Trouble I cannot ask, nor peace,
> Nor toil, nor rest, nor gain, nor loss,
>   Nor joy, nor grief, nor pain, nor ease,
> Nor life, nor death—but ever groan,
> *Father, thy only will be done.*"

"No selfish indulgence," says Dr. Merrick, "in dress, sleep, or any of the appetites injurious to health is compatible with entire consecration; while health, and even life itself, must be cheerfully sacrificed at the command of God. He who, to preserve his health, shrinks from the discharge of known duty, or to save his life denies his Saviour, shows that he has not given up *all* to the Lord. None may choose his own profession or calling regardless of God's will. What God appoints he must do. Where God directs there he must go. If called to the ministry, he must 'obey the voice divine.' If the providence of God points him to some heathen land as his appropriate field of labor, thither he must direct his steps. His own ease, convenience, pecuniary interest, and aggrandizement, must yield to the claims of God. 'For none of us liveth to himself, and no man dieth to himself.'"

Moreover, an entire consecration implies *a cheerful submission to sufferings.*

We shrink instinctively from pain. Loss, suffering, and anguish of body and soul, break down and subdue the bravest hearts. The trials of life will, in the end, quench the most fiery spirit, unreplenished by the grace of God. Most persons find, with Lady Maxwell, that it is much easier to do than to suffer the will of our heavenly Father. In doing, there is much to engage our attention, to excite the flow of the animal spirits, and to rouse all the powers of the mind for the successful accomplishment of our work. But there is no romance in suffering. It simply requires endurance. It calls for patience and resignation to the divine will, and we are slow to discern the greatness of these passive virtues. And when clouds and darkness are round about us, when we are taken from the active duties of life to be laid away in a chamber of sickness, when our possessions are wasted and friends alienated, when we bow down in utter desolation over our dead, or stand by the open grave ready to swallow up our loved ones, it is so hard to see that we can serve and honor our Master in these things, or that the gracious purposes of his providence can be accomplished through such ministrations of sorrow! And yet one whole side of Christian character, and a side of great beauty and power, has its development chiefly through the agency of afflictions and adversities. Consecration is *sacrifice*, and to be complete it must be submissive; it must consent to whatever God appoints, and it must yield up the most precious things at his requirement. We must give ourselves into the hands of God, to do or to suffer as he may order. There was a device on an ancient medal, which has been adopted by a modern missionary society, that represents a bullock, standing between a plow and an altar, with this inscription, "Ready for either"—ready either to drag and swelter in the furrow, or to bleed on the altar of sacrifice. And this is precisely the posture of the truly consecrated soul. He is ready for the divine will; and though he may prefer to be an active laborer in the Lord's vineyard, yet if he is hindered or laid aside by sickness or afflictions he is cheerful in the midst of sufferings; he rejoices amid flowing tears; he praises God when his heart is torn, and he welcomes the cross and the thorns, while he hopes for the crown and the harp of praise.

When Mrs. Sigourney, the American poetess, had lost her only son at the age of nineteen, in the depth of her anguish she said: "God's time and will are beautiful, and through blinding tears I would fain give him praise." This is entire consecration in the furnace of affliction. And Dr. Stephen Olin has left on record the fact that it was through a discipline of suffering that he was brought into the enjoyment of the grace of Christian perfection. "I sunk into it," is his testimony. "My children, my wife, my health, my entire prospects on earth, all were gone—God only remained: I lost myself as it were in him; I was hid with Him in Christ, and found, without any process of logic, but by an experimental demonstration, 'the perfect love that casteth out fear.'" And every man who has obtained this great salvation has complied with this condition—he has accepted and sunk into the perfect will of God. He has prayed, with the Psalmist, " Lord, choose thou mine inheritance for me;" he has exclaimed, with the suffering Son of God, " Not my will but thine be done." And he has not gone regretfully and murmuringly to the place of sacrifice, but he has learned to esteem it an honor and a pleasure to suffer for Christ. What a touching picture to the eyes of angels was that, when a devoted mother, as the receding ship bore away her only son to missionary labor in a heathen land, knelt on the sands, and, with uplifted hands and streaming eyes, exclaimed: "O, Jesus, I do this for thee!" And the time will come when we shall desire, more than all things on earth or in heaven, to be able to say to the Lord Jesus that we have done or suffered something for him. There will gather around the throne consecrated souls who will say to the glorified Lamb: " Lord Jesus, I gave my fortune for thee; I gave my home and friends for thee; I was an exile from my father's house for thee; I was hunted to the mountains and to the caves of the earth for thee; I passed weary years in vile and loathsome dungeons for thee; I went joyfully to the scaffold and the flames for thee!" And will not those be esteemed happiest who can present the longest and most thrilling record of cheerful suffering for Jesus? And all the afflictions which come to us in the order of divine providence may be borne cheerfully and heroically for

Jesus' sake, and so as to be rewarded and honored in the everlasting kingdom.

Under the appropriate caption, "Ready for Service or Sacrifice," a correspondent of the Detroit "Tribune" tells the following incident, as illustrative of the spirit of the brave men who fought the battles of freedom against treason and oppression:

"A New Hampshire regiment had been engaged in several successive battles—very bloody and very desperate—and in each engagement had been distinguishing themselves more and more; but their successes had been very dearly bought, both in men and officers. Just before 'taps,' the word came that the fort they had been investing was to be stormed by daybreak next morning, and they were invited to lead the 'forlorn hope.' For a time the brain of the colonel fairly reeled with anxiety The post of honor was the post of danger; but, in view of all circumstances, would it be right, by the acceptance of such a proposition, to involve his already decimated regiment in utter annihilation? He called his long and well-tried chaplain into counsel with him, and asked him what was to be done; and the chaplain advised him to let the men decide it for themselves.

"At the colonel's request, he stated to the regiment all the circumstances. Not one in twenty, probably, would be left after the first charge. Scarcely one of the entire number would escape death, except as they were wounded or taken prisoners. No one would be compelled to go, if he did not go with all his heart. 'Think it over, men, calmly and deliberately, and come back at twelve o'clock, and let us know your answer.' True to the appointed time, they all returned. 'All?' said I. 'Yes, sir, all, without exception; and all of them ready for service or for sacrifice.' 'Now,' said the chaplain, 'go to your tents, and write your letters; settle all your worldly business, and whatever sins you have upon your consciences unconfessed and unforgiven, ask God to forgive them. As usual, I will go with you, and the Lord do with us as seemeth him good.' The hour came; the assault was made; on these noble spirits rushed into 'the imminent deadly breach,' right into the jaws of death. But, like Daniel when he was thrown into the lion's den, it pleased God that the lions' mouths should be shut. Scarcely an hour before the enemy had secretly evacuated the fort, and the 'forlorn hope' entered into possession without the loss of a single man!"

Rev. J. T. Gracey, who has rendered the Church effective service in her foreign fields, writing for the *Northern Christian Advocate* of the consecration and sacrifice manifested in this great missionary work by those who have confronted paganism with all its horrors in the name of Jesus, says: "We know of those who, for Christ's sake, have endured what no wealth nor fame would have tempted them to begin; who have suffered unutterable things in the seas, and escaped only with their lives; who, in their ordinary work, have traveled amid wolves, tigers, and other wild animals, continually compelled to realize, by the destruction of others, the peril to which they themselves were exposed; who have been beaten, bruised, and prepared for hanging; who have preached, alternately keeping guard against suspected assassins in their audience; who, when cartridge was dealt out to British soldiers because of an assured attempt at general massacre, quietly conducted their native worship with their native families, removed from all protection; who persisted in preaching at large fairs when warned that they and theirs would be murdered the same night; who tried to plant colonies of native Christians, and, rather than abandon their Master's work, remained amid fever and pestilence, exhibiting Christian fidelity and all graces, till the colony melted away by death, and they were dragged off more dead than alive, never after to recover from the ill effects to their constitutions. We know of women who have participated in all this, and who have traveled for as much as two days without any but the coarsest food, throughout roadless tracks, and sat them down all night, wet to the skin, by the banks of swollen streams. We know of such things as a father reading the burial service over members of his own family, among heathen desolation; mothers seeing their offspring die in camp whole days' march away from medical means which might have readily recovered them; parents' hearts wrung with intensest torture, as their children's lips dropped foulness never heard but in heathendom, and, who yet rather than abandon their posts, have sent their children half a world away from them, fainting as they said, 'O Christ it is for thee, else would we die rather than do this, and but for thee we would die in doing it.' We know of missionaries who have buried their wives in darkness and storm, or seen them sicken and waste in a foreign clime, and then die almost in sight of the home-land. We know of—well we had as well have done with it or write a volume of the incidents that flood our individual recollection, of what our missionary force has done and suffered, only for Christ, and because it seemed necessary to establish his kingdom in the ends of the earth."

Let us make this entire consecration our steadfast aim. The very endeavor to be wholly the Lord's will enrich our Christian experience and intensify our spiritual life. And if we walk in the light we shall prove the sufficiency of the atoning blood to cleanse us from all unrighteousness. Are we not persuaded that *entire* consecration is a plain demand of the Gospel? Can we, then, retain what grace we have, except we go on to perfection? But if we let go of every thing for Christ, Christ will be to us a satisfactory and unfailing portion.

III.

CONSECRATION A CONSTANT SERVICE.

"If any man serve me, him will my Father honor."—JOHN xii, 26.

It is a great mistake to suppose that consecration is a work which can be done or consummated at any given time. The obligation is constant and life-long. Every moment the covenant is to be renewed and ratified by a willing, obedient, and cheerful soul. There is, to be sure, a sense in which one can say,

> "'Tis done—the great transaction's done;
> I am my Lord's, and he is mine:"

but in what sense? The young man who enlists as a soldier in the service of his country, or the maiden who stands at the hymeneal altar and plights her vows, may say, "The great transaction's done." And so it is; but what significance has this act for all the future? Henceforth the enrolled soldier must obey the orders of his captain, stand on perilous guard, make the weary march, or rush into "the imminent, deadly breach," just as he may be directed, without question and without hesitation; yea, with cheerfulness and enthusiasm. And this obligation will continue during the whole period of his service, till he shall receive his "muster out," and retire upon his honors. The betrothed maiden must henceforth be dead to all other men; must leave her father's house, and, perhaps, her girlhood friends and associates, and cleave unto her husband and his fortunes in prosperity and adversity, through good report and evil report, till death disrupts the sacred relation into which she has solemnly entered.

Thus it is with the Christian. He is consecrated to Christ as a soldier to his flag, as a wife to her husband. He has enlisted under the banner of the cross, and he must follow whithersoever that victorious banner leads him. He must not be ashamed of his colors—of Bethlehem's star rising in the east, of the descending dove, of the emblazoned cross, nor of the royal inscription, "HOLINESS UNTO THE LORD." For that banner he must stand, march, fight, suffer, endure the loss of all things, and, if need be, die. He cannot permit it to be struck down for a single moment without treason to his Lord. No matter how long he has been in the ranks, he must not grow impatient for release. There are no furloughs in Christ's war, but the King of saints, in his own good time, grants a discharge and calls his faithful servant home. Or, in other words, the Christian is espoused to Jesus, and must be *faithful* to the end. There can be no dalliance with the world, no lusting after former lovers, no "aid and comfort" given to Christ's enemies, without essential dishonor, and damning sin. Every moment the consecrated soul must be ready to exclaim, "I am not my own: I belong to Jesus. I feel, purpose, speak, act, suffer for him. I have no life but in him. I am in the world, mingling with men, transacting the business of the world, but I am not of the world. The strong undercurrent of my being flows constantly toward God, and to magnify

Jesus, whether by life or death, is the master-passion of my soul."

Certainly, if we are under obligation to be able to say this at any moment, then, also, at every moment; if the grace of God is sufficient for this consummation at any time, then, likewise, for every time,'and to the end of time. "I am jealous over you," said Paul to his converts in Corinth, "with godly jealousy: for I have espoused you to one husband, that I may present you as a chaste virgin to Christ. But I fear lest by any means, as the Serpent beguiled Eve through his subtilty, so your minds should be corrupted from the simplicity that is in Christ." Sacred as love and sweet as heaven is this constant, loyal repose in the bosom of Jesus. And if we maintain our *simplicity*, "intent on *one* object most tender;' if we guard, cherish, and preserve the virgin purity of our perfect love—we shall not go after "another Jesus," nor shall we "receive another spirit;" but we shall triumph over all the arts and devices of our great enemy, and keep ourselves constantly on the altar of sacrifice, and "in the love of God." Let us ever bear in mind, then, that our consecration must be life-long; that we are perpetually under obligation to reckon ourselves dead indeed unto sin, but alive unto God; and that it is our privilege always to know that we are *all the Lord's*.

Consecration must also be *active*. There is a kind of passive, quiescent, sentimental offering, which some souls seem to make of themselves to God. But the consecration which the Gospel contemplates is a consecration of *service*. It demands that time, talents, possessions, strength of body, brain, and heart, and all our capacities, of whatever character, shall be constantly used in the work of Jesus Christ. The Lord requires us to "serve him with a perfect heart and with a willing mind;" and he hath delivered us "out of the hand of our enemies," that we "might serve him without fear, in holiness and righteousness before him, all the days of our life." "If any man serve me," said Jesus, "him will my Father honor." It is plain, then, that an active consecration is demanded. It is not enough to say, "I am the Lord's:" we must *be* the Lord's. It is not enough to say, "I give up my will:" the will must be engaged in recording decisions for Jesus. "My property." says one, "is on the altar;" and it would seem that it remains there; for it is not employed in building churches, sustaining missions, multiplying means of usefulness, or in ministering to the necessities of saints.

If we consecrate body and soul to Christ, it is that body and soul may be used, as Christ used his body and soul, in works of love and beneficence. If we behold him instructing the ignorant, healing the sick, comforting the despondent, relieving the wretched, counting it more than his meat and drink, more than all earthly advantage, to do the will of his Father, and yearning even for the baptism with which he was to be baptized—the baptism of tears and sweat and blood, in the garden and on the cross, that he might accomplish the world's redemption—then we shall discover the class of labors to which we are called as the servants of Jesus, consecrated to his will and work, and coveting, above all things, the advancement of his kingdom and the revelation of his power. Did Jesus leave behind him the glory which he had with the Father before the world was, and suffer and die a malefactor's death—a sacrifice and oblation for a guilty, thankless race—that he might save souls from guilt and ruin; and shall we, if consecrated to his service, refrain from manifold labors, or shrink from heavy crosses, or fail in any effort, expenditure, or endurance, which may be necessary to bring these same redeemed souls to the knowledge of sins forgiven, or to the higher life of holiness and heaven? The consecration of Jesus was positive and practical. Is it not enough for the disciple to be as his Master? Since he left heaven itself for the work of redemption, is it too much for us to leave the heaven of our closets and our contemplations, and go into the vineyard, and work with him for the restoration of paradise to man?

There seem to be many persons who have obtained the grace, but who do not apprehend the process of entire consecration. To be wholly dedicated to Christ is manifestly their desire, but they do not discern how they may reach the coveted consummation. They have often endeavored to consecrate themselves wholly to God, but they have no such evidence of success, no such witness of acceptance, and no such realizations of experience as they had anticipated. The offering lacks something, the fire does not fall from heaven, and their hearts are still restless and troubled. The process of consecration is not understood. It appears to be a quite common opinion that the work can be done by one wholesale act. This is an error which has hindered and stumbled thousands. We may *begin* the consecration instantly. and we ought to do so the moment Christ's claim is recognized, and to the very extent of the Gospel demand, and the whole process need not occupy any considerable length of time; but there must be distinct mental acts, and detailed and considerate sacrifice and oblation, in order to fullness and completion. Our all, however little, embraces many particulars, and it is *our all* which we purpose offering up to God. How much this includes we cannot know without detailed examination. It is like attempting a conception of distance or numbers; it cannot be done at once, but only by a gradual, step-by-step process. You think, for instance, of the distance from New York to Liverpool, and your mind passes from one point to the other in a flash, but you have a very imperfect conception of the intervening space. If, however, you have ever crossed the ocean, you will go back in your thoughts, and traverse the whole distance, numbering the days and nights of your voyage, recalling the various incidents which took place, the sunshine and storm, the health and sickness, the ships spoken, the friendships formed, the messages exchanged, the longing for the shore, the joy of arrival, and so by a prolonged consideration of incidents and details you will form something like an adequate conception of the width of waters separating continents. So of numbers. You attempt to think of a million of men, but there is not room in your mind for such a host. You must think of them in detail. They must pass in review before your mind. You must see the divisions, brigades, regiments; the long line of march, the extent of country covered, the time occupied in passing a given point; and so, at length, your mind takes in the stupendous whole.

These illustrations may help us to apprehend the necessity of detailed and deliberate consecration. It cannot otherwise be complete. The mind must be directed to every specific thing, and every part, of which the whole is composed, must be laid on the altar of sacrifice. We must, to speak commercially, make a complete inventory of our possessions, and on every item of person and property must be written in unmistakable characters, *This is the Lord's.*

Take the following historical illustration. When the people of Collatia surrendered to the power of Rome, they were asked, "Do you surrender all?" and they said, "Yes." But the answer was not satisfactory, and the question was presented in detail, thus: "Do you deliver up yourselves, the Collatine people, your city, your fields, your waters, your bounds, your temples, your utensils, all things that are yours, into the hands of the people of Rome?" and on their replying, "We deliver up all," they were received. The presumption was that they might shrink from the surrender required upon a full and detailed presentation of the case.

It was needful that they should distinctly understand how much was included in the act. So, in regard to the demand which the Holy Spirit makes for service and sacrifice in the kingdom and patience of Jesus. "Do you surrender all to Christ?" "Yes." The answer is honest, but it may not be intelligent, comprehensive, sufficient. "Do you surrender yourself, your body, mind, soul, time, talents, influence, acquirements, possessions, household, honors, expectations, *all things that are yours*, to be the property of

Christ, to do or suffer, to labor or sacrifice, for his kingdom and glory henceforth and forever?" If on the most minute, particular, and exhaustive presentation of what is required, the soul can still say, "*Blessed Jesus, I am in thy hands; I would be nowhere else; I am thine, fully and forever,*" then the sacrifice is complete, and faith will soon bring the crowning grace of salvation—the baptismal fire from heaven.

This detailed and entire consecration does not suppose that all these things, presented on the divine altar, should absolutely pass out of our hands, but only that we acknowledge the fullness of the divine claim, and cheerfully acquiesce in the divine orderings in respect to ourselves, and in respect to all things appertaining or belonging to us. It may be the will of God that we should continue to employ our wealth in business, making money for him; and it certainly is his will that we continue to cherish our homes, maintaining in all purity our domestic relations, but making those homes his sanctuary, recognizing wife and child as his gift, and constantly presenting to him, as a sweet offering and incense, our purest affections.

Wesley has furnished us "a method of expression" for this specific and all-including consecration in one of his "Forms of Prayer," as follows:

"To thee, O God, Father, Son, and Holy Ghost, my Creator, Redeemer, and Sanctifier, I give up myself entirely; may I no longer serve myself, but thee, all the days of my life.

"I give thee my understanding; may it be my only care to know thee, thy perfections, thy works, and thy will. Let all things else be as dung and dross unto me for the excellency of this knowledge. And let me silence all reasonings against whatsoever thou teachest me, who canst neither deceive nor be deceived.

"I give thee my will; may I have no will of my own; whatsoever thou willest may I will, and that only. May I will thy glory in all things, as thou dost, and make that my end in every thing; may I ever say with the Psalmist, 'Whom have I in heaven but thee? and there is none upon earth that I desire beside thee.' May I delight to do thy will, O God, and rejoice to suffer it; whatever threatens me, let me say, 'It is the Lord, let him do what seemeth him good;' and whatever befalls me, let me give thanks, since it is thy will concerning me.

"I give thee my affections; do thou dispose of them all; be thou my love, my fear, my joy; and may nothing have any share in them, but with respect to thee and for thy sake. What thou lovest, may I love; what thou hatest, may I hate; and that in such measure as thou art pleased to prescribe me.

"I give thee my body; may I glorify thee with it and preserve it holy, fit for thee, O God, to dwell in. May I neither indulge it, nor use too much rigor toward it; but keep it, as far as in me lies, healthy, vigorous, and active, and fit to do thee all manner of service which thou shalt call for.

"I give thee all my worldly goods; may I prize them and use them only for thee; may I faithfully restore to thee, in the poor, all thou hast intrusted me with, above the necessaries of life; and be content to part with them too whenever thou, my Lord, shalt require them at my hands.

"I give thee my credit and reputation; may I never value it, but only in respect of thee; nor endeavor to maintain it, but it may do thee service and advance thy honor in the world.

"I give thee myself and my all; let me look upon myself to be nothing, and to have nothing out of thee. Be thou the sole disposer and governor of myself and my all; be thou my portion and my all."

This is a particular and comprehensive consecration, embracing the understanding, will, and affections; the body, worldly goods, reputation, and all, without any reserve or limitation whatever. Happy is he who can, in sincerity and truth, offer this prayer to God.

James Brainard Taylor, speaking of the time when God fully sanctified his soul, says:

"At this very juncture I was most delightfully conscious of *giving up all to God.* I was enabled in my heart to say, 'Here, Lord, take me, *take my whole soul,* and seal me thine, thine now, thine forever.' I have had keener sorrows for indwelling sin," he adds, "than I ever experienced before conversion. O the distress which I have felt on account of pride, envy, love of the world, and other evil passions which have risen up and disturbed my peace and separated between God and my soul! I felt that I needed something which I did not possess. There was a void within which must be filled or I could not be happy. My earnest desire then was, as it has been ever since I professed religion six years before, that all love of the world might be destroyed, all selfishness extirpated, pride banished, unbelief removed, all idols dethroned, every thing hostile to holiness and opposed to the divine will, crucified ; that Holiness to the Lord might be engraven upon my heart, and evermore characterize my conversation."

The consecration which President Jonathan Edwards made of himself to God he has stated in these words :

"I have been before God, and have given myself, all that I am and have, to God, so that I am not in any respect my own ; I can challenge no right in myself; I can challenge no right in this understanding, this will, these affections that are in me ; neither have I any right to this body or any of its members ; no right to this tongue, these hands, nor feet ; no right to these senses, these eyes, these ears, this smell or taste. I have given myself clear away, and have not retained any thing as my own. I have been to God this morning, and told him that I give myself wholly to him. I have given every power to him, so that for the future I will challenge no right in myself in any respect. I have expressly promised him, and do now promise Almighty God, that by his grace I will not. I have this morning told him that I did take him for my whole portion and felicity, looking on nothing else as any part of my happiness, nor acting as if it were ; and his law for the constant rule of my obedience ; and would fight with all my might against the world, the flesh, and the devil, to the end of my life : that I did believe in Jesus Christ, and receive him as a Prince and a Saviour, and would adhere to the faith and obedience of the Gospel, how hazardous and difficult soever the profession and practice of it may be : that I did receive the blessed Spirit as my teacher, sanctifier, and only

Comforter, and cherish all his motions to enlighten, purify, confirm, comfort, and assist me. This I have done. And I pray God, for the sake of Christ, to look upon it as a self-dedication, and to receive me as entirely his own, and deal with me in all respects as such, whether he afflicts me, or whatever he pleases to do with me, who am his.

"Now henceforth I am not to act in any respect as my own. I shall act as my own if I ever make use of any of my powers to do any thing that is not to the glory of God, and do not make the glorifying him my whole and entire business; if I murmur in the least at afflictions; if I grieve at the prosperity of others; if I am in any way uncharitable; if I am angry because of injuries; if I revenge; if I do any thing purely to please myself, or if I avoid any thing for the sake of ease; if I omit any thing because it is a great self-denial; if I trust to myself; if I take any of the praise of any good that I do, or rather which God does by me; or if I am any way proud."

Mark the minuteness, particularity, and completeness of this consecration. Wesley and Edwards widely differed in their theological views, but how certainly did their hearts throb in holy unison! And how marvelously does the prayer we have quoted from the former correspond to the experience which we here cite from the latter. Thus are all saints, by consecration and experience of divine love, one in Christ Jesus:

> "Dear Lord, only thee!
> Only thee, I pray;
> Fill my heart with only thee
> Till I pass away.

Many do I love,
  And many do love me,
But thou—thou all above—
  'Thou knowest I love thee.'

"Dear Lord, be thou my guide;
  I give my hand to thee!
By day and night, through time and tide,
  I know thou wilt keep me.
The fairest love is mine
  Which in this world may be;
Dear Lord, let ever mine be thine;
  'Thou knowest I love thee!'"

Jesus has taught us, in the twenty-fifth chapter of Matthew, that *beneficent activity* will be the standard of judgment in the last great day. The faith and holiness, if such there be, which do not lead to service and sacrifice, are of no value. In other words, the power of the Gospel is proved *by the service rendered to man in the name of Christ.*

And even in that world in which there is no more curse; in which grows the tree whose leaves are for the healing of the nations; in which flows "a pure river of water of life, clear as crystal;" in which the throne of God and the Lamb pale the light of the sun, and make everlasting day—in that world, " His servants shall serve him ; and they shall see his face, and his name shall be in their foreheads."

IV

THE CONSECRATION OF SELF.

"And this they did, not as we hoped, but first gave their own selves to the Lord, and unto us by the will of God."—2 Cor viii, 5.

The apostle celebrates the liberality of the Churches in Macedonia. Such was the greatness of their poverty and the abundance of their afflictions that he had not anticipated from them any very considerable offerings. But the grace of God moved them to a free, earnest, generous contribution for the poor saints in Judea. "And," adds the apostle, "not as we hoped;" or, rather, "not as we expected;" that is, they went entirely beyond our expectations. And the reason of it was found in the underlying principle. They first gave themselves to the Lord, and then unto us, as the apostles and ministers of Christ, the agents and representatives of his cause by the will of God; that is, as the will of God indicated their duty and the extent of the offering which they ought to make.

I do not propose, to-day, to discuss Christian liberality; but rather its principle, its root. "The giving themselves means here," says Olshausen, "the bestowing every thing, and retaining nothing for themselves." Bloomfield says, " Giving themselves to the Lord is a strong expression to denote the devoting themselves and whatsoever they possessed to his service." Barnes' note is, "They first made an entire consecration of themselves and all that they had to the Lord. They kept nothing back. They felt that all they had was his. And where a people honestly and truly devote themselves to God, they will have no difficulty in having the means to contribute to the cause of charity."

This, then, is the theme: *The root consecration is the consecration of self.* What God requires is not gifts, services, sacrifices, but our own selves.

Now, we are ready to do any thing rather than give up self. Men will submit to the most exacting ritualism; will make the richest charitable offerings; will walk according to the straightest moral code, provided only that the denial of self is not required. But the indispensable condition of Christ's service is to deny self; that is, not merely to practice self-denial in some things, or in many things; but, as some one has expressed it, to deny self itself; or, in other words, to give ourselves to God.

What, then, is it to give one's self to God? What is self-hood? What is essential to our own proper, personal life? What is there which belongs to us, which, I may say, constitutes us, which we can give to God?

"Moral good," says M'Cosh, "lies in the region of the will. It is the region, and the exclusive region of moral good. It is in voluntary acts that the conscience discerns a moral quality, and it is upon such acts, and no others, that it pronounces its decisions." Again he says, "It is from the exercise of will that we get our very idea of freedom. It is in the sanctuary of the will that freedom alone is to be found." To surrender one's free, conscious self to Christ, then, is to give up absolutely one's will to Christ, and to take Christ's will for the government of our hearts and lives.

I say of our hearts, for the will controls the affections. "Give me thy heart," is the divine command ; and that which we can give or withhold is subject to the control of the will. "Because," saith the Lord, by the Psalmist, "he hath set his love upon me, therefore will I deliver him." "Set your affection on things above, not on things of the earth." The margin reads, "Mind;" set your mind on things above. The Greek word means to think, discern, judge, conclude, and then, by implication, to approve, esteem, covet, delight in.

This order of meaning shows conclusively the control which the will has over the affections. And with this accords the common-sense judgment of mankind ; for we hold men responsible for low tastes, corrupt affections, and groveling dispositions.

We must also take Christ's will for the government of our lives ; for the regulation of our conduct is within the scope of our own free agency And this extends not only to moral action, or to those things which relate to duty, but to our order of life, our business pursuits, the government of our households, the disposition of our time, the use we make of our talents and possessions, and, in a word, to all our possibilities.

Scripture illustrations of this law of self-sacrifice abound. We are represented as servants ; and the servant is not to do his own will, but the will of his master. He is to study the pleasure, interest, and purposes of his employer or lord.

We are exhorted to endure hardships as good soldiers of Jesus Christ; and if we are soldiers, we must obey the orders of the great Captain of our salvation. We must march, stand on the weary sentinel guard, or storm the imminent deadly breach, just as we are directed, without the least consideration of our own wishes or feelings in the matter. To raise the question as to what would be in accordance with our personal views or relishes would be an impertinence akin to treason.

And now what motives can I present to you, to labor and aspire for this sublime life of self-sacrifice and utter devotion to God?

1. Christ gave himself for this world. He was rich in all heavenly possessions; but for our sakes he became poor. He took on him the form of a servant. He submitted to the cross. He was obedient to death. Suppose he had given of the immense riches of his universe, as some wealthy Christians give a small fraction of their gold and silver, and then plume themselves on their devotion to Christ's cause; would that have won the heart of the world? Suppose he had sent some bright and gifted angel, as we send others to represent us in perilous and distasteful missionary fields, and then pride ourselves on our liberality; would that have sufficed for human redemption? "Do not call yourselves Lutherans," said the great Reformer to his followers; "call yourselves Christians. Who and what is Luther? Has Luther been crucified for the world?"

Now it is just because Jesus *was* crucified for the

world that he is able to draw all men unto him. And if you would know what it is, precisely and unmistakably, to give yourself to God, think of Christ in the garden of Gethsemane, praying, "O my Father, if it be possible, let this cup pass from me," but adding as in his agony he sweat great drops of blood, falling down to the ground, "Nevertheless, not as I will, but as thou wilt." Early in his career he asked, "Wist ye not that I must be about my Father's business?" and this question was the key-note to his whole life and ministry. Consecrated Christians are like Christ in the world; they are about their Father's business.

2. Nothing so much as self-sacrifice dignifies and ennobles human nature.

Our poor humanity is never lifted up so high as when it reaches the altitude of self-forgetfulness. The men whom we honor have not lived selfish but consecrated lives; honest laborers, who have toiled to give sustenance and comfort to wives and children and aged parents; colonists, like those who came over in the Mayflower, carrying the fortunes of a continent in their storm-tossed ship, and who said of themselves in the midst of their hardships and sufferings, "It is not with us as with men whom small things can discourage;" patriot soldiers, who have given their lives for the liberties of men; or brave martyrs, who have gone to the stake or the scaffold in honor of their religion, singing all the while triumphal hymns.

"That," says Froude, "which especially distinguishes a high order of man from a low order of man —that which constitutes human goodness, human greatness, human nobleness—is surely not the degree of enlightenment with which men pursue their own advantage, but it is self-forgetfulness; it is self-sacrifice; it is the disregard of personal pleasure, personal indulgence, personal advantages, remote or present; because some other line of conduct is more right."

3. This high devotion of body, soul and all to Christ, beyond any thing else, demonstrates Christianity to the world. It is evidence which cannot be turned aside, which confronts the popular gaze, and which is within the grasp of the commonest apprehension.

Referring to Mr. Buckle, Goldwin Smith says: "He will scarcely deny that the ethical doctrine of self-sacrifice is a peculiarly, if not an exclusively, Christian doctrine, and that it was Christianity that first effectively filled society with this aspiration." And that religion which demands and creates an unselfish devotion, and which enables men to sacrifice every thing else rather than the truth of God, which subdues passion and overcomes even the love of life, so as to make possible the lofty heroism of martyrdom, must be divine in its origin, and pregnant with blessings of inestimable value for the human race.

4. It is the way to usefulness, and usefulness is the chief thing in this world. How much God can make of a man can never be known till he is wholly given up to God. "The eyes of the Lord," it is said, "run to and fro throughout the earth, to show himself strong in the behalf of them whose heart is perfect toward him." That is the perfect heart which is wholly turned unto the Lord, and completely filled

with his presence and love. The eyes of the Lord run to and fro for such souls, and in their behalf he stands strong—strong as only God can stand.

"I have concluded," said one, "that the best thing I can do is to let Christ have his own way with me." That is it exactly. Let Christ take you, my hearer, with all your powers and purposes and possessions, to do the most he can with you, and he will make your life a grand opportunity, the seed-time of a golden harvest, the warp and woof of a resplendent immortality.

5. This life of consecration will be a life of rugged sacrifice, it may be, of privation, of tears; and yet it will be an exalted, ennobling, and satisfactory portion.

Froude, speaking of England's forgotten worthies, "indomitable, God-fearing men, whose life was one great liturgy," says: "Life with them was no summer holiday, but a holy sacrifice offered up to duty, and what their Master sent was welcome. Beautiful is old age; beautiful is the slow-dropping, mellow autumn of a rich, glorious summer. In the old man nature has fulfilled her work; she loads him with her blessings, she fills him with the fruit of a well-spent life, and, surrounded by his children, and his children's children, she rocks him softly away to a grave, to which he is followed with blessings. God forbid we should not call it beautiful. It is beautiful, but not the most beautiful. There is another life, hard, rough, and thorny, trodden with bleeding feet and aching brow—the life of which the cross is a symbol, a battle which no peace follows this side of the grave, which the grave gapes to finish before the victory is won, and, strange that it should be so, this is the highest life of man."

Such a life was that of John Wesley Walking over the grounds of an English nobleman, he exclaimed, "I also have a relish for these things, but there is another world;" and, under the inspiration of that grand thought, he went on his way to confront opposition, encounter mobs, and experience hardships of every kind, expecting to fight the battle out and seize at last the fadeless crown.

6. Finally, this is a practicable thing; you *can* give yourself to Christ. You may not have a fortune to lay on his altar, but you have what is of infinitely more value in his eyes, a will and a heart. In the domain of your own soul you are supreme, and here you may invite Christ's reign. You may not have great talents or high culture to employ in the Lord's service, but Christ will accept you just as you are, and little as you are, and put you to honorable use in his service.

And the greatest gift is the gift of yourself. If you had an empire to lay at the Lord's feet, it would not be so much as the offering of yourself. Men gave their wealth, their honors, their party prospects, their high places in the nation, to the country in the hour of its need; but did any of these give so much as the humblest soldier in the ranks, who gave himself?

And this consecration to Christ disposes of all other questions which might be perplexing or embarrassing. These Macedonian Christians, says the Apostle, "first gave their ownselves to the Lord and unto us by the will of God." They saw plainly the path of duty in the light of their great consecration. He who gives himself wholly to God escapes all questions of casuistry and all difficulties in regard to the measure of his obligations. In his business, household, political relations, every-where, he is Jesus Christ's man, and that shows him at once what he ought to do, and what he ought not to do. He does not seek to please himself, or men, but Christ. And Christ, my brethren, is easier to follow than either ourselves or the world. The most practicable, successful, honorable and satisfactory life is the Christian life.

And to live thus for the Lord is to be owned by the Lord, to be kept by him, to have his care, guidance, protection, and blessing. And the Lord will acknowledge his own when the world is on fire, will approve them in the presence of an assembled universe, and will exalt them to share his kingdom and throne— his presence and glory—forever.

V

THE SEPARATING POWER OF THE DIVINE PRESENCE.

"For wherein shall it be known here that I and thy people have found grace in thy sight? Is it not in that thou goest with us? So shall we be separated, I and thy people, from all the people that are upon the face of the earth."—EXOD. xxxiii, 16.

THE Jewish people were the peculiar people of God. They were distinguished in many ways from the surrounding nations. The chief fact, however, in their history was the unusual, transcendent and glorious manner in which Jehovah manifested himself to them as their God, Guide, and Portion. The nations round about, as Moses affirmed, had heard that the Lord was among his people, that he was seen by them face to face, that the cloud stood over and went before them which enshrined the divine presence, and that he had promised to bring them through the wilderness into a land which they should possess for an inheritance forever.

In like manner, the spiritual Israel is "a chosen generation, a royal priesthood, a holy nation, a peculiar people," who have been called out of darkness into the marvelous light of God.

In the verses preceding the text, Moses remonstrates against going up into the promised land at the head of the host which he had led out of Egypt, except he could be assured of the divine presence, and the text may be considered the argumentative part of that remonstrance: "For wherein shall it be known here that I and thy people have found grace in thy sight? Is it not in that thou goest with us? So shall we be separated, I and thy people, from all the people that are upon the face of the earth." The argument is, "If thou goest with us, we shall be separated from the heathen nations, and they will know that we have found grace in thy sight." The theme of our discourse, therefore, is, *The Separating Power of the Divine Presence.*

That the Church of God is to be separated from the world, and is to be no more of the world than was its divine Master, is a plain doctrine of the inspired word, and is in accordance with the general religious convictions of men. The only question relates to the cause and manner of the separation. What separates? What distinguishes the followers of Jesus from other men? What makes God's people a peculiar people? How do they most effectually show forth the divine praises? These are questions of great practical importance. Let us consider them.

1. Nothing merely external sufficiently marks the line of distinction between God's people and the people of this world. Christians are not separated, in the sense of this passage, by dress, visage, deportment, or any thing of this character.

Church-membership, faith in a creed, and the partaking of the sacraments, indicate certainly no more than nominal Christianity.

Simplicity and modesty of apparel become the followers of Christ, but an unholy heart may throb beneath the most saintly vestments. A serious deportment is to be commended, but he who supposes that a sanctimonious face and a godly character are synonymous terms, will often be the victim of the wiles of the hypocrite. Membership of the Church is a plain Christian obligation, but it is greatly to be feared that there is a wide disparity in the rolls of members in the visible and in the invisible Church. Every man who belongs to the earthly does not belong to the heavenly Zion. So some men are orthodox who are also reprobates, and some partake of the sacraments who also partake at the table of devils.

2. It should be observed, in the second place, that it is not by going out of the world or society that this true separation is realized. The monastery and the nunnery have no warrant in the Scriptures, nor in the philosophy of the human mind. The ideas underlying them are antagonistic to the ideas of the Gospel. Christianity is not a sickly hot-house plant which will wilt in the fervors or be chilled by the rigors of the world. Men are to be none the less business men because they are Christians, but they are to be Christian business men. Society is not to be abandoned, but sanctified, by the followers of Jesus. The monasticism of the heart, the closet, the select religious circle, is opposed to the whole genius of Protestantism. Methodism never had a particle of sympathy with any exclusiveness of religious thought or experience. Its mission was, and is, to spread Scripture holiness, and to bring as many sinners as possible to repentance. And living Christian men are wanted every-where, in the schools, on 'Change, in the halls of legislation, in the caucus, in the work-

shop, and by the fireside, as well as in the sanctuary, and in the evangelical and missionary work of the Church.

3. Spirituality, the divine presence, the indwelling of the Holy Ghost, the life of consecration and faith—these separate and make God's people a peculiar people.

This truth is best illustrated by the life of Jesus our Lord, who was in the world, among men, mingling with society in its various phases, at the weddings, feasts, and funerals, in the market-places and in the synagogues, and yet was "holy, harmless, undefiled, separate from sinners," and who has left us an example that we should follow his steps. He said of his disciples, "They are not of the world even as I am not of the world;" and, "As the Father hath sent me, so have I sent them." O, to be like Jesus, and to do the work of Jesus—to walk in his blessed footprints and to reproduce his life—these things will separate, and make us a peculiar, because a holy and beneficent people.

4. For this separation, one's own act, concurrent with the divine, is necessary. You remember the apostle's exhortation, and the divine promise of graciousness and fatherhood: "Wherefore come out from among them, and be ye separate, saith the Lord, and touch not the unclean thing: and I will receive you, and will be a father unto you, and ye shall be my sons and daughters, saith the Lord Almighty." "Come out," "Be ye separate;" that is your work. "Touch not the unclean thing," that is, make your renunciation of sin and impurity utter and absolute. Then the divine promise can be

claimed, and the presence and power of the Most High experienced. So, in like manner, when Paul affirmed that he was "separated unto the Gospel of God," might it not be said, That separation, Paul, is because you were "not disobedient to the heavenly mission," because you did "not frustrate the grace of God," and because you so yielded yourself to the Spirit's guidance as to be able to exclaim, "The law of the spirit of life in Christ Jesus hath made me free from the law of sin and death?" The manifestation of the divine presence to our souls and in the midst of us as a Church will be according to the degree of our devotion to Christ and to his work.

5. It is very important that this separation should be "known." This is the thought of Moses in the text: If God be with us, we shall become a teaching power to the nations round about us. These heathen will detect the tokens of the divine presence, and will magnify the name of Jehovah. And a spiritual Church is God's testimony to the world. Spirituality is luminous, and a holy Church shines for the same reason that the sun shines, because it is full of light. A spiritual Church is a transforming, evangelical, and missionary Church. It does two things which are demonstrative of its life and power—it produces integrity, striking down to the very roots of a man's nature and conforming him in passion and purpose to God, and it creates in the soul a profound satisfaction, such as the world cannot give, and such as makes men superior to losses and trials. These are mighty victories, and demonstrative of the power of the Gospel.

6. The advantages of the divine presence are man-

ifold and great. The perils of transgression are discerned, the needs of the Church are understood, the range of the promises is perceived, and the prophetic spirit which discovers revivals afar off and realizes their approach, as the fevered brow feels the first touch of the reviving breeze, is experienced, and holiness becomes a matchless power for the conviction and conversion of sinners in this out-beaming splendor of the divine presence.

And this spiritual power is our surest defense against error in doctrine or practice. We must maintain the vital force; then we can throw off disease and escape contagion. We must have spiritual life; then we shall become strong and able to thrive on any regimen. But the healthiest digestive fluid will not transmute food into chyle in the stomach of a dead man. And even the blessings of God seem lost on a formal and worldly Church.

Lord Dufferin thus describes the cataract of Van Jayen, in the icy region of Spitzbergen: "It is like a river larger than the Thames," he says, "plunging down hundreds upon hundreds of feet; every wreath of spray and tumbling wave frozen in a moment, stone stiff, rigid as iron, awful, everlasting death-in-life, staring up at the sun and the stars in their courses, and never meeting the Norland winds and the washing waves with the thunder music of its waters."

So, I have thought, falls the ceaseless stream of divine love upon a formal, worldly Church. Its very energy is stiffened into rigid, ritualistic shapes, and its warm life is frozen over, and frozen in, by irresistible and eternal frosts. What need we under such circumstances? More of the river of life, more of the warm stream from above, more of the breath of heaven breathed upon us, till the frosty spray and the mountains of ice melt and flow away in the music of rippling waters.

There is, it is said, a certain convent on the coast of Spain which is a monument of the time when Spain was the Spain of Columbus. That convent has a strange chapel. It is a marble ship about to weigh anchor. Masts of marble serve for columns; ropes and cables of marble are quaintly wound about them. Not far off the Atlantic breaks upon the coast, and the free winds shout forever across the waters. And yet that marble ship launches not forth upon the deep, and brings no treasures from distant lands.

Such is a formal Church, unchanging, rigid, fixed; perfect, it may be, in form, admirable as a work of art, splendid in its adaptations, imposing and solemn in its ritual, and complete in its doctrinal statements; but accomplishing, in no essential respect, the end for which a Church was instituted. It lacks the mighty enginery which, despite winds and waves, would impel it on its way, freighted with the treasures of all seas, and bearing frankincense and myrrh from the ends of the earth, to make fragrant the ivory palaces of the great King.

A Church, having the unction of the Holy Ghost, is rather symbolized by the popular idea of the old ship, Zion, walking the water like a thing of life, every sail spread to catch the breezes of heaven, jubilant with happy voices and songs of praise, bounding on its way toward the coveted shore even amid storm and tempests, floating joyously over sunny seas, borne by every current and by every gale that blows nearer and nearer to the celestial haven, and landing its redeemed thousands on the happy shores of a glorious immortality.

And yet this popular religious conception hardly symbolizes the endowed and powerful Church of Jesus Christ. That Church depends not on wind or wave, nor on any external circumstances whatever. It has an internal force, an unction of divine power, an inexhaustible spiritual energy, which cannot be suppressed or counteracted, and which brings it on its way majestic and triumphant.

One day last summer I stood, with some friends, on a bold headland of the Atlantic, looking out on the sea. The day was beautiful, the afternoon sun shone soft and resplendent, the sea glowed like a mirror, and within the range of our vision we counted over eighty ships, with sails all spread to catch the light breeze, but seeming to make scarcely any progress. As we gazed, another craft came into view. It had no sails spread, but it moved forward rapidly and powerfully The waves foamed and tumbled at its prow, and far backward could be traced its pathway across the waters. It passed beyond one proud sailing craft after another, and soon disappeared from our view, with its prow toward the distant shore.

Such, I exclaimed, is the Christian and the Christian Church. Like the steamship, the great driving power is within; like the steamship, the Christian holds on his way, reckless of winds and waves, leaving far behind the little sailing smacks which perpetually trim their sails to catch the favoring breezes of popularity and worldly prosperity; and, like the steamship, the Christian launches forth into the deep, in calm assurance of reaching the distant shore and safely entering the coveted harbor.

VI.

FORMER FAITH CALLED TO MIND.

"But call to remembrance the former days.—HEB. x, 32."

THERE is a speculative element in religion, as there is a ritualistic form, and a dogmatic utterance of truth; but that which is vital to Christianity comes within the realm of experience, and so of certainty "We know that we are of God." We do not know that our creed is faultless, that our forms are the best that could be devised, or that no morality or virtue can be found beyond our portals; but we *do* know "that we are of God." We know that we have passed from death unto life, that our sins have been forgiven, that Jesus is our divine Lord and Saviour, that prayer is a prevalent and glorious reality, that the Holy Spirit is an abiding comforter, that we are not deceived in our religious experiences, that our record is on high, and that our budding faith will bloom in a resplendent immortality. And this is in accordance with Christ's promise: "At that day ye shall know that I am in my Father, and ye in me and I in you." As Whedon adds, "It shall be by experience. There shall be no guess, or mere expectation, or *hope so* about it. The religion of the Spirit is not a *hope*, but an *enjoyment*." In other words, it amounts to certainty. Nothing attests itself like a religious experience. It is a revelation to the inner consciousness. Here, if anywhere, men may say with propriety, *We cannot be mistaken.*

In the fullest sense, the Christian faith brings certainty—brings the strongest conviction, and brings an ever-growing assurance that this conviction rests on immutable grounds, and has a basis which is as deep and strong as the Infinite.

Nor is it any argument against this assurance that men of thought and culture are not able to perceive the foundation on which it rests; for, as the apostle argues, it is a matter of spiritual discernment, and in what relates to experience nothing is reliable but testimony. "The natural man receiveth not the things of the Spirit of God; for they are foolishness unto him; neither can he know them, because they "are spiritually discerned." But he that is spiritual has this discernment, compares spiritual things with spiritual, and has the revealing light of that Spirit which searcheth all things, even the deep things of God. "Now we have received, not the spirit of the world, but the spirit which is of God, *that we might know the things which are freely given us of God.*"

And that this is truly a revelation of God to the soul we are certain; because it accords with the promise of the Inspired Word; because it is given to us in answer to prayer; because it produces a divine transformation of our natures; because it is adapted to the constitution, temperament, and necessities of each individual man; because it satisfies the heart in its longings for full and unwasting joys; because it meets every variety of human condition; because it inspires the purest morality and the most unselfish beneficence; because it creates a genuine missionary spirit, leading to sacrifice and labor for the instruction and salvation of every soul for whom Christ died; and because, in a word, it advances every human interest, gives sanction to law, purity to domestic life, power to civilization, support to the bereaved, training to childhood, exaltation to woman, and songs of triumph to the lips of the dying. "A preparatory faith," says Whedon, "comes by testimony; the fullness of faith, by experience." And when we have heard Jesus ourselves, then, like the Samaritans who had listened to his instructions, we know that he is, indeed, the Christ, the Saviour of the world. Bengel, speaking of the expressions of the beloved apostle, *to know him, to be in him, to abide in him*, observes that they are synonyms with a gradation, *knowledge, fellowship, constancy*. O happy soul, that in this unbroken fellowship of a Saviour's presence and love has this certain knowledge of acceptance and salvation!

How great the consolation of this assurance! Every Christian may exclaim, as the apostle, "I know whom I have believed, and am persuaded that he is able to keep that which I have committed unto him against that day." In this certain confidence there is triumphant joy Hence the pertinency of Rutherford's exhortation, "Die believing; *die with Christ's promise in your hand*." And that promise, firmly clasped, will buoy up the soul in the darkest and most troubled waters. "And this is the confidence that we have in him, that if we ask any thing according to his will, he heareth us; and if we know that he hear us whatsoever we ask, we know that we have the petitions we desired of him."

"With a man of faith," says Buckminster, "not an affliction is lost, not a change is unimproved. He studies even his own history with pleasure, and finds it full of instruction. The dark passages of his life are illuminated with hope; and he sees that although he has passed through many dreary defiles, yet they have opened at last into brighter regions of existence. He recalls with a species of wondering gratitude periods of his life when all its events seemed to conspire against him. Hemmed in by straitened circumstances, wearied with repeated blows of unexpected misfortunes, and exhausted with the painful anticipation of more, he recollects years when the ordinary love of life could not have retained him in the world. Many a time he might have wished to lay down his being in disgust, had not something more than the senses provide us with kept up the elasticity of his mind. He yet lives, and has found that light is sown for the righteous and gladness for the upright in heart." "If any man will do his will, he shall know of the doctrine whether it be of God." In the path of obedience and truth he will realize a growing faith, unwavering certainty, unfailing consolation, and an everlasting assurance of that love of Christ which passeth knowledge.

In 1769 Mr. Wesley records in his journal that he spent "a comfortable and profitable hour" with Whitefield, who was then near the close of his remarkable career, in *"calling to mind the former times,"* and the manner in which God had prepared them for "a work which it had not entered into their heart to conceive."

There is, perhaps, a tendency in old men, as in

soldiers returned from the wars, to consider the past, to re-fight the battles of other days, and to look backward rather than forward, for inspiration and the ardor of hope.

Certainly, the past is not to be forgotten, nor its lessons unheeded. Wisdom is born of observation and experience. Second sight is clearness of sight; and those who have looked long into the heavens, look deeply, and discern what to others are unknown worlds. Knowledge of the past brings knowledge of the future,

"Till old Experience doth attain
To something like prophetic strain."

"Thou shalt remember all the way which the Lord thy God led thee these forty years in the wilderness," was God's command to his ancient people; and he confidently appeals to them, on this wise: "Ye know in all your hearts and in all your souls, that not one thing hath failed of all the good things which the Lord your God spake concerning you; all are come to pass unto you, and not one thing hath failed thereof." This command and appeal suppose and require a remembrance of the past, an examination of the covenant, and a comparison of what had been promised with what had been received. It is, in one word, a demand that former things be called to mind.

So the apostle, arguing with the Hebrew Christians against apostasy, to which they were peculiarly liable because of their persecutions, reminds them of their former trials and their patient endurance of them. Soon after they were enlightened they had a severe trial of their faith, and endured a great fight of afflictions. They suffered the spoiling of their goods; they were "made a gazing-stock, both by reproaches and affliction," that is, they experienced the greatest contempt and contumely from the world, even as criminals who became a spectacle in the theater, and were insulted and outraged by the populace; and, when they personally escaped, yet they were "companions of them that were so used," in their tenderest and holiest sympathies and brotherly identity with them, and so experienced the common trial. But their faith did not fail. They knew for themselves that they had in heaven a better and a more enduring substance, and they rejoiced in their fadeless and everlasting possessions.

It is to this time of wasting persecution that the apostle refers, when he asks them to "call to remembrance the former days;" and he does it for their encouragement, for the quickening of their faith and the inspiration of their hopes. If this seem strange to us, we have need to consider that trials passed through successfully in a good cause are not unpleasant to recall to remembrance, and that the consciousness of having endured hardship and grief with fortitude steels and strengthens the soul for present and future conflicts. Those addressed, as Olshausen states, "had already, at an earlier period, endured manifold trials of their faith; in this lies a double motive for them not to fall away from their faith now: first, because thereby all their former sufferings would be rendered vain; and, secondly, that suffering itself was an experimental testimony to the power of faith."

It is as if a military force had carried one line after

another of an enemy's works, but others yet remain to be carried. If they fall back they will lose what they have gained; but, on the other hand, what they have accomplished is proof of their sufficiency to go forward and gain a complete victory, if their courage does not fail. It is thus that Christian soldiers, timorous at first, are made veterans by experience. Every successful conflict through which they pass increases their confidence in the Captain of their salvation, in the completeness of their impenetrable armor, and in the power of the sword of the Spirit to strike through every defense of their artful and implacable enemy.

In order, therefore, to nerve the soul for its conflicts, former faith and former triumphs may be appropriately called to mind. The same promises remain, the same grace abounds, and the same Guide still holds our hand and directs our way. Moreover, "He hath said, I will never leave thee, nor forsake thee; so that we may boldly say, The Lord is my helper, and I will not fear what man shall do unto me."

This assurance, springing from the remembrance of a former faith, is, however, a very different thing from a disposition to rest in an old experience as the ground of present acceptance. To assume that we are now in the favor of God because we once had tokens of his love, that former activity in his service condones for present sluggishness, and that the recollection of early joys may compensate for dearth of comfort, faintness of hope, and littleness of strength in our actual, living experiences, seems like a species of madness. A business man might as well boast of his former success, though at the present driven into bankruptcy and ruin ; or a soldier exult in the victories which he once gained, though now prostrate beneath the feet of an insulting foe; or a criminal rejoice, in the darkness of his dungeon and amid the clanking of his chains, in the sunny memories of an innocent childhood, or a manly career of integrity and honor.

If we have not, to-day, Christian constancy and the light and joy of the divine approval, our former experiences of a Saviour's presence and love are only an occasion of shame and reproach, and should excite bitter self-condemnation, and profound humiliation of soul. The memory of former days, in such a case, should only lead to pungent sorrows and many tears. God's word of precept to such persons is : " Remember therefore how thou hast received and heard, and hold fast, and repent ;" and his word of promise, that then shall their offering " be pleasant unto the Lord, as in the days of old, and as in former years."

This calling to mind of a triumphant faith does not lead one to inquire, in a croaking, misanthropic spirit, " What is the cause that the former days were better than these ? " but rather it may be, "What is the cause that my faith is not as strong, my consecration as complete, my diligence as great, my zeal as intense, my concern for souls as consuming, and my success in doing the Lord's work as manifest, as in former days ? " And though one may not inquire wisely in regard to former days, yet a contrast of present with former experience, for the purpose of admonition, instruction, encouragement, or inspiration, must always be a source of substantial and enduring profit; for it will certainly bring before the mind the faithfulness, the sufficiency, and the loving-kindness of a covenant-keeping God. "Remember the former things of old," saith the Lord by the prophet, "for I am God, and there is none else; declaring the end from the beginning, and from the ancient times the things that are not yet done; saying, My counsel shall stand, and I will do all my pleasure."

Sometimes the saints of God may be induced to inquire, as the Psalmist, "Lord, where are thy former loving-kindnesses?" but a contemplation of the divine goodness will customarily excite that strain of holy rapture and conscious triumph which the sweet singer of Israel reaches in the final note of his song, "Blessed be the Lord for evermore. Amen, and amen."

Former faith called to mind, ought not only to inspire present confidence, but also large expectations of future success and ultimate victory. The law of divine manifestation is that of development, revelation, and progress. The glory of the latter house was to be greater than that of the former. "Behold," saith the Lord, "I create new heavens and a new earth; and the former shall not be remembered, nor come into mind." He who "spake in time past unto the fathers by the prophets hath in these last days spoken unto us by his Son." The ministration of death, written and engraven in stones, was glorious, but the ministration of the Spirit is rather glorious: "for even that which was made glorious had no glory in this respect, by reason of the glory that excelleth." An increase, therefore, of light, wisdom, strength, and glory, and joy of the divine presence, in the processes of Christian experience, is in perfect accordance with the whole history of the divine manifestations, and in harmony with the entire analogy of the faith. Precisely what we ought to expect is, that "the path of the just" will be "as the shining light, that shineth more and more unto the perfect day." However beautiful the morning of our Christian experience, when the day star of a Gospel hope rose on the darkness of our benighted natures, a noon-day more luminous may be justly anticipated; and even the clouds which gather around life's close may become gorgeous with the reflected light of a glorious immortality

The remembrance of former days will awaken many troublesome questions in our minds, except we have learned the great truth, that "a man's life is where the kingdom of heaven is—within him," and that the purpose of the Infinite Goodness is always, by whatever sorrow or sacrifice of other things, to bring us to the noblest type of character, and the completest conformity to the image of his Son. Trench, discussing the question whether the tribulations visited on the Church in Smyrna were to be regarded as the gracious trials of God or the temptations of the devil, says, "It is, indeed, perfectly true, that the same event is oftentimes both the one and the other—God sifting and winnowing the man to separate his chaff from his wheat; the devil sifting and winnowing him in the hope that nothing else but chaff will be found in him." And he adds, "God makes trial of his servants to show them what of sin, of infirmity, of unbelief, is in themselves; and, showing them this, to leave them holier than before this temptation found them." Let us be grateful, then, that if in former times we have been sifted and winnowed, in ways which we could not comprehend, and for reasons which to our finite understandings were inscrutable, we have not been found wholly chaff, but that the existence of some genuine wheat has been demonstrated. Let us learn to regard every thing as a mercy for which God is to be devoutly praised, which has been calculated to bring us nearer to Christ, to make us more like him, and to prepare us more fully to reproduce his life in the earth.

The sustaining power of a former faith called to mind is aptly illustrated in the following narrative, which will be found, at length, in the first volume of Stevens' History of Methodism. John Haime was one of Mr. Wesley's most successful lay preachers. He was the victim of nervous disorders, morbidly conscientious, inclined to solitude and sentimental sadness, and often, before his conversion, contemplated suicide. Seeking relief for his troubled spirit, he enlisted in the army as a dragoon, but serious thoughts and gross excesses alternated in his life from day to-day. Walking by the side of the Tweed, he cried aloud, "being all athirst for God, 'O that thou would hear my prayer, and let my cry come up before thee!'" "The Lord," he wrote, "heard; he sent a gracious answer; he lifted me up out of the dungeon. He took away my sorrow and fear, and filled my soul with peace and joy in the Holy Ghost." That day was never forgotten. He went into the battle of Dettingen, exclaiming, "*In Thee have I trusted; let me never be confounded.*" He adds: "My heart was filled with love, peace and joy, more than tongue can confess. I was in a new world." His comrades for seven terrible hours fell on either side of him, but he came out of the battle safe and triumphant in his faith. Afterward, in the more sanguinary contest at Fontenoy, Haime was in the hottest of the fire for several hours. He did not believe that he should die that day. He trusted in the same Lord who had delivered him. His horse was killed under him. An officer cried out, "Haime, where is your God now?" He answered, "Sir, he is here with me, and he will bring me out of this battle." Presently, a cannon ball took off the officer's head. Haime disengaged himself from his fallen horse and walked on, praising God. "I was exposed," he says, "both to the enemy and to our own horse; but that did not discourage me at all; for I knew the God of Jacob was with me. *Surely I was in the fiery furnace, but it did not singe a hair of my head.* The hotter the battle grew, the more strength was given me; I was as full of joy as I could contain." A quarter of a century after the battle of Fontenoy an aged preacher wrote to John Wesley that "all the promises of Scripture were full of comfort to him, *particularly this, 'I have chosen thee in the furnace of affliction.'*" It was the brave and trustful John Haime, who had been so marvelously delivered, and who now called to mind his former faith. The promises of God so often tried and proved, had become, he said, as "precious to his soul as rain to the thirsty land." He died in his seventy-eighth year, exclaiming with a confident and triumphant faith, "When my soul departs from this body, a convoy of angels will conduct me to the paradise of God."

In heaven, I may add, there will be no forgetfulness of earth, but the former days will often be called to mind. Even the things which have passed away will not sink into oblivion. They will be still remembered, and celebrated in glowing songs ; for they will have become a part of the great history of redemption. He who stands at the head of the sacramental host is "the first begotten of the dead, and the Prince of the kings of the earth." And the triumphant song, from hallowed lips, chanted by glorified saints, and swelling around the eternal throne, will commemorate the praises of God the Father Almighty, and of the Lamb, fountain of redemption and salvation. And these ransomed souls will recall the fact that they were washed from their sins, made kings and priests unto God, brought out of great tribulation, "arrayed in fine linen clean and white, for the white linen is the righteousness of the saints," and made inheritors of the new earth and heavens, through the mercy and love of Jesus Christ, the Son of man, who died on Calvary for the sins of the whole world. The former faith, therefore, will constitute the warp and woof of their exalted and imperishable being. That former faith, indeed, was the bud which blossomed into their heavenly experiences. And as their first illumination was the dawning blush of the glorious and eternal day, so "the former days" are now recalled as key-notes to their immortal songs.

VII.

GIVE THE CHOICEST THINGS TO JESUS.

"And when they had opened their treasures, they presented unto him gifts; gold, and frankincense and myrrh."—MATT. ii, 11.

GOLD was early known, highly esteemed for ornamental purposes, and reckoned a desirable treasure, long before it was coined into money, employed as a medium of exchange, or made a standard of commercial values. Frankincense is a vegetable resin, brittle, glittering, and of a bitter taste, formerly used for the purpose of sacrificial fumigation. It is obtained by successive incisions in the bark of a tree called the *arbor thuris*. It is a product of the East, emits a pleasant odor, and is an appropriate offering to a royal or divine personage. Incense conveys the idea of adoration; it is the breath of praise. Myrrh is the Arabic of a thorny tree, like the acacia, from which flows a white liquid that thickens and becomes a gum. It is used as a perfume, but especially for embalming. We are told, for instance, that Joseph of Arimathea, and Nicodemus, who at first came to Jesus by night, embalmed the body of our crucified Lord in a mixture of myrrh and aloes, winding it in linen cloths with the spices, as the manner of the Jews is to bury.

In one word, then, this presentation to Him who was born King of the Jews, of gold, frankincense, and myrrh, was an acknowledgment on the part of the Magi that he into whose presence the light of a journeying star had mysteriously guided their steps was entitled to their homage, service, and affection— was entitled to their most costly and most tenderly loved treasures; and that unto him tribute must be paid, fealty avowed, and incense offered. In like manner it is our privilege to give our best things to Jesus. Our gold and incense can be brought gladly to his altars. Our time, talents, possessions, reputation, capacity for service and suffering, may all be rendered to our royal Master. Such an offering is demanded at our hands.

Our Lord deserves this grand recognition. He is the Prince of peace and the Lord of life. His wisdom is infinite, his goodness is inexhaustible, his love and mercy boundless and free. He is a most princely Prince, and a most loving Lover. All his garments smell of myrrh and cassia out of the ivory palaces. He has shown his favor to us. He has loved us with a great love and ransomed us with a great price. For us he left the glory which he had with the Father before the world was. He was rich, yet for our sakes he became poor. He bore our sins in his body on the cross. He triumphed over death and hell in behalf of our imperiled souls. He is our Mediator, our living Intercessor before the throne. Can we recall what he is and what he has done for us, and not render unto him our best thoughts, our fullest energies, our purest affections, our choicest possessions, our tenderest relations, our grandest consecration of purpose, and our most comprehensive devotion of life, with all its powers and possibilities? Can we do too much for such a Saviour? Can we deny ourselves too rigidly for him who was made in sinful flesh and endured the agonies of Calvary for us? Can we render too precious an offering to the Lover of our souls, who offered his life for our redemption? Can we live too constantly and utterly for him who lives in heaven, " the prime and blossom " of our glorified humanity, to be our Representative and Advocate?

Bring gold, bring incense, bring the heart's best offering to Jesus. Give life, love, friends, and fortune to him. Learn to employ the mind for him. Think of his cause and its necessities. Ask yourself, How can I do more for him? How can I deny myself more fully and economize more closely that I may give more to his cause? How can I lead men whose eyes are closed and whose ears are stopped to discern his beauty and to listen to that voice whose music makes the melody of the heavens? A heart full of love will long to express it. A life given up to a grand purpose will yearn for the opportunity of heroic devotion. And a soul, lifted to something like a just conception of the extent of redeeming mercy and love, will desire above all things to manifest, by sacrifice and service, its boundless attachments, its heroic ardors, and its utter and unmeasured consecration. To know and to love Jesus when he is truly discerned is the soul's most cherished privilege and passion.

O Son of God! thou art worthy; there is none like thee; thou art a tender, loving Saviour; thou art our Brother, and yet the Divinity shines through thy human nature; thou art a Prince and a Deliverer, and worthy of our homage and love! We bring our all to thee. We give thee our gold and our incense, our hearts and our homes, our fortunes and our future. Accept us, for thy mercy's sake, our Lord and King!

We owe this fullness of consecration to ourselves. No man is fully a man till he is fully the Lord's. The treasures we withhold are moth-eaten; the sacrifice which we do not present on the divine altar becomes a stench; the choice things reserved to ourselves are transmuted into curses; the incense which we do not offer to Jesus ministers to self-love, vanity, and idol-worship; the disloyalty and treason to heaven's King produce anarchy, misery, and a dreary desolation and darkness of death in the soul. No man is ever a gainer by any thing withheld from Christ. On the contrary, the intellect consecrated to him is henceforth a brighter intellect, the heart given to him is a purer and happier heart, and the life devoted to his service is a nobler and sublimer life. How precious is the gold which has been laid on his altar! How sweet the incense, diffusing royal perfumes through every chamber of the soul, which has been breathed in prayer before the Lord! How delightful the possession which is held and enjoyed, as belonging to Jesus, sanctified by his acceptance, and used only for his kingdom and glory! How exalted the privilege of doing or suffering something, in some way, for that Saviour who every moment gives us himself and makes us sharers in his immortal inheritance! The will grows stronger, the aim higher, the life more heroic, just as we are able to count all things loss for the excellency of

Jesus. Our relations to others are better understood and the ways of Providence are plainer, the more complete and constant our consecration to Christ.

We may not have much to give; but the whole, however little, is never a small offering. The two mites become a royal gift, which heaven stamps as munificent and rewards with a kingdom, *when it is all one's living.* If we have not gold we can bring incense—the incense of grateful, loving, consecrated hearts. The sincere desire to pour our all at the feet of the Saviour, to give him ten thousand times more than we have to give, to love him with a perfect love, and to serve him with unselfish and faithful souls, is what chiefly commends us to the Father of all goodness and grace. "Richer by far" than all the splendors which wealth can show, "is the heart's adoration." "Dearer to God" than all the munificence of princes, the gifts of genius, or the endowments of learning, "are the prayers of the poor." We may not be able to offer "odors of Eden," "gems of the mountain," "pearls of the ocean," "myrrh from the forest, or gold from the mine;" but a broken, contrite, and loving heart he will not despise, but will assuredly accept, beautify, and ennoble with his presence and salvation.

VIII.

CONSECRATION OF MONEY AND INFLUENCE.

"If riches increase, set not your heart upon them."—PSA. lxii, 10.

IN his letter to "Zion's Herald," "From Detroit to Duluth," Bishop Gilbert Haven recites an incident which occurred in the former city, as follows:

"A new chapel dedicated in the afternoon revealed a new sight to me in Church-begging—that of a rich man doing the solicitation. David Preston was the man that did it, and admirably was it done. He held that house full, with hardly a leak, for two whole hours, and gave them a clear receipt for $7,000 of indebtedness as its pleasant *finale*. You never heard of David Preston? Well, you ought to. He should have many imitators in giving and in begging. He is a banker of Detroit, not very wealthy as wealth goes nowadays—a quarter of a million or so—who loves his Church, and shows his love by his works and words. He took the platform, opened the offertory services with a song by Chaplain M'Cabe, promised another when $5,000 should be raised; started off the $500 subscriptions with one for himself and one for his wife, and worked on and down till he got the whole amount raised. It was a delightful service. Every body enjoyed it. He gave about $3,000 of the whole, and rode home the happiest man of all the crowd. How I wished and prayed that other Davids who are bankers, and others of all names and callings, would go and do likewise in free chapel building, and other benevolences. Brother Preston promises thirty, and even forty, churches in Detroit in not many years, and he will make his promise sure."

David Preston ought to have many imitators in every city. This kind of active, leading, inspiriting beneficence on the part of rich men is the great need of the Church in our time. The greatest boon our Methodism could receive from heaven in any city would be a David Preston. Not that our rich men are not generous, and have not cheerfully sustained the institutions of the Church. There is little ground for complaint in these regards; but leadership, organizing power, and inspiring example in beneficence and home missionary labors on the part of our wealthy men we deplorably lack. What we want in every city is a layman of intelligence, business capacity, ample resources, and *utter consecration to Christ's cause*, who will put himself in the front and cry, "Come on." We could build a church edifice in any growing city every year, if we had a single man among all its men of wealth who would say, "I make my money for Christ; this is Christ's work, and it must go forward; I do not propose to live in a fine house and have Christ's cause turned out-of-doors, to ride in a fine carriage and have Christ's cause go on foot, to be honored by my fellows, and enjoy the fullness of commercial and political distinctions, and have Christ's cause reproached by gainsayers and infidels, and trodden under foot of men. And I ask you who have corresponding ability with myself to assist me in this work, and I ask every body to help, to give their money in however small sums, and their prayers with unrestricted liberality, and let us build up the cause of God in this city." No bishop coming to reside in a metropolitan center, with whatever measure of learning, eloquence, and sanctity, could by any possibility do so much for Christ's cause as one such layman. The Church will never realize her full measure of prosperity till her wealthy and cultured laymen take hold of her enterprises of beneficence, as they take hold of bank and railroad enterprises, *putting themselves into them* with all their resources of energy and capital, resolved to make them a success. And what is chiefly wanted in order to the realization of this state of things is *lay leadership*, which is clear-headed, full-handed, and large-hearted. It is not necessary that such persons should themselves give such extraordinary sums—not more, perhaps, than they might under other circumstances—but that they should give as a privilege, as their mode of preaching the Gospel, and that they should be originators, inspirers, organizers, leaders, John-the-Baptists of benevolence, preparing the way for one to come after them baptizing with fire.

There are two or three considerations bearing on this subject which I ask you, my wealthy brethren, to consider:

1. *Property has its duties.* You will not deny this proposition. If God has given you wealth, and talent for making wealth, he will call you to account for the use of these gifts. He has not given you money for luxury, for selfish indulgence, for worldly show, or for the ends of your personal ambition. You will say

that such men as Haven and Whedon and Simpson and Bowman are bound to consecrate their power of intellect, splendid erudition, practical wisdom, and thrilling eloquence, wholly to the service of our divine Lord; in the same manner, for the same reason, and *to the same extent*, you are bound to devote your property, and your talent for accumulation, to the advancement of the Redeemer's cause and kingdom in the world.

2. *Property has its perils.* As wealth furnishes facilities for indulgence, and gives opportunities for wrongs which could not otherwise be committed, its possession may be regarded as a constant temptation. How few fail to become vain, exacting, consequential, luxurious, pompous, overbearing, and foolishly ambitious who pass under its influence! And how seldom, when parents escape these blighting effects, do children also! In how great a majority of instances is parental wealth a curse rather than a blessing to the sons and daughters of opulence! How few persons who have become rich are happier than when they were poor, or had only a competency! This ought not to be. Every added power or possession should increase our joys, and certainly would, if they were faithfully consecrated to Christ. But that which is wrongfully withheld from God is a curse not only to our own souls, but also to our children after us.

How few wealthy men enjoy as much of the love of God in their hearts as they did when they were poor! They should enjoy more; and would, if they were diligently employing their means and opportunities to spread the Gospel of the Son of God in the earth. "If riches increase, set not your heart upon them." But how difficult not to set the heart upon them! and how certainly will they become the object of an idolatrous affection if they are regarded as a selfish possession, and not simply as trust funds, received for the use of Christ's homeless and churchless poor in this land and in all lands! But how dignified and important the position of Christ's steward—the almoner of God's gifts to perishing men! On the other hand, our Saviour has distinctly taught us that the man is a fool—a moral fool, a fool in respect to spiritual things, that is, the highest kind of a fool—who "layeth up treasure for himself, and is not rich toward God." And "they that will be rich," according to the apostle, "fall into temptation and a snare, and into many foolish and hurtful lusts which drown men in destruction and perdition."

3. *Property brings great possibilities of usefulness to its possessors.* Wealth is not power in the sense in which Bacon made this affirmation of knowledge, but it is an agency which may be successfully employed for the noblest ends. Property is often a kind of blind force in this world, grinding impotently at the mill of the Philistines, or madly wrenching away the pillars of the temple, to its own destruction, or used by ignorance and superstition to acomplish ends which it never contemplated. But money and brains and devout souls can inaugurate revolutions, and lay the foundations of empires. And men who have wealth, and talents, and opportunities for acquisition, should be very grateful to Almighty God, should employ these resources diligently, and should consecrate all their growing gifts on the altars of a Saviour's love

and a world's necessities. Then how much can wealth accomplish, especially when organized, inspired, and aggregated! To what needs will it minister, what necessities relieve, and what sorrows assuage! What wrongs, outrages and oppressions will yield to its beneficent power and pass away! What continents of moral waste will it fertilize, and what fountains of joy and blessing will it open for the refreshment of millions of perishing souls! What institutions of charity, education, and religion will spring up beneath its golden touch, and how vast the results it will accomplish for humanity and God!

"Charge them that are rich in this world, that they be not high-minded, nor trust in uncertain riches, but in the living God, who giveth us richly all things to enjoy ; that they do good, that they be rich in good works, ready to distribute, willing to communicate ; laying up in store for themselves a good foundation against the time to come, that they may lay hold on eternal life."

Let us not envy the rich who use their riches for selfish ends, inasmuch as they lose life's grand opportunity, and have a fearful account to render ; but how distinguished, how favored, how truly enviable the condition of those who, having wealth, can resist its blandishments ; who, possessing an abundance, realize their constant dependence on the Great Giver ; who are rich in good works, ready to distribute and willing to communicate ; who pave with gold the streets of the New Jerusalem, garner up for themselves stores of immortal riches, by transmuting their perishable into imperishable and fadeless possessions, and who lay hold on God's great gift of eternal life, praising and magnifying the grace of that Saviour who was rich, and yet for our sakes became poor, that we through his poverty might be rich!

"I counsel thee," saith Jesus to every man of property in the Church, "to buy of me gold tried in the fire that thou mayest be rich," spiritually rich, rich in faith, and heirs of the eternal kingdom. "I know several rich men," says Bishop Haven, "who would make admirable beggars;" and those who become such for Christ's cause will reign as princes before the throne of God in heaven.

IX.

RICHES IN POVERTY.

"I know thy poverty, but thou art rich."—Rev. ii, 9.

So said the First and the Last to the angel of the Church of Smyrna. In poverty, in tribulation, and in prison, the suffering saints in Smyrna had a right to claim the compassion of their fellows; but He who was alive from the dead, and beheld their works, esteemed them rich, and worthy of congratulations. "Be thou faithful unto death" is the word of Jesus to this tried and persecuted minister, "and I will give thee a crown of life." "He that overcometh," said the Spirit to the Churches, "shall not be hurt of the second death."

"How much better this," says Trench, "poor in the esteem of the world, but rich before Christ, than the condition of the Laodicean angel, rich in his own esteem, but most poor to the sight of Christ? Men saw nothing there save the poverty, but He who sees not as man seeth saw the true riches which this seeming poverty concealed—which, indeed, the poverty, rightly interpreted, *was;* even as He too often sees the real poverty which may lie behind the show of riches; for there are both poor rich-men and rich poor-men in his sight."

Manifestly the teaching is, that while men are

poor, in the sense of not possessing earthly treasures, which are usually supposed to constitute riches, they may be rich in some higher and better sense, in the heirship and possession of a spiritual opulence more golden than gold and more princely than princedoms. There are no such riches as riches of goodness, the wealth of a noble nature, the abundance of a generous heart ; and there is no such poverty as the poverty of a mean soul—a sinful, selfish, sordid character and life. "A little that a righteous man hath is better than the riches of many wicked."

The majority of men are, and must always remain, relatively poor, although the poor of one period and country may enjoy many more advantages and comforts than the rich of another age and land. "The poor," said the Lord to his ancient people, "shall never cease out of the land ;" and the word of Jesus was, "Ye have the poor always with you." Since, then, this is a condition of society which must always exist ; since only the few can, in the very nature of things, be opulent, it is important to consider the hardships, advantages, and opportunities of the poor.

1. *Poverty has its peculiar trials and temptations.* There are manifold privations to be endured. For how many things do the poor vainly sigh ! Not for food and drink only, or chiefly ; but for knowledge, opportunities for culture, for travel, for the gratification of esthetic tastes and benevolent impulses, and for all those things which enrich manhood and ennoble the soul. The necessity of daily toil is not so great a hardship as are the privations born of that necessity. It is hard to feel that there are mines of inestimable value beneath our feet which we can

never fathom; that there are promised lands, flowing with milk and honey, on the other side of us which we can never explore; and that there are heavens above us, glowing with resplendent beauty, into which we can never rise. We are confined, by an iron necessity, to a daily routine of labor. Poverty deprives us not only of wings, but of hands and feet. We can neither fly nor go. We are bound, like galley slaves, to our tasks. We see the needs of the Church and the world, and we cannot supply them. We look on sufferings which we are not able to relieve. The wolf howls at our hearth-stones, and we cannot drive him away. Our children sicken and die, and we can neither minister to their comfort in sickness, nor lay them in their lowly graves, in a manner consonant with the yearnings of our hearts. Who but those who have experienced such trials know how to appreciate their severity? "The destruction of the poor is their poverty."

And of such trials are born temptations. Agur's prayer has generally been regarded as a model of wisdom: "Remove far from me vanity and lies; give me neither poverty nor riches; feed me with food convenient for me; lest I be full, and deny thee, and say, Who is the Lord? or lest I be poor, and steal, and take the name of my God in vain." To trespass on the property rights of others, and to blaspheme the name and providence of God, are the pressing temptations of those who are in circumstances of indigence. How greatly liable also are they to envy of the rich, and discontent with their own condition! Poverty often breeds selfishness, coarseness, and sensuality. Men feeling that the heights are beyond their reach, will often plunge madly into the depths.

But let it be considered that many who are rich are wrongly rich, by extortion, fraud, and violence; and that no Scripture is truer, or more abundantly confirmed by observation, than this: "As the partridge sitteth on eggs, and hatcheth them not; so he that getteth riches, and not by right, shall leave them in the midst of his days, and at his end shall be a fool." Why envy the rich fool? "Labor not to be rich," saith the word of Inspiration, "cease from thine own wisdom. Wilt thou set thine eyes upon that which is not?" that is, having no reality, and not even worthy of being mentioned; "for riches certainly make themselves wings; they fly away as an eagle toward heaven." Even when honestly acquired, they are, by no means, a secure possession. And if they abide, they are often a drag on the soul—a source of corruption, degradation, and ruin. "How hardly shall they that have riches enter into the kingdom of God."

Riches are not transmissible to children, like the blessing of a covenant-keeping God. Men, by much toil and sacrifice, heap up riches, but they know not who shall gather them. "Be not afraid when one is made rich, when the glory of his house is increased; for when he dieth he shall carry nothing away; his glory shall not descend after him." And who is so poor as the man who dies in spiritual insolvency, and goes empty-handed into eternity? "But the mercy of the Lord is from everlasting to everlasting upon them that fear him, and his righteousness unto children's children; to such as keep his covenant, and to those that remember his commandments to do them." And this blessing of a covenant-keeping God is the richest inheritance which any man can transmit to his posterity. And this is the possibility and the privilege of the poor.

2. *Poverty has its advantages.*

It is a source of *physical* profit. "The sleep of a laboring man is sweet, whether he eat little or much." A good digestion, hardness of bone and muscle, and a strong vitality, are blessings not to be despised.

It is a source of *mental* profit. "Better is a handful with quietness, than both the hands full with travail and vexation of spirit." One of God's promises to Zion is, "I will satisfy her poor with bread." His special providence is vouchsafed to the needy.

It is a source of *spiritual* profit. "The poor have the Gospel preached to them;" and this was its joyful evangel, as it fell from the lips of the Son of God himself: "Blessed be ye poor; for yours is the kingdom of God." And the inquiry of the apostle, which is equivalent to the strongest affirmation, is in the same strain: "Hath not God chosen the poor of this world, rich in faith, and heirs of the kingdom which he hath promised to them that love him." The poor are exempted from many temptations and trials which beset the rich; and the struggles which they have to make, the privations which they have to endure, and the conflicts through which they have to pass, are calculated to produce in them the noblest elements of character, to chasten, subdue, and purify their souls, and to lead them into the richest experiences of the things of God. Beneath the garb of poverty treasures more precious than gold are often concealed. Spiritual princes walk the earth disguised as beggars. The world passes them by in contempt, but angels throng their paths. Men say, "They are poor;" but Christ says, "I know their works, and their tribulations, and their poverty; *they are rich.*"

"If the end and the key of history," says Goldwin Smith, "is *the formation of character by effort*, the end and the key of history are the same with the end and key of the life of man. Certainly, if we believe in a Creator, it is difficult to imagine him making such a world as this, with all its abysses of misery and crime, merely that some of his creatures might with infinite labor obtain a modicum of knowledge, which can be of use only in this world, and must come to nothing again when all is done. But if *the formation of character by effort* is the end, every thing has a meaning, every thing has a place." "*Character*, indeed," he observes elsewhere, "seems to be the only thing, within the range of our comprehension, for the sake of which we can conceive God having been moved to create man. Our hearts acquiesce, too, in the dispensation which, instead of creating character in its perfection, leaves it to be perfected by effort. We can conceive no character in a created being, worthy of affection, which is not produced by *a moral struggle;* and, on the other hand, the greater the moral difficulties that have been overcome, the more worthy of affection does the character seem. Try to conceive a being created morally perfect without effort, you will produce a picture of insipidity which no heart can love."

Now the trials of poverty are directly calculated

to develop character. They demand effort, endurance, power of resistance, the grace of contentment, and every thing, in a word, which beautifies and aggrandizes character. They make the whole life a moral struggle; and with the victory come strength, purity, the loftiest manhood, and the most radiant immortality. Through the discipline of such trials, by the help of God's grace, selfishness and Satan are overcome, and the kingdom of Christ is established in the soul.

3. *Poverty has its duties, and its possibilities of great achievement.*

The poor must help the poor, and furnish an example to the rich. It was Lady Maxwell who said that God had taught her, not only that her conveniences must give way to other people's necessities, but also her necessities to other people's extremities. And this grace need the poor. They must learn to do the little they can do, to yield their necessities to the extremities of those poorer than themselves. They must come to the apostle's measure, "As poor, yet making many rich." Those who have nothing, comparatively, must practice benevolence. In the old law it is written, "The poor shall not give less than half a shekel, when they give an offering unto the Lord;" and Jesus taught that the poor widow who cast two mites into the treasury had cast in more than many rich, because, while they had cast in of their abundance, she had cast in all her living. It will often be the privilege of the poor thus to give their whole fortunes to God. And they will win, by such offerings and sacrifices, their proudest distinctions in the kingdom of Christ.

Blessed is that soul of whom Jesus shall say, "I know thy poverty, but thou art rich"—affluent in all spiritual things; for spiritual riches are, after all, the most fruitful source of influence and power existing in this world. They insure access to God, and answer to prayer. They produce sanctity of character, and the outbeaming beauty of holiness. They create that sublime content and profound peace, in the midst of life's conflicts and trials, which is the mightiest argument ever addressed to the understanding of men in favor of the religion of Jesus. And they are of the nature of that treasure in heaven which will enrich the soul forever.

"Of great riches," says Bacon, "there is no real use, except it be in the distribution; the rest is but conceit. So saith Solomon: 'Where much is, there are many to consume it; and what hath the owner, but the sight of it with his eyes?' The personal fruition in any man cannot reach to feel great riches; there is a custody of them, or a power of dole and donative of them, or a fame of them; but no solid use to the owner."

Let us be grateful, then, that if God has not given us riches, neither has he made us responsible for the distribution of them; and let us learn the sublime lesson that "godliness with contentment is great gain," and that he who is faithful in the least things, shall, by no means, lose his reward.

> "Whate'er our willing hands can give,
>   Lord at thy feet we lay;
> Grace will the humble gift receive,
>   And grace at length repay."

X.

THE INSPIRATION OF A GREAT PRESENCE.

"I am the Almighty God; walk before me, and be thou perfect."—GEN. xvii. 1.

WHATEVER resources we may have within ourselves, we are more or less affected by the presence and power of others. Great minds, especially, awe, excite, and uplift our souls. The Infinite mind, therefore, must be a source of unfailing life and inspiration. The divine presence must always be a quickening influence to creature capacities. "I am the Almighty God," or "God, all-sufficient," as Bush renders the Hebrew. All life, power, blessing, completeness, fullness, are in him in infinite sufficiency; so that he can perfectly satisfy all the necessities of his creatures, in all possible unfolding of their powers, and through the whole period of their duration. He is a God of rich, abundant and immeasurable resources.

And God's first requirement is that we should discern his presence, that we should set ourselves diligently to order our ways so as to please him, and that each one of his creatures should realize the poet's aspiration—

"As ever in my great Taskmaster's eye."

And in order that we may come to know him, God

has not only revealed himself in all his works, from every blade of grass and every flower beneath our feet to the fiery stars which glow resplendently in the heavens above our heads, but he has also wrought within us a quick and strong sense of the need of the infinite, so that our souls perpetually yearn for the unseen, the unattained, and the inexhaustible.

Mrs. Livermore is said to be the author of these two memorable sentences: "A divine discontent must pursue all human lives;" and "Life is lonely to every soul." And Dr. Thomas Chalmers, on one occasion, exclaimed, "What a wilderness this world is to the heart, with all it has to inspire happiness;" and he adds, "What a marvelous solitude every man bears about him; and then that other and mysterious seclusion, the intervening veil between us and the Deity." Now, who does not realize that there is something in the human soul which finds no creature companionship, and which therefore makes life lonely, even amid the throng of great cities, and excites that "discontent" of which Mrs. Livermore speaks? How many idiosyncracies of life and eccentricities of conduct have their root in that "marvelous solitude every man bears about him," and into which the world cannot enter? Did any one ever look at a flower, and think how it came up out of the cold earth, or gaze on the clayey yet lovely features of a dead child, marveling whither its little life had gone, without a certain sense of loneliness? Can one behold the ocean in its vastness, or lose himself in the limitless prairie, or roam, in thought, through the infinite heavens, finding no bounds, and not be oppressed and overwhelmed? The truth is, that in all our experiences of nature, of life, of death, we do constantly pass beyond the domain of the finite, and come into a realm, vast, solitary, dreadful, except as it is filled with the light and glory of the divine presence. To walk before God, then, in his conscious nearness, in the realization of his love, in the knowledge of his fatherly care and blessing, in the mysterious fellowship of his infinite nature, is to find a fullness, a companionship, and a sufficiency which nothing but the Gospel of our Lord Jesus Christ ever makes a reality in any human experience. Henceforth the solitude is filled by one glorious presence, and the loneliness is cheered by voices such as make melody in heaven.

To those who walk before God, the uprightness, sincerity, and completeness which the Gospel requires, come to be realizations, almost in the way of natural consequences. That is, if one will set God always before him, he will be self-denying, honest, pure, devoted, even without deliberate determination. His sins and corruptions will fly the divine presence, as owls and bats the light of the sun. If the heaven of his soul glows with the manifest God, his virtues and graces will spring up like grass and flowers in the spring-time, and will come to ripeness and maturity, like the golden grain of summer. Integrity is what is required of us—that is, a *whole* and not a *fractional* life; and, as Bush has said, "Integrity is true scriptural perfection, and without that every thing is defective, and all profession vain."

"Noah," we are told, "was a just man, and perfect in his generations, and Noah walked with God;" and because he walked with God, he was just in character, and perfect in his generation. His obedience was not hypocritical, but sincere; not partial, but complete; not fitful, but constant; not formal, but fervent; not deficient, in a word, but perfect. And such is ever the character of the obedience inspired by the consciousness of the divine presence.

Whedon, commenting on Matthew v, 48, "Be ye therefore perfect, even as your Father in heaven is perfect," says: "Neither St. Paul nor St. James expected that the Christians they addressed would be perfect like angels, or even ideally perfect men; nor perfect performers of God's absolute law. But they did expect *that the law of love might possess a perfect power in their hearts,* and in that would consist the perfected character of their piety." And if the law of love—a law which lives and operates and governs only in the light and under the sanction of the recognized presence of God—does possess a perfect power in our hearts, then our repentance will be deep and thorough, and our abhorrence of sin strong and constant; and then our consecration to Christ and his work will be complete and perpetual. It is reported of Charles XII., of Sweden, that, when he ascended the throne, he wrote on a map of Sweden: "God has given me this kingdom, and the devil shall not take it away from me." In like manner, we shall be able, if the law of love rules in our hearts, to write on body, soul, and possessions: "These are Christ's, and neither self nor Satan shall pervert them to base and unholy uses." Then, too, faith will grasp all the promises of the inspired word, and rely with fullest confidence on the covenant love of God. Then the choice of God's way and work will be cheerful and absolute. Then all malice will be expelled from the heart, and gentleness, kindness, forbearance, patience, and resignation will dwell there like angels. Then service and sacrifice for Jesus and his cause will be rather sought than shunned. Then hope will be exultant, the victory over sin and Satan constant, and the confident assurance of a final triumph over death and hell an abiding and glorious experience.

XI.

THE PERFECT MAN.

"If any man offend not in word, the same is a perfect man."
JAMES iii, 2.

BEHOLD, then, that rarest of sights, the completed Christian character. And what is, at once, the test and the proof of manhood's perfection? A bridled tongue, a mouth in which there is no guile, that supreme knowledge and sanctity which "out of a good conversation" show forth "meekness of wisdom." Nor shall we marvel at this if we consider that the tongue of the unsanctified "is a fire, a world of iniquity," that "it setteth on fire the course of nature, and is set on fire of hell," that it is more untamable than any beast or serpent, that "it is an unruly evil full of deadly poison," and that it is impossible to estimate the waste and desolation which it has wrought in the earth. As the great ships "driven of fierce winds," so are the mightiest souls tempest-tossed and rudderless on life's ocean when speech is perturbed and passionate. As with a bit in a horse's mouth, so does a wise man, by a godly restraint on his tongue, "bridle the whole body" of his life and conversation.

The Psalmist characterizes the sinner as one "whose mouth speaketh vanity," and our Lord teaches that the soul is defiled by that "which cometh out of the mouth." "Not physical touch, but moral action," says Whedon, "makes a man truly impure before God." The irremissible sin against the Holy Ghost seems to be impossible without *utterance*. "Whosoever *speaketh* against the Holy Ghost, it shall not be forgiven him, neither in this world, neither in the world to come." Of so great significance, in Scripture estimation, are *words!* The bad feeling, the wicked disposition, the impious thought, must find expression in order to reach its consummation. The subjective must become the objective. The soul must body itself forth by speech, and behold its creation, and acknowledge it, and feel its retroactive influence and excitive power, and so become intensified in its feeling and purpose, before the moral quality reaches its highest type of sin or holiness.

The propriety of making an ability to keep the tongue under constant government a proof of perfect Christian manhood is manifest from two considerations:

1. The state of the appetites and passions is clearly indicated, on the whole, by the drift of our conversation. There may be deceit and hypocrisy, but the stream, however disguised, will not fail to exhibit the character of the fountain from which it flows. "The tongue," says Benson, "is an index of the heart, and he who does not transgress the law of truth, or love, or purity, or humility, or meekness, or patience, or seriousness, *with his tongue*, will, with the same grace, so rule all his dispositions and actions as to manifest that he has in him the mind that was in Christ, and walks as Christ walked."

"The mouth of the righteous," says David, "speaketh wisdom, and his tongue talketh of judgment;" and he immediately adds, as a reason, "The law of God is in his heart;" and the moral force within determines the wisdom and judgment with which he speaks. Moreover, David's King and Lord has asserted the same general principle in the following plain and unmistakable words: "A good man out of the good treasure of his heart bringeth forth that which is good; and an evil man out of the evil treasure of his heart bringeth forth that which is evil: *for of the abundance of the heart his mouth speaketh.*" Our speech, therefore, bewrayeth us. Our words are exponents of our affections. And nothing will meet the exigencies of our spiritual state but that grace which, "casting down imaginations and every high thing that exalteth itself against the knowledge of God," brings "into captivity every thought to the obedience of Christ."

2. Our words are prophecies of our actions. The evil deed will not be performed if the speech can be restrained. He who can subdue the angry word will not strike the vengeful blow. The victory which we obtain over ourselves is complete when the tongue is bridled. In this triumph are the seeds of a thousand triumphs. Golden speech will fructify in golden deeds. When no corrupt communication proceeds out of our mouth, nothing but "that which is good to the use of edifying," and calculated to "minister grace unto the hearers," then we may be sure that in walk and conduct we shall be examples of purity, beneficence, and Christian consecration. Gracious words on the lips are the blossoms which indicate gracious

seed in the heart and gracious fruitage in the life. "Let the word of Christ dwell in you richly in all wisdom; teaching and admonishing one another, in psalms and hymns and spiritual songs singing with grace in your hearts to the Lord. And whatsoever ye do, in word or deed, do all in the name of the Lord Jesus, giving thanks to God and the Father by him." Now observe that in this passage the word of Christ in the heart, the language of teaching, admonition, and praise on the lips, and the will of the Lord done in the whole ordering of the life, closely and beautifully correspond. If any one, therefore, "seem to be religious, and bridleth not his tongue," manifestly he "deceiveth his own heart." The finger of inspiration points at such a man derisively, as the Holy Oracle affirms for the instruction of mankind, "*This man's religion is vain.*"

Speech, the crowning gift of God to man, is capable of the grossest perversion and the most shameful abuse; but it is also a weapon of great power. The lips of a good man are as honey and the honeycomb. They drop sweetness. They charm while they admonish, and they attract while they rebuke. There are words of wisdom and faith which linger in our memories like the tones of bells which we heard in childhood. On words of prayer and sacred song we rise even to the golden gates of the New Jerusalem. A sanctified speech is at once the proof and prophecy of Christ's kingdom in the world; and not to stumble in word is the indisputable demonstration of the perfect man.

It is a striking remark of the author of "Ecce Homo," that "The door of heaven, so to speak, can be opened only from within." Whoever would speak the words of God must be consciously in the presence of God. The message of Jesus, to reach the hearts of men, must be delivered in the spirit of Jesus. A young minister said in a religious assembly, "There is an old gentleman present who gave out a hymn in a meeting which I attended, and during the reading of that hymn I was convinced of my sins and moved to seek the salvation of my soul." What sermon and prayer and exhortation had failed to accomplish, was thus mysteriously wrought. How evident that it was rather the manner than the matter of the performance which produced the result! The old gentleman opened the door of heaven *from within*, and so the common words of Christian song rang with the melodies of the celestial world. It was as if the familiar strain had been chanted with the accompanying notes of angels. Here is a great lesson to be mastered by Christian workers. They must stand inside the gates of the New Jerusalem, while they proclaim the words of life to the weary wanderers who are far off in sin and misery. Thus the commonest speech will be instinct with divine love, and will charm and attract with a strange eloquence. There is a touch of tenderness, a melting of compassion, a yearning of sympathy which is not taught by art, which is never learned from books, which is not the gift of genius, and which cannot be acquired in the schools, but which comes inevitably with the glowing realizations of Christian experience. There is no eloquence like that which blazes forth from the hidden fires of a sanctified soul. There is no logic like the logic of a holy heart. There is no argument like that which

Christ has inspired by his presence. There is no such language of persuasion as that which has been learned in view of the cross and the saintly Sufferer.

How, my brethren, can we tell of the sweetness of the heavenly manna, except we have the taste of it in our mouths? It is said of the evangelical M'Cheyne, whose pulpit was such a throne of power, that "he fed on the Word, not in order to prepare himself for his people, but for personal edification." And yet no technical preparation for lecture or sermon could have been worth so much to his hearers as this constant communion of his own soul with the precious truth of God's word. Personal edification is, in its results, Church edification also. If fountains of salvation are unsealed in our souls, some beneficent streams will flow forth to gladden the weary wastes of lives blasted by sin, and to refresh the spirits of saints whose lips are feverish with desire for the waters of life.

"Not the words he spoke," says the biographer of M'Cheyne, "but the holy manner in which he spoke, was the chief means in arresting souls." Now it is not within the reach of many of us to speak words of extraordinary eloquence and power, but all of us can speak in a gracious manner, with a holy earnestness, and with evident sincerity and fervor of desire. The richest gifts of heaven are the commonest—the most attainable. The highest endowment for a Christian worker is a genuine, irrepressible love of souls; and tender concern for the perishing, jealous regard for Christ's cause, fullness of consecration to the work of an evangelist, and longing desires for the prosperity of Zion, are sources of influence and power which are freely dispensed at a throne of grace by the munificent Head of the Church. This precious baptism all of us may receive who wait and long for it.

In Rutherford's "Rules of Holy Living," the very first is, "That hours of the day, less or more time, for the word and prayer, be given to God." Was it not in those "hours" that he learned the freedom, sweetness, and strength of Christ's love? Hear him exclaim, as he comes from his place of holy communion, "How little of the sea can a child carry in his hand; as little am I able to take away of my great Sea, my boundless and running-over Christ Jesus!" It is not a strange thing that a minister who *felt* that Christ's love was an inexhaustible sea, and that it was boundless and running over in the experience of his soul, should have that tender yearning for the unsaved, leading him to affirm, "I would lay my dearest joys in the gap between you and eternal destruction. My witness is in heaven, your heaven would be two heavens to me, and your salvation two salvations." And it is not strange that this *inside touch* should have opened the gates of heaven to many perishing souls.

And what we most need in our great life business of finding sinners and bringing them to Jesus, is not, perhaps, more ability or better appliances, but *the advantage of position.* We need to stand where we can open the door of heaven *from the inside.* Then the light will stream forth to illumine the darkness of sin and unbelief; and then voices, terrible as the thunders of the Apocalypse, but sweet as those which announced a Saviour's birth, will startle and charm the sinner's heart, and multitudes will be led to accept life and salvation.

XII.

PURPOSE OF HEART.

"Who, when he came and had seen the grace of God, was glad, and exhorted them all that with purpose of heart they would cleave unto the Lord."—Acts ii, 23.

GREATHEART is one of the noblest conceptions of Bunyan's genius. He was a hero of the grandest type, incapable of fear or discouragement. He was the helper and deliverer of all weak and imperiled Pilgrims. It was Greatheart who cheered and guided the timorous women and children, who defied the lions, and who struck down Giant Grim with a great blow, despite his hideous roaring and bloody threats. Greatheart, in a word, was always valiant, and was always a conqueror. He led the Pilgrims to the Palace Beautiful, and he conducted their trembling steps through the Valley of the Shadow of Death. No man has ever come, with songs of Christian joy and triumph, to the gates of the Celestial City without his aid.

It shows how deeply Bunyan had drunk from the fountains of Inspiration, and how genuine and thorough had been his Christian experience, that he makes Greatheart not only a source of consolation, but also of strength and victory. Power and prevalence in the religious life come not of the brain but of the heart. Hence the Psalmist exclaims: "Thou hast proved my heart; thou hast visited me in the night; thou hast tried me and shalt find nothing; I am purposed that my mouth shall not transgress." And this *purpose*, which embodies victory, was born of the visitation of the heart—of its trials and proof, under searching and solemn circumstances. It had its deep root in purified affections.

In like manner, we are told, when Barnabas visited, with apostolic authority, the infant Church at Antioch, and saw the grace of God and was glad, he exhorted them all "that with purpose of heart they would cleave unto the Lord." The genitive of the noun in regimen has here, as often, according to Bloomfield, the force of an adjective, and signifies "with hearty and determined purpose and intent;" and with such purpose or determination of heart the apostle moves these believers to cleave unto the Lord, clinging unto him *with affectionate regard;* "for the original word," continues Bloomfield, "signifies properly to remain by, and, with a dative of a thing, to persevere in, but with that of a person, *to continue attached to.*" Or, as Dr. Clarke expresses it, "To be a Christian is to be united with Christ, to be of one spirit with him: to continue to be a Christian is to continue in that union. It is absurd to talk of being children of God, and of absolute, final perseverance, when the soul has lost its spiritual union; there is no perseverance but *in clinging to the Lord.*"

But this affectionate clinging unto the Lord is only realized when there is a purpose in the soul, which wells up from the great deep of the affections; or, in other words, it is *the purpose of the heart* which secures practical perseverance in the Christian life.

The will is the regal faculty in the human constitution. Men are not saved by their understandings or their affections, except they will to be saved. Knowledge, desire, conviction of duty, sense of need, fear of loss, nor all of them, will bring a man to Christ. When he says, from the very throne of his being, "I *will arise* and go to my Father," then the mighty transformation begins. And the light which the Holy Spirit sheds on the understanding, the sense of guilt which it excites in the conscience, the deep spiritual necessities which it discloses to the soul, and the clearness with which it reveals the path of duty, interest, and happiness, are only so many arguments for that supreme decision of the will, which, more than any thing else, governs conduct, determines character, and shapes destiny. God works in us *to will* and *to do*—that is, to lead us to decide and act—in order that his good pleasure may be accomplished in our salvation.

But how shall the soul be kept up to its high purpose? There is opposition to meet, a warfare to wage, discouragement to be overcome, painful and protracted duties to be discharged, and a great life-work for immortality to be accomplished. Can one constantly review the grounds of his decision? Can he consider perpetually the great argument for rectitude and a holy life? Can one, by strength of purpose, walk every moment as in eternity? Powerful as is the will, it must have supports. It does not act capriciously and tyrannically. Its throne of dominion must have some adequate basis. There must be some reason for its decisions, or they will not stand. Especially is this the case in the religious life, because the will is weak in that which is good, being touched like every other faculty of our being with the blight of depravity.

Now it may be said that there are many things to hold the will to its high purpose of loyalty to heaven and service to man. There are duty, right, interest, happiness, obligations assumed, the fear of condemnation, and the hope of heaven. But the trouble is, that these are things which have *to be kept in mind*, and just at the moment when we most need to remember them they are forgotten. It is not thus with *the purpose of the heart.* That is our life. The inspiration of our love is an abiding power. The chief affection makes the soul's atmosphere. The patriot does not need the great argument for patriotism resting on duty, obligations incurred, and interests involved, to move him to the front when his country is in peril. He *loves* his country, cherishes its institutions, and hopes for its future, and that love determines his purpose and conduct. The child does not need to say, "I am under obligation to my parents, I owe them every thing, and it will be a shame if I do not honor and obey them." The truth rather is, that the filial affection governs the child unconsciously. Because it loves, it chooses, constantly, the very things which its parents choose for it. And so obedience is not a yoke, service is not a burden, and the loving child is not duty's slave.

And thus it is with a genuine Christian life. It is an exalted patriotism, an experience of filial love, a loyal attachment, kindling to an ardor of enthusiasm, for a Prince and Saviour whom we have enthroned in our hearts. The Christian man not only says,

> "Let thy will, not mine, be done,"

but also,

> "Let thy will *and mine* be one;"

and in this *oneness of purpose,* this communion of soul, this perpetual choosing of Christ, as a bride chooses perpetually her husband and lord, he finds the grandest realizations of life and the surest pledge of immortality.

XIII.

SALVATION THROUGH GOD'S FORBEARANCE.

"And account that the long-suffering of our Lord is salvation."
2 Pet. iii, 15.

It is not only true that there is wickedness in the world, but also that in many cases it is long-continued and prosperous. "Doth God know?" is the exultant infidel inquiry. Does he concern himself in regard to human interests? Does he hear the sighs of the oppressed? Does he consider the ignorance, superstition, poverty, and wretchedness which are in the world? In one word, what is the meaning of the divine forbearance? There is no question in regard to the fact. God bears long with men. He is slow to anger. "Forbearance," according to Macknight, "is that disposition in God by which he restrains himself from instantly punishing sinners." But why does he restrain himself? These mockers, described in the context, said that the divine delay meant *slackness;* but the apostle insists that its significance is *salvation.* They said, "Where is the promise of his coming?" "And scoffers, walking after their own lusts," have kept up the refrain to the present hour, shouting incessantly, "All things continue as they were from the beginning of the creation," and affirming vehemently, "God is not observant of these matters, and it is safe to live in sin and for the rewards of pleasure and power." The apostle, on the other hand, is bold to declare, "The Lord is not slack concerning his promise, as some men count slackness," and "the day of the Lord *will come*," in which every earthly possession will perish, and there will be "a day of judgment and perdition of ungodly men;" and there is no wisdom or safety but in "all holy conversation and godliness," and no inheritance in the new earth and heavens, "wherein dwelleth righteousness," except for such as are found of him "in peace without spot and blameless."

Because judgment against an evil work is not executed speedily, men conclude, in numerous instances, that it will not be executed at all. They despise the riches of God's goodness, forbearance, and long-suffering, which are designed to lead them sweetly, but effectually, to repentance and a life of holiness, by making it an excuse for continuance in sin, and so treasuring up unto themselves wrath against the day of wrath and the revelation of the righteous judgment of God. "By goodness," says Bengel, "God restrains his wrath; by forbearance, he keeps himself, as it were, unknown until he is revealed; by long-suffering, he delays his righteous judgment." But it is certainly a great abuse of the divine mercy to suppose that this hiding of his power, and restraint upon his wrath, and slowness to punish, mean indulgence of sin, laxity of government, disregard of the ends of justice, and indifference to the facts of human condition. Let us rather conclude that the long-suffering of our Lord is salvation. "Reckon, as you justly may," says Bloomfield, "that this long-extended waiting and forbearance of the Lord is meant to be our salvation ; that is, to promote it, by giving us opportunity for *working it out.*" By the use of all moral means and spiritual persuasives, in infinite forbearance and love, the Lord would lead us to repentance and the formation of holy characters. His long-suffering is gracious, designed to give us space and opportunity to escape from sin and condemnation, to prepare for the solemn scenes of judgment and retribution, and to grow up into his image and the fellowship of his love. The result will be, if our opportunities are properly improved, the salvation of our own souls, and the salvation, through our instrumentality, of the souls of many others. This is in accordance with the whole scheme of redemption. Jesus Christ is set forth, as a propitiation, to declare the divine righteousness for the remission of sins through the forbearance of God. And it is through this forbearance, through the space allotted for repentance and for the remedial agencies of the Gospel, that the just God is enabled to become the justifier of the believer in Christ.

The God of Israel proclaimed himself unto Moses as "The Lord God, merciful and gracious, long-suffering and abundant in goodness and truth, keeping mercy for thousands, forgiving iniquity, transgression, and sin, and that will by no means clear the guilty." Again and again is it declared that this God, "full of compassion and gracious, long-suffering and plenteous in mercy and truth," will, though he delay long, most assuredly mark every offense against his character and government, and overwhelm with his wrath the finally impenitent and incorrigible. "The long-suffering of God waited in the days of Noah;" but the delay was not slackness, or remissness in the divine government. The patriarch, believing in God's word, and having faith's vision of things "not seen as yet," "condemned the world," while he became himself an heir of the righteousness which is by faith.

The forbearance of God is not, therefore, any just ground for continuance in sin. It is no encouragement to impurity and rebellion. On the contrary, it is the highest dissuasive. Terrible must be the anger of infinite Love when it shall finally blaze forth to consume the sinner! Fearful beyond expression is the wrath of incensed holiness! When the forbearance and long-suffering of God, provoked and outraged by persistent impenitence, made an excuse for high-handed wickedness, and abused and insulted by a scoffing infidelity, shall at last arise for judgment and vindication, inconceivably awful must be the doom of its blasted and helpless victims!

The forbearance of God is the ground of our hope of life and salvation. But for his long-suffering mercy we should long since have perished. May that forbearing goodness lead us to repentance! May it melt our hearts into genuine contrition! May it lead us now to turn unto him with full purpose of soul!

The forbearance which God shows to us, we ought, in our poor measure, to show to our fellow-men. If we have the genuine Christian spirit we shall bear much with men, and through many weary years, in order to secure their salvation. By long-suffering, as well as by pureness, knowledge, and love unfeigned, do we commend the grace of God. Goodness, faith, meekness, temperance, are not more certainly the fruit of the Spirit. We must reprove, rebuke, exhort; but with all long-suffering and doctrine.

In all this Jesus is our perfect example. He endured the cross, despising the shame, in order to the salvation of a perishing race. He carries our griefs and is touched with all our sorrows, when we enter into his spirit and reproduce his life of ministering and forbearing love. May he fill us with his grace, and make us his messengers to the world!

XIV.

THE PERFECTION OF BEAUTY.

"Out of Zion, the perfection of beauty, God hath shined."—Psa. l, 2.

GOD himself is the standard of all excellence. There can be no higher reason for a certain type of character than that God has chosen that type of character. There can be no completer justification of any course of conduct than that it is in accordance with the divine mind. In every respect, theologically, spiritually, and esthetically, God is the standard. Whatsoever things are true, just, good, honest, lovely, worthy of admiration and praise, are so because of their harmony with the nature, choice, purpose, and delight of the infinite Mind. All the elements of beauty, as they are stated by Ruskin, exist in perfection in the divine Being. In him is infinity, comprehensive unity, sublime and eternal repose, perfect symmetry, living, energetic, spiritual purity, and that absolute self-completeness which in its lower forms, in men, is revealed as equipoise, moderation, restraint, and superiority to passion, pride, or changefulness. Completeness is, beyond all question, the crowning element in beauty. And this supposes not only the perfection of every part, function, and quality, but also incapacity of growth, accretion, or development in the future, or under any other circumstances. That only is entirely beautiful which can be no more so, by any possibility, through any change, combination, unfolding, or revealment. God is the supreme loveliness. He can never be any more beautiful than he is at this moment, and has been from eternity. But all creatures, enjoying his presence and having a discernment of his excellences, will discover more and more of his infinite beauty, and will have increasing satisfaction in the grandeur and glory of his character, through the eternal ages.

To dwell in the house of the Lord all the days of his life, that he might behold, as revealed in his sanctuary, *the beauty of the Lord*, was, in the estimation of the Psalmist, the one grand object of life and endeavor. Nothing so purifies, quickens, exalts, and ennobles the human soul as such visions of the beauty, the infinite loveliness, of the divine nature. The beauty of the Lord is the beauty of holiness— *wholeness;* truth, purity, integrity, without any deviation or deficiency.

This infinite beauty is indescribable—inconceivable. If, as Rutherford says, " the discourses of angels, or love-books written by the congregation of seraphim," would not suffice to tell the love of Christ, then who shall picture, by word or symbol, that faultless loveliness which is the splendor and glory of the adorable Jehovah?

And yet it is said, "Thine eyes shall see the King in his beauty," and, "In that day shall the Lord of hosts be for a crown of glory, and for a diadem of beauty, unto the residue of his people." "Blessed are the pure in heart, for they shall see God." The extent and clearness of our vision of the Infinite One will depend on the measure of our spiritual purity and love. "The belief of truth," says Bacon, "is the enjoying of it;" and the discovery and enjoyment of the celestial beauty of our divine King will closely correspond. If we find satisfaction in God, and love to meditate on his goodness, we shall, with growing distinctness, discern "how excellent is his name in all the earth." A man, as Emerson argues, "in proportion to the energy of his thought and will, *takes up the world into himself.*" He possesses so much of earth and sky as he is able to appropriate. No man is charmed by voices which he does not hear, or enraptured by visions which he does not see, albeit the air may throb with melody, and the heavens glow with beauty. And there are men who are esthetically *atheists—without God.* Having eyes, they do not see; and having ears, they do not hear; and having hearts, they do not perceive, nor understand. The beauty of the Lord is nothing to them. They have no vision of faith which is as the breaking of the morning. And they have no revelation of God as a crown of glory and a diadem of beauty. How invaluable that spiritual energy of thought and will which seizes on God, and, in some poor sense, takes him in, makes him the portion and delight of the soul, and exults in him as "a joy forever!"

> "I would not ask to climb the sky,
>   Nor envy angels their abode;
> I have a heaven as bright and high
>   *In the blest vision of my God!*"

Zion is declared to be "the perfection of beauty." because, as Horne observes, "There that glory first arose and shone which, like the light of heaven, soon diffused itself abroad over the face of the whole earth." It is God in the Church which makes the Church beautiful and glorious, and that despite poverty, persecution, and reproach. When Sir Harry Vane was dragged up the Tower Hill, sitting on a sled, to suffer death, as the champion of English laws and liberties, one of the multitude cried out to him, "*You never sat on so glorious a seat!*" It was the cause which he represented that made his humble seat glorious; and it is the cause which she represents, and the wonderful Being who has chosen her as a dwelling-place, which lead men to exclaim, "The perfection of beauty! the joy of the whole earth!" "The glory of Lebanon," God said of Zion, "shall come unto thee, the fir tree, the pine tree, and the box together, to beautify the place of my sanctuary; *and I will make the place of my feet glorious.*" "Beautiful for situation" is "the city of our God, the mountain of his holiness."

"Churches exist in this world," says Froude, "to remind us of the eternal laws which we are bound to obey. So far as they do this, they fulfill their end, and are honored in fulfilling it."

And Churches which do not remind men of the eternal laws of this spiritual kingdom, fail to accomplish the object for which Jesus Christ instituted his Church in the world. They may have a grand historic record, venerable traditions, an imposing ritual, an orthodox faith, and a position of high culture and great social respectability; and yet be without that measure of moral power and spiritual energy which are the only infallible tests of a true Church of Jesus Christ. "We are the circumcision," says Paul, "which worship God in the Spirit, and rejoice in Christ Jesus, and have no confidence in the flesh." In the position, influence, and history of such a Church, the prayer of the Psalmist will certainly be answered: "Let thy work appear unto thy servants, and thy glory unto their children. And *let the beauty of the Lord our God be upon us*, and establish thou the work of our hands upon us; yea, the work of our hands, establish thou it."

XV

WELLS WITHOUT WATER.

"These are wells without water."—2 Pet. ii, 17.

The Lord complains of his ancient people, by the prophet, "They have forsaken me, the fountain of living waters;" and Jesus declares of the soul enriched by his grace, "The water that I shall give him shall be in him a well of water springing up into everlasting life." The Psalmist, lifting his longing soul to the Father of all goodness, exclaims, "All my springs are in thee." Every stream which gladdens life flows from the infinite Fountain. The Lord Jehovah is the strength, the trust, and the song of his people; therefore, with joy shall they draw water out of the wells of salvation. The old prophetic promise to such as perform the fast which the Lord hath chosen, and accomplish in the earth the beneficent work of the Gospel, is, "The Lord shall guide thee continually, and satisfy thy soul in drought, and make fat thy bones; and thou shalt be like a watered garden, and like a spring of water whose waters fail not." Joel predicted that a fountain should come forth from the house of the Lord—an inexhaustible spring of happiness and prosperity from the divine presence. And with this accords

Christ's promise, that the Holy Spirit in the soul of a believer should be as rivers of living water. And the assurance which the Son of God sends, ringing like an anthem of celestial music, down from heaven, as the Apocalyptic vision closes, is in the same exalted strain: "I will give unto him that is athirst of the fountain of the water of life freely." To which we may add the words descriptive of the supreme happiness of the saints, as they stand, in their stainless robes, in the place of loftiest vision, "The lamb which is in the midst of the throne shall feed them, and shall lead them unto living fountains of waters;" or, as Bengel renders, to "the life-water fountains"— infinite depths of life and joy.

In our present experience, therefore, and in our prospective reward, the Holy Spirit is a fountain of life to our souls, full of inspiration and refreshment.

> "The well of life to us thou art—
> Of joy the swelling flood;
> Wafted by thee, with willing heart
> We swift return to God.
>
> 'We soon shall reach the boundless sea;
> Into thy fullness fall;
> Be lost and swallowed up in thee—
> Our God, our All in all."

What, then, are we to understand by wells without water, and clouds driven by the tempests, but Christians who promise by their professions what they do not supply in their lives, disappointing just and reasonable expectations? "A most lively comparison," says Bloomfield, "to designate the persons in question as promising much, but constantly disappointing expectation; specious but deceiving, as wells destitute of water, and clouds which bring no rain; than which no disappointment can, in Eastern countries, be greater; and of which the former sometimes not merely disappoint, but lure travelers to destruction."

"Wells without water;" such are destitute of spiritual life, although they have come into nominal relations with Christ and his Church. There are two classes of these—hypocrites and backsliders. The former are like wax flowers, vainly striving to represent an inimitable original; the latter are the genuine blossoms, dried and withered, reminding us of a fragrance and beauty which have hopelessly departed. The form of godliness is maintained, sentiments of piety are cherished, orthodoxy in belief is zealously upheld, and the garb of a respectable godliness is ostentatiously flaunted in the face of the world; but the power of faith, the warmth of love, the sincerity and earnestness of desire for the salvation of souls, the tender concern for Christ's cause which weeps over the desolations of Zion, the spirit of consecration and sacrifice, and that fullness of the blessing of the Gospel of Christ which overflows to a perishing race, near and remote, even to the ends of the earth—these are unknown or forgotten experiences. And yet, as Bishop Foster has observed, "it is holiness, not the profession of it, that will give us influence both with God and men; winging our prayers with faith and our counsels with power, deriving power from above, and sending out from us currents of power through the earth. 'God in us, the hope of glory,' shining out in the even and resplendent beauty of a holy life, will give us, unperceived, it may be, and unknown to ourselves, an influence which will draw many after us, to brighten in our crown of rejoicing forever."

"Wells without water;" such were these teachers, comments Macknight, "wholly void of knowledge." And how could they teach what they did not know? How can those break the bread of life to others who have not themselves been fed? Every genuine Christian is a prophet, that is, a teacher of righteousness. He knows something which he has received directly from the great Head of the Church. He is a witness to the saving power of divine grace. He has proved the sufficiency of the Gospel for the remission of sins and the sanctification of the soul. He can take any trembling sinner by the hand and lead him to Jesus. He can teach the great lessons of repentance, faith, and trust in God's promises. He is a guide to the blind, and a light to those who are in darkness. He has not learned speculative divinity, it may be, or the theology of the schools; but he has heard the voice of the Spirit, he has apprehended the plain teachings of the inspired word, and he has proved, by his experience, the power of prayer, the excellence of worship, and the beauty of the way of holiness. Those who call themselves by the Christian name, and yet are without this knowledge, or incapable of imparting its savor of life to others, are "wells without water." Such Christians and Christian Churches are like the mirage of the desert, which gladden the eyes of travelers with visions of refreshing waters, but furnish for their parched lips no joyous streams.

"Wells without water;" having the form but lacking the power of godliness. Alas, how many march under the banner of Christ who lack that divine earnestness of soul which brought our Lord from heaven, and which, to a greater or less extent, characterizes all his genuine followers! What we chiefly need is that white heat of enthusiasm, which rather burns than glows, which makes us restless with desire to work for Jesus, and which, whether we purpose it or not, flames forth, like the morning, on the darkness of the world.

"Wells without water;" such are all who lack true beneficence of life. If the soul be a fountain of love, it will overflow in genuine charity to the bodies and souls of all who need. If Christ dwells in his saints it is as a well of water, or, as the word means, an up-springing fountain, and it cannot be shut up in its own narrow bounds, but out-gushes with life and love, irrigating and gladdening all earth's desert wastes. A genuine Christian experience is as the sea, reaching to all shores, fresh, flowing, and forever.

"Christ," says the author of "Ecce Homo," "held that a despicable Christianity which flung to the poor some unregarded superfluity: he valued more the mite which the widow spared out of her poverty;" and the same writer argues that the most effective means of Christian propagandism was found in the fact that "there worked within the Church, and outward round its whole circumference, the living, diffusive, assimilative power of the Christian Humanity." And this large, uncalculating beneficence has, in every age, characterized the Church of Jesus Christ in the earth. That Church is not only an organization for conquest, but also an institution of benevolence. If it carries in one hand the sword of the Spirit, and in the other the torch of truth, its bosom is filled with loaves for the perishing, and joys bloom along its onward and triumphant march, as flowers in the pathway of Spring.

"We dwell far from the well," says Rutherford, "and complain but dryly of our dryness:" no marvel, then, that we become as "wells without water." But with Jesus is "the fountain of life," and we shall act wisely if we sing the song which Israel sang, "Spring up, O well," till the Lord God shall bring us "into a good land, a land of brooks of water, of fountains and depths."

> "With me, I know, I feel, thou art;
>   But this cannot suffice,
> Unless thou plantest in my heart
>   A constant paradise.
>
> My earth thou wat'rest from on high—
>   But make it all a pool:
> Spring up, O Well, I ever cry;
>   Spring up within my soul.
>
> Come, O my God, thyself reveal;
>   Fill all this mighty void:
> Thou only canst my spirit fill;
>   Come, O my God, my God!"

But to prayer must be added Christian activity. It is the workers in the Lord's vineyard who are most abundantly refreshed with the streams of life and salvation. And the gifts of grace which earnest Christians impart to others, do, by no means, impoverish their own souls. Then go, break thy bread to the hungry, and point a lost world to its Redeemer, and thou shalt receive, in largest measure, the "gift of God," the living water which satisfies the thirsty soul, forever.

> "Work for the good that is nighest,
>   Dream not of greatness afar;
> That glory is ever the highest
>   Which shines upon men as they are.
> Work, though the world would defeat you,
>   Heed not its slander and scorn;
> Nor weary till angels shall greet you
>   With smiles through the gates of the morn.
>
> "Offer thy life on the altar;
>   In the high purpose be strong;
> And if the tired spirit should falter,
>   Then sweeten thy labor with song.
> What if the poor heart complaineth,
>   Soon shall its wailing be o'er;
> For there, in the rest which remaineth,
>   It shall grieve and be weary no more."

XVI.

THE MOUNTAIN OF MYRRH.

"Until the day break and the shadows flee away, I will get me to the mountain of myrrh, and to the hill of frankincense."—CAN. iv, 6.

THE purpose expressed in this passage, if literally interpreted, is to pass the night-watches in the fragrant mountains, from whose odoriferous trees myrrh and incense were extracted. Metaphorically, it conveys the idea of charming privacy, delightful communion, and perfect content and satisfaction, till the shadows of night shall flee away, and the beams of the Orient golden the heavens. A night in the mountain of myrrh and in the hill of frankincense is a night of wakefulness and watchfulness, in prayer and holy fellowship with the Redeemer and Lover of our souls. Perfumes afforded great refreshment to the inhabitants of the east, and so naturally came to express, in a figurative way, whatever was pleasing to the mind or enrapturing to the soul. They soothed, excited, and gratified the weary senses with aromatic odors, so that rest, stimulation, and recovered strength were possible to the exhausted body. Any thing, therefore, producing a corresponding effect on mind or heart—comforting, inspiring, arousing to continued exertion, and bringing, mediately, fresh vigor to the prostrated powers, and increased energy for life's conflicts, may be tropically described as a mountain of myrrh and a hill of frankincense.

For the Christian, this mountain of myrrh and hill of frankincense is his place of secret prayer—of intercourse and communion with the God and Rock of his salvation. Here he is rested, quieted in spirit, strengthened, aroused to fresh activities, comforted as a mother comforteth her child, exalted by contemplation of the Highest and Holiest, and prepared for the duties, trials, and combats which await him in life.

We read of our divine Master, not only that he was often "alone praying," but that "he withdrew himself into the wilderness and prayed," and that going up into a mountain for that specific purpose he "continued all night in prayer to God." And, on another occasion, "rising up a great while before day, he went out, and departed into a solitary place, and there prayed." "The day after the Sabbath," says Whedon, "He retired from the crowds to find a place of prayer. It was as if to recruit his spiritual strength, that had been expended upon such a number of miracles, preachings, and debates, *by communion with God.*" He went from the city to the mountain, from the thronged ways to the solitary places, from intercourse with man to fellowship with God. It was not the forgiveness of sins which he craved, or purging from corruption, or a fuller consecration, or a larger baptism of the Spirit; for there was no guile in his heart or life, and he had said, "Lo, glad I come to do thy will, O God," and the Holy Spirit was not given by measure unto him; but, turning for a season from throngs, and duties, and miraculous works, he sought the fullness of his Father's presence, undisturbed contemplation of the infinite perfections, and all "the silent heaven of love," in closest communion with its chosen object. What a mountain of myrrh, and what a hill of frankincense, were those lofty Galilean ranges, when turned into temples and oratories by the immaculate Son of God! And if He who was without sin, "the prime and blossom of our race," needed such privacy of religious worship, such undisturbed and protracted fellowship with the Father, such early-morn and all-night seasons of prayer, how much greater is our necessity, who have been weakened, corrupted, and darkened in our spiritual vision, by transgression?

I make no argument for secret prayer. It is enjoined directly and emphatically in the Scriptures; it is sanctioned by the highest examples, even that of the Son of God himself; it has been practiced by good men in every age of the Church, and it is an indispensable necessity to the devout soul. No man has ever maintained a Christian experience without it. Its obligation and expediency are things not to be questioned, among the followers of Jesus.

That for which I plead is *purposed, prolonged communion with God.* No soul is so self-complete or self-contained, or so richly furnished in creature associations, or has such princely opportunities for rendering adoration and homage to God in a public way, as not to need altar-places for sacrifice and prayer, where the worship is solitary, except as angels throng the spot, and God's presence makes it as the gates of heaven. Every Christian *must have*, in order to overcome the world, the corrupt tendencies of his own fallen nature and the power of the prince of darkness—in order to growth in grace, the enrichment of his soul in spiritual things and sufficiency of wisdom and strength to meet the high responsibilities imposed on him, his mountain of myrrh and hill of frankincense.

It is the place of refreshment, enlargement, and triumph. "So, Mrs. Kitty, my dear," says Betty in the diary of Mrs. Trevylyan, "I'll leave you alone with HIM. You'll find it better; for all the great fights, it's my belief, *have got to be fought out alone with the Almighty*. And you'll find, when you kneel down and give yourself up to him heartily, that you don't want any more promises than He has given—not one. For all the words in the world end somewhere, and leave something they cannot reach; but the love of the Lord ends nowhere, but flows right down to the bottom of every trouble." This is the experience of all those who dwell in the secret place of the Most High, and abide under the shadow of the Almighty. God is to them a rock and a fortress and a hiding-place, a shield and buckler, an all-sufficient portion. "It is not years or griefs," some one has said, "that make us old, nor poverty that makes us poor; but looking down instead of up, and being shut up alone with self instead of with God." O, it is dreadful to be shut up alone with self, to the exclusion of God's creatures, even the meanest, or, worse still, of God himself! It is poverty, barrenness of soul, desolation, death. But to be shut up with God! That shames selfishness out of sight, rebukes worldliness and shows the tinsel and nothingness of its gifts and honors, reveals the loathsomeness of sin and sinful indulgence, and humiliates the soul at the remembrance of its unfaithfulness and cowardice. That, also, brings marvelous light to the understanding, quickening power to the conscience, purity to the affections, purpose of integrity to the will, and dignity and grandeur of life and character to the whole manhood.

"We are liable in this world," says Andrews Norton, "to continual delusion; to a most extravagant over-estimate of the value of its objects." This delusion is dispelled, and this false estimate corrected, in the place of lofty vision; and we learn not only the relative insignificance of sublunary things, but also the incomparable value of those which are spiritual and eternal.

But the great advantage of this prolonged communion with God is in its purifying, energizing, and transforming influence on our own nature. We become like Him whom we adore and love; for "we all, with open face beholding as in a glass the glory of the Lord, are changed into the same image from glory to glory, even as by the Spirit of the Lord. And to be changed from the image of the earthly, sensual, and devilish, into the resplendent image of Christ's holiness, is the loftiest privilege and richest endowment of a sinful man. "It does us good," we are told, "to admire what is good and beautiful; but it does us infinitely more good to love it. We grow like what we admire; but we become one with what we love." Admiration, however, belongs to the finite, not to the Supreme; we reverence and adore, with prostration of soul, with a deep sense of our own nothingness, and with some faint discernment of the infinite glory, the transcendent greatness and goodness of Jehovah. And to dwell on His perfections, to contemplate His character, to meditate on His wondrous works, to pour out our souls in gratitude for His mercies, to consecrate our powers and possessions to His service, to commit ourselves, interests, ambitions, loves, all to which our hearts cling, to Him, as to a faithful Creator, is to grow divine in our inner life, to be exalted in every sentiment of our being, to be lifted to a nobler plane of experience, and to attain to a peace and purpose of soul not to be realized in any other way, and in which, as Ruskin expresses it, " the rest is one of humanity instead of pride, and the trust no more in the resolution we have taken, but *in the hand we hold.*"

The vision of God is a joyful vision. It is the rapture of the saints. It is the source of strength and consolation in the midst of their trials. It brightens dying eyes, and brings unfailing comfort to the soul in the last great conflict. Over the wreck of mortality it awakens shouts of victory. This manifestation of God is a vision of heaven. In the light of the divine presence, saints behold their future inheritance. If " thine eyes shall see the King in his beauty, they shall behold the land that is very far off," also. The Spirit reveals, in the mountain of myrrh, the things which God hath prepared for them that love him. And those who have this enrapturing view do not think it long to tarry, " till the day break and the shadows flee away." " The saints," says Rutherford, " have a sweet life between them and Christ. There is much sweet solace of love between Him and them, when He feedeth among the lilies and cometh into His garden." And, perhaps, even in glory, the "golden vials full of odors, which are the prayers of the saints," will remind them of their oft-time secret communion with their Lord and King, while probation lasted, in the Mountain of Myrrh and in the Hill of Frankincense.

XVII.

HELP ONLY IN GOD.

"O Israel, thou hast destroyed thyself; but in me is thy help."—
HOSEA xiii, 9.

RATIONALISM, which is the prevailing form of infidelity, asserts just the contrary of this passage, namely: "I am not destroyed, and my help is in myself." In other words, the divergence between Revelation and Rationalism begins with respect to the fact of human condition. Is man a sinner? Is he destroyed? Is he a spiritual ruin? Have we to deal with such a fact as sin? If we admit sin, and have any adequate conceptions of its true character, our need of a Saviour, and of an almighty Saviour, will at once become manifest. If, on the other hand, we deny sin, or regard it as an inconsiderable matter, how shall we account for moral disorder and human misery? Must not sin exist, and must it not be an agency of tremendous power, a contagion of deadly virulence, an enginery as fierce and terrible as hell to produce those fearful, continuous, and wide-spread results of desolation and death which confront us on every side? "Sin," some one has said, "is the one mystery which makes every thing else plain." We have only to glance around us in the world to behold the evidence of the ravages of sin. The facts of human condition attest its reality. Poverty, superstition, physical and moral disorders, ignorance, crime, are so many poisonous streams flowing from the baleful fountains of transgression. That is, we cannot suppose these things to exist, under the government of a wise and good God, as facts and experiences of a race of innocent beings. Sin explains their existence, although the mystery of its own dark origin may remain unsolved.

But if sin exist, it is not only objective but subjective; it is not merely an external fact, it is an internal reality. Rationalism discards revelation, and asserts the full competency of the mind to discover religious truth for itself; while Christianity teaches that the understanding is darkened by the influence of sin, and needs to be enlightened by that true Light which lighteth every man that cometh into the world.

Now what is the fact? Does reason teach us all that we need to know of God? Does it teach His existence, His character, His relation to us? Without revelation, what can I learn of the Most High? What is His character? What is the object of His government? How does He regard *me?* Is He angry with me? If not, why does He subject me to loss, trial, misery, and death? If He is, then how can I appease or escape His wrath? With the simple knowledge of God, or Deism, how could I be other than wretched, shivering in the grasp of an unknown and terrible power?

Again, what of the future? The idea of another world, a world of judgment and retribution, is in the minds of men; it has somehow originated. Heaven and hell are possible, are actual realities, for all I can show to the contrary. Then what relation do I sustain to them? May I hope for the one, may I escape the other? Does reason give me sufficient light? Does its light shine at all beyond the tomb? And yet here is the grave just before my feet, and my path lies inevitably that way. Is there any thing beyond, and, if any thing, what is its character? Can I, ought I, to be satisfied, except I *know*?

Is there not a hunger in the human soul for the truths of revelation? Do we not instinctively, in the high necessities of the spiritual life, seek for guidance? Do we not go out of ourselves for truth? and in the great exigencies of our life is not prayer the natural language of our souls? But Rationalism does not satisfy the moral and spiritual sense, and does not comfort the heart in its griefs and trials. Infidelity at the grave of buried love cries, "This is an eternal sleep!" But Jesus stands and weeps, calls the afflicted soul to himself, and points to the compensations and rewards of an eternal state. Robert Hall said that he buried his rationalism in the grave of his father; and many a man, when the dark shadows have fallen across his pathway, has found cheer and comfort in the bright beams of the Sun of Righteousness scattering all his gloom, and filling his soul with Heaven's own light.

Take another view. Has any nation in darkness ever groped its way into the light? Do any people ever obtain that knowledge of God, and of the facts of His spiritual kingdom, on which our civilization rests, except it is brought to them, except they are the fruit of missionary labor, except, in other words, they receive the revelation which God has given to us by his Son? And yet the world has always been groaning for the truths of the Gospel. Look at Paganism, with its altars, sacrifices, and temples! What are they but its confession of guilt, and of the need of expiation? The one great question which has seemed to burden the soul of man in every age and land is substantially this: *How shall a sinner come into the presence of a holy God?* Paganism always comes to this, and every religious system in the world has this significance. It is the cry of human need in its depth of conscious moral degradation. It is the question which Christianity answers, fully answers, answers to the perfect satisfaction of every believing soul; and as the oracle, to meet human necessity, must be of divine origin, Christianity is thus demonstrated to be a revelation of God.

Again, it must be admitted that *authorized objective teaching* is included among the possible sources of knowledge. If so, revelation is at least possible, and if it be given, may be *authoritative* in its character. An authoritative revelation from God, therefore, is within the range of human experiences, and any system claiming to be such a revelation is not to be rejected as absurd or impossible, but received with the utmost candor, and examined with all seriousness and earnestness.

And here the question arises, What is the legitimate office of Reason in Religion? I answer,

1. To examine the facts of so-called natural religion.

2. To examine the evidences of any system asserting itself to be a revelation from God.

3. To determine the rules of exegesis and historic investigation, and so to apply them that falshoood may be detected and the truth demonstrated.

4. To prevent any thing being received as revealed and authoritative which is in conflict with *known* truth, because, as God is the author of all truth, every truth must be in harmony with every other truth.

5. To interpret and harmonize the Holy Scriptures in their different parts, and in their teachings on various subjects.

6. To determine the relative value of Christian doctrines, all having manifestly the same divine origin.

But it is utterly absurd to reject a doctrine or revelation as irrational because mysterious and incomprehensible to a finite mind. The human reason must, of course, be limited by its possibilities. There are bounds which it cannot pass. There is nothing in the universe of God which we can comprehend in its essence. We know the existence of matter, and such facts as growth and gravitation, but we cannot tell what they are. In the last analysis they elude us. They are just like the facts of God's spiritual kingdom, capable of being known only by their phenomena. Besides, those things which are easy of comprehension and without mystery are short-lived, and neither satisfy the soul nor stir the emotions.

There is, moreover, perfect harmony betwixt philosophy and theology in their processes and results. Philosophy starts with the facts of human consciousness; theology with the facts of historical Christianity, including man's sinful condition. Each employs its own methods; but the conclusions, which are legitimately reached, do not contradict each other. Both find sin, misery, mystery, hungering for the infinite, a religious nature in man, a disposition to worship, a conscience and a soul lifting man above the brutes, and a possible cognition of the Unknown and Absolute. Neither can comprehend God, explain the origin of evil, or bring the whole domain of truth within the range of our finite powers. Learning and philosophy are the handmaids, not the enemies, of religion, though sometimes, like a blind Samson, they are made to grind in the mill of the Philistines. And yet it was the Church which established and endowed the great universities, which reduced language to writing, which made literature a necessity by maintaining the religion of *a Book*, which preserved the lights of learning amid the lamps of the monasteries and at the altars of religion when barbarism deluged Europe, which, despite some bigoted exceptions, has been the steady patroness of science, and which has given to the world our high, enlightened, and beneficent civilization.

A fair test of a religion is its fruits, and we are not unwilling that Christianity should be thus judged. Does Christianity save men? Is it the light of the world? Is it the salt of the earth? Does it reform society? Is it the antidote of corruption and decay? Could we get along without it, and maintain our homes, our liberties, and our systems of education? If it were banished from the midst of us, would not the very structure of civil society perish, and our boasted civilization become a night of barbarism, if not an utter pandemonium of guilt and shame?

"Thou hast destroyed thyself;" sin is man's darkness, misery, ruin. The one thing to be shunned, loathed, hated, and escaped from, at whatever cost, sacrifice, or peril, is sin.

"In Me is thy help." The Lord is our strength and our salvation. "The law of the spirit of life in Christ Jesus," saith the apostle, "hath made me free from the law of sin and death." And again, "I am crucified with Christ, nevertheless I live, yet not I, but Christ liveth in me; and the life which I now live in the flesh, I live by the faith of the Son of God, who loved me and gave himself for me."

The whole history of the Church glows with such testimony.

"In Me is thy help." The light, the help, the power, the wisdom, the sufficiency, the love greater than the world's needs, the uplifting, the sanctification, the redemption, the victory over sin and death and hell, the everlasting triumph, the exaltation, enthronement, and glorification of the soul forever— all must come from God; and to him, Father, Son, and Holy Spirit, be endless praise.

XVIII.

THE JOY OF OUR LORD.

"These things have I spoken unto you, that my joy might remain in you, and that your joy might be full."—JOHN xv, 11.

JESUS is described as a man of sorrows. His position in life was humble. He trod the stormy pathway of a reformer, enunciating truths for the future ages. He was serious, earnest, consecrated, bearing a great burden on his heart, till he cried, "It is finished!" And yet no man can read the record of the Evangelists without perceiving that Jesus was upborne by some mighty consolation—that there was in him some spring of perennial comfort, and that light shone on his pathway from beyond the heavens.

What were the elements of this joy?

We know that it did not consist in external things. When we think of Jesus we do not think of wealth, or honors, or ambitious rewards—of the splendor of place and power—of elegant leisure for study and travel and the enjoyment of home and friends, or even of a satisfaction springing from great mental endowments. "Intellectual gifts," says Froude, "are like gifts of strength, or wealth, or rank, or worldly power—splendid instruments, if nobly used; but requiring qualities to use them nobler and better than themselves." Conscious of such brilliant intellectual powers, we see Milton seeking "fit audience, though few," for his immortal song, and exulting, even in his blindness, that he had lost the light of vision " in Liberty's defense, that noble task, with which all Europe rang from side to side ;" or Bacon, lifting himself above his own times, and, in the proud self-assertion of genius and greatness, bequeathing his fame to the "future ages." But no such strains of exultation fall from the lips of Jesus. He glories not in conscious superiority, nor in the assurance of immortal fame. He yearns for the baptism with which he is to be baptized ; but it is a baptism of tears, sweat, and blood, in the garden and on the cross, for the world's redemption.

In what, then, did the joy of Jesus consist?

1. *In the power given unto him in earth and heaven* —the power to dethrone Satan, to ransom a race, to abolish death, to bring in everlasting righteousness, to extend the offers of salvation to lost sinners on terms of possible acceptance, to become the second federal Head of humanity, to restore the lost Eden, to vindicate the authority of the divine government, to reveal God to the human consciousness, to demonstrate the justice, sovereignty, and infinite beneficence of the Almighty Father, and to gather around the throne millions of ransomed souls, to shine in the divine image, and to sing the song of the Lamb through the eternal ages.

2. *His personal character was a source of joy.*

Character is the quality of manhood, or, as one has said, it is what a man is in the sight of God. A character which is pure, noble, beneficent, and harmonious, has a pulsation of joy in its every throb of life, and exults in the midst of all earthly desolation, of all hellish malice, in the consciousness of its own purity; and such a character insures a life of unfailing joy.

Jesus says of himself, "I am meek and lowly in heart;" and he declares that those who learn of him this meekness and lowliness shall have rest to their souls. The meek, says Mr. Wesley, are "they that hold all their passions and affections evenly balanced." In the light of this definition, Jesus was emphatically *The Meek*. There was no disturbance, no perturbation, no fever of anxiety, no pulsation of impurity, no torture of apprehension, no bleeding of a lacerated heart, "no restless seeking after rest." All the passions and affections were evenly balanced. Lowliness of heart, moreover, prepares us for any and every condition in life. The soul crowned with this grace is alike content in poverty or opulence, in adversity or prosperity, in obscurity or renown. No circumstance of human condition, therefore, could disturb the joy of Jesus.

Consider also his humility, as seen in the fact that he girded himself and washed the feet of his disciples; his tenderness, weeping with the afflicted sisters of Bethany at the grave of buried love, and weeping over the doomed city in which he was betrayed and crucified; his beneficence, so constant and active that his whole life is pictured in the words, "He went about doing good;" his regard for childhood, taking the little ones up in his arms and blessing them; his veracity and courage, exposing the hypocrisy and lies of the Pharisees, and blasting them with the most terrible denunciations; his divine temper and soul, praying, as he hung on the cross, for the murderers who mocked his dying agonies. Now must not a character so pure, simple, beneficent, sympathetic, and courageous have had great resources of joy and satisfaction in itself? Can we think of the humility, tenderness, child-love, friendliness toward man, and magnanimity—genuine greatness of soul—toward his enemies, displayed by our Lord, without feeling that such a nature must have realized a joy kindred to the joy of heaven? The joy of Jesus was, then, in part, the result of right manhood.

3. *His joy also consisted in his perfect accord with the will of the Father.*

To do and suffer that will was his delight. "My meat," he said, that is, my very life, "is to do the will of him that sent me, and to finish his work." "And he that sent me," he affirmed, "is with me"—source of unfailing and eternal joy—"The Father hath not left me alone"—O infinite satisfaction of the divine presence!—"for I do always those things that please him;" and so he always manifests himself to me in approbation and love. He expresses this perfect accord with the Father in the words, "We are one." This close and constant communion of his soul with God was the source of unfailing satisfaction. It thrilled his human consciousness with divine joy.

4. *He had joy in his beneficent work.*

At his approach the blind saw, the deaf heard, the lame leaped, the sick recovered, and the dead walked forth among living men. Our Lord showed the beneficence of his heart and his tender regard for man by choosing to prove himself the Son of God, not by arresting the course of the orbs of heaven, but by performing works of mercy on the sorrowing and wretched of earth. And this work was his joy.

5. *He never despaired of his own cause.*

He saw Satan fall like lightning from heaven. He knew the strength of sin, the malice of hell, and the fierceness and duration of the conflict; but he knew also the matchless resources of infinite love, the greatness of the power given him, the stupendous achievements of Providence touching all interests, public and private, extending through all ages, and changing the destinies of men and nations, and he knew how much would be accomplished in the illumination and transformation of the human soul by the power of the Holy Ghost. This was "the joy that was set before him." Through the inspiration of this joy he "endured the cross, despising the shame," and in anticipation of its fullness he "is set down at the right hand of the throne of God," carrying forward his work in the earth, till all shall know him, from the least to the greatest. How great the joy of Jesus in anticipation of that full and glorious triumph, when "he shall see of the travail of his soul, and shall be satisfied!"

The Christian is permitted to have the fullest fellowship with Jesus in his joy. The conditions are renunciation, consecration, faith in the Son of God. The conditions are indispensable; the renunciation must be absolute; the consecration whole and complete; and the faith constant, active, and reliant. But the conditions being fully and always met, the follower of Jesus may rejoice, as did his Master, in the power given to him—power over sin, the world, and Satan;

in his personal character, beautified, ennobled, and (relatively) perfected by the grace of God ; in his oneness with the Father, through Jesus, and in the consciousness of the divine presence and love, so that he can always say,

> "May thy will, not mine, be done;
> May thy will and mine be one;"

in the delightful work of love and beneficence, gladdening the hearts and brightening the destinies of his fellow-men ; and in the assurance of final victory over sin and death and hell, so that at last it shall be said of him, "Well done, good and faithful servant; thou hast been faithful over a few things, I will make thee ruler over many things ; ENTER THOU INTO THE JOY OF THY LORD."

XIX.

THE LORD'S PECULIAR TREASURE.

"For the Lord hath chosen Jacob unto himself, and Israel for his peculiar treasure."—Psa. cxxxv, 4.

Solomon, describing his earthly splendor, the glory of his kingdom, and his vain attempts to find a satisfactory portion in the world, says: "I gathered me also silver and gold, and the peculiar treasure of kings." He had the gold of Ophir, and "of spices very great store, and precious stones;" he had "harps also, and psalteries for singers," and gardens, and vineyards, and orchards, and pools of water, and "great and small cattle," and whatsoever his eyes desired, or his longing heart coveted; and so he was great, and his wisdom also remained with him. These things, according to Oriental ideas, constituted the peculiar treasure of kings.

The great King, the Lord Jehovah, has also his peculiar treasure. He hath chosen Israel to be "a special people unto himself, above all other people that are upon the face of the earth." He said thus, by Moses, to the house of Jacob and to the children of Israel: "If ye will obey my voice indeed, and keep my covenant, then ye shall be a peculiar treasure unto me above all people: for all the earth is mine: and ye shall be unto me a kingdom of priests, and a holy nation." "For the Lord's portion," it is said, in language still more marvelous, "is his people; Jacob is the lot of his inheritance." Hence, saith the Lord, by the prophet, "Thou, Israel, art my servant; Jacob, whom I have chosen; the seed of Abraham, my friend." And so dear is this chosen seed to the heart of the Most High that he exclaims: "Fear not: for I have redeemed thee, I have called thee by thy name; thou art mine. When thou passest through the waters, I will be with thee; and through the rivers, they shall not overflow thee: when thou walkest through the fire, thou shalt not be burned; neither shall the flame kindle upon thee. For I am the Lord thy God, the Holy one of Israel, thy Saviour: since thou wast precious in my sight, thou hast been honorable, and I have loved thee." "For thou art a holy people unto the Lord thy God, and the Lord hath chosen thee to be a peculiar people unto himself, above all the nations that are upon the earth." We are also taught by the great apostle to the Gentiles that our Saviour, Jesus Christ, "gave himself for us, that he might redeem us from all iniquity, and purify unto himself a peculiar people, zealous of good works." And Peter testifies, in the same strain: "Ye are a chosen generation, a royal priesthood, a holy nation, a peculiar people; that ye should show forth the praises of him who hath called you out of darkness into his marvelous light: which in time past were not a people, but are now the people of God; which had not obtained mercy, but now have obtained mercy."

The conditions and blessings of this covenant relation are worthy of our consideration:

1. *On what condition may we become* the *peculiar people of God?*

The first, manifestly, is, *obedience*. God must be accepted as Lawgiver and King. His voice must be heeded, and his covenant remembered.

The Lord must be *served*. If Jacob is chosen, it is as a servant. We are not to do our own will, or seek our own pleasure, but the will and pleasure of our heavenly Father.

Again, it is only a *holy* or *consecrated* people which the Lord will acknowledge as his own. They are separated from the world, redeemed from all iniquity, that is, actually delivered from its power, purified in affections and life by an application of the atoning blood, and called out of darkness into the marvelous light of the Gospel—from sin, ignorance, and misery, unto righteousness, knowledge, holiness, and happiness.

The chosen generation of the Most High are also zealous of good works. They delight in charity, benevolence, and deeds of Christian faith and love. "This being the great end of Christ's death," says Macknight, "how dare any person, pretending to be one of Christ's people, either to speak or to think lightly of good works as not necessary to salvation?"

This people, which is for a possession of the Most High, having been called out of darkness into the marvelous light of the divine presence, *show forth the praises*, or, as Macknight renders it, *declare the perfections* of their Redeemer, the Lord. The light into which they have come is marvelous, because, to use Leighton's words, "it is a pure, undecaying, heavenly light," scattering all the darkness of the sinful soul. "Let us not, therefore, think it incredible," adds the Archbishop, "that a poor unlettered Christian may know more of God, in the best kind of knowledge, than any the wisest and most learned natural man can do; for the one knows God only by man's light, the other knows him by his own light, and that is the only right knowledge. As the sun cannot be seen by its own light, so neither can God be savingly known but by his own revealing." But whoever does thus know him, will declare him, or show forth his praises. The imparted illumination makes the recipient at once a revelator of God. When the prophetic fire burns in his soul it will glow on his lips. He will turn a shining face on his fellows, who comes to them from the thick cloud of the divine presence. He will show forth the praises of Jesus, whose heart is musical with the grace of redemption. The peculiar people of God walk, white-robed, with harps and crowns and shining faces, even in this world. In a thousand ways, they make manifest the excellency and glory of their Lord and King. They are his witnesses; they magnify his grace; they make mention of his goodness, and they show forth to earth and heaven his praises.

2. *What are the blessings of this chosen generation?*

The Lord espouses them unto himself as his own, his peculiar treasure, throws around them his protecting arm, and vouchsafes unto them the guidance of his unerring wisdom and the blessings of his infinite love. The Lord makes them a kingdom of priests, or a royal priesthood. He gives them the right of approach into the divine presence, he accepts their gifts and offerings, he hearkens to their requests, he bestows on them a measure of his own royal power, and exalts them to thrones of dominion in the world to come. He bestows on them a "profusion of blessings, temporal, spiritual, and everlasting, of which the crown of all is, that ·they should be *an appropriation unto himself.*"

On the words, "A peculiar treasure," in Exodus xix, 5. Bush comments as follows: "Hebrew, *segullah*, a word of which we do not find the verbal root, *sagal*, in Hebrew, but in Chaldee; it signifies, *to gain, to acquire to one's self, to make one's own, to appropriate.* Wherever the name occurs in Hebrew it denotes a *peculium*, a possession or treasure of which the owner is peculiarly choice, one on which his heart is set, and which he neither shares with others nor resigns to the care of others. It has an obvious relation to the Latin word *sigillum, seal*, and is especially applied to such choice possessions as were secured with *a seal*, as gold, silver, jewels, precious stones, etc."

The same word occurs in Malachi iii, 17, "And they shall be mine, saith the Lord of hosts, in that day when I make up my *jewels*"—that is, my *choice, peculiar, and invaluable treasures.*

The Lord even represents himself as choosing his people for an inheritance; they are, he says, "the seed of Abraham, *my friend,*" and so to be remembered with special mercies. He declares that they are precious in his sight, honorable, and the objects of his peculiar regard—that the waters shall not overflow them, nor the fire kindle its flame upon them. "I am thy Saviour, thou art mine," expresses, in fewest words, this sublime and glorious covenant relation. And the Lord promises to make Israel, because, by consecration and covenant, they had become his own peculiar people, "high above all nations in praise, and in name, and in honor."

Those who accept the invitations of the Gospel, and enter into covenant with God, to be his and to live for his glory, experience the redemption of power, are purified by the blood of the Lamb, become, through sovereign grace, "a chosen generation, a royal priesthood, a holy nation, a peculiar people," are called out of darkness into God's marvelous light, and show forth his praises in the earth.

How great, then, are the privileges of the children of God! How happy are all those who are identified with the Redeemer's cause and kingdom in the earth! And how superlative the folly of such as turn their backs on the Church, and forfeit its covenant blessings! O the indescribable felicity of being consciously the treasure, the precious possession, the peculiar care of the King of kings! To have the shelter of the arm, and the love of the heart, and the covenant mercy and grace of Him who suffered on Calvary, but who lives in glory, is the rapturous height of Christianity.

"If God has given you the earnest of the Spirit," says Rutherford, "as part of payment of God's principal sum, ye have to rejoice; for our Lord will not lose his earnest, neither will he go back, nor repent him of the bargain. If ye find, at some time, a longing to see God, joy in the assurance of that sight, (howbeit that feast be but like the Passover, that cometh about only once a year;) peace of conscience, liberty of prayer, the doors of God's treasure thrown open to the soul, and a clear sight of himself looking out, and saying, with a smiling countenance, 'Welcome to me, afflicted soul,' this is the earnest that he giveth sometimes, and which maketh glad the heart, and is evidence that the bargain will hold."

XX.

THE HOLY HATRED OF GOD.

"Thou hatest all workers of iniquity."—PSA. v, 5.

No being loves like God, and no being hates like God. The latter fact corresponds with the former, and both root in the infinite nature of Jehovah. God hates sin; he hates sinners, considered as such; he hates the devil; he hates all workers of iniquity. He does not merely look on them with disapprobation; he *hates* them. He has no pleasure in wickedness, evil shall not dwell with him, and the foolish shall not stand in his sight. But this is not all; he *hates* all workers of iniquity, and he *abhors* the bloody and deceitful man.

As God, beyond any other being in the universe, discerns the true character, relations, and consequences of sin, so, beyond any other being in the universe, he looks on sin with loathing, detests transgressors, and arrays the whole strength of his nature against that which is evil.

We are taught, at least in our hymnal theology, that we ought to hate the sin and yet the sinner love; but no man, in the whole range of human experience, has ever loved or hated an abstraction. And God, as we are so strongly assured in this Fifth Psalm, hates all *workers* of iniquity, and not merely iniquitous *works;* and abhors the bloody and deceitful *man,* not merely the bloody and deceitful *thing.* The wicked blesseth the covetous, it is said, that is, the covetous person; but "the Lord abhorreth," looks with a strong emotion of horror, upon this same character. "No objects of the senses," says Horne, "can be so nauseous to men as the various kinds of sin are in the sight of God."

In the strongest terms, the Almighty expresses his deep detestation of the hypocritical observances with which a backslidden people maintained the forms of religion: "Your new moons and your appointed feasts my soul hateth; they are a trouble unto me; I am weary to bear them." "For I, the Lord, love judgment, I hate robbery for burnt-offering." "I hate, I despise your feast-days." "I have no pleasure in you, saith the Lord of hosts, neither will I accept an offering at your hand."

And God's utter abhorrence of immorality, falsehood, treachery, idolatry or devil-worship, and all wicked devisings and imaginings, is expressed with a certainty and emphasis quite as marked and unmistakable. When Israel forsook God, and sacrificed unto devils, and forgot the Rock of their salvation, the Lord, we are told, saw it and abhorred them, and said, "They have provoked me to anger with their vanities." When Israel was in desolation and wasted, the testimony of the Lord is that he besought them not to burn incense to other gods, "rising early and sending, saying, *O do not the abominable thing that I hate!*" but that this entreaty, which seems a burst of passionate remonstrance from a heart of infinite love, availed nothing, so that his fury and anger were poured forth.

"Speak ye every man the truth to his neighbor," saith the Lord by another prophet, "execute the judgment of truth and peace in your gates; and let none of you imagine evil in your hearts against his neighbor, and love no false oath, for all these are things which I hate, saith the Lord." And again we read: "These six things doth the Lord hate; yea, seven are an abomination unto him: A proud look, a lying tongue, and hands that shed innocent blood, a heart that deviseth wicked imaginations, feet that be swift in running to mischief, a false witness that speaketh lies, and he that soweth discord among brethren."

The angel of the Church at Ephesus is commended because he hated the deeds of the Nicolaitanes, "which," the Lord adds, "*I also hate.*" And to the angel of the Church of Pergamos it is said: "So hast thou also them that hold the doctrine of the Nicoliatanes, which thing *I hate.*" From which it appears, that both the doctrine and the deeds of the Nicolaitanes, whatever they may have been, excited the hatred—the utter moral abhorrence—of the gentle Jesus.

And he who thus avows his detestation of the doctrine and deeds of the Nicolaitanes has obtained the lofty title of SON OF GOD, is worshiped by angels, occupies a throne of everlasting dominion, is fairer than the children of men, stands at the head of the renovated universe, girds on his thigh the sword of almightiness with his glory and majesty, and wields a scepter which can never be broken, because of him, emphatically and pre-eminently, can it be said, "Thou lovest righteousness and hatest wickedness: therefore God, thy God, hath anointed thee with the oil of gladness above thy fellows"—because, as one observes, "the sermons, the example, and above all the death of Christ, for the expiation of sin, demonstrated his love of righteousness and hatred of wickedness." And just as certainly as he loves righteousness, and just as constantly, and just as intensely, he hates all iniquity. He could not die to bring in everlasting righteousness, except he had an infinite horror of wickedness.

Now if God so hates iniquity, we ought to hate it. "Abhor that which is evil," is the injunction; not simply disapprove it, oppose it, discountenance it, but *abhor* it. The whole tide of our moral nature must be turned against sin if we would feel as God feels in respect to it. "Hate the evil and love the good, and establish judgment in the gates," is God's word by his prophet. "The fear of the Lord is to hate evil," that is, such is its legitimate fruit, its certain results. Accordingly, we find the angel of the Church at Ephesus commended because he could not bear them which are evil, and because he tried those claiming to be apostles, who were not, and proved them liars. In the work of saving souls a compassionate difference is demanded; but some are to be saved with fear, "pulling them out of the fire, hating even the garment spotted by the flesh," or the slightest approach to contact and contamination.

The Psalmist describes the sinner who has no fear of God before his eyes as one who "abhorreth not evil," and this is presented as the very crown and climax of his iniquity and deceit; and he rather plumes himself on his piety, because he had "hated the congregation of evil-doers," "hated them that regard lying vanities," hated "every false way," hated "vain thoughts," and hated and abhorred "lying," which hearty hatred of specified and abominable vices may be supposed to argue the existence of as genuine and earnest love for the opposite virtues. "Ye that love the Lord hate evil," is the comprehensive direction of the inspired word. "Do not I hate them, O Lord, that hate thee?" inquires the Psalmist, "and am not I grieved with those that sin against thee?" "I hate them," he adds, "with perfect hatred; I count them mine enemies." As a servant with his master, a subject with his king, a child with his father, so he is in thoroughest sympathy and fullest identification with God and his cause.

"No man loves," said Bacon, "where he ought to love, who has not first hated where he ought to hate." And the clearer our discernment of God and truth and holiness, the more odious will sin appear, the more we shall dread its slightest touch, the more persistently shall we antagonize it with all our moral force, the more shall we hate it, somewhat, at least, as God hates it, and the more earnestly shall we labor and pray for its destruction, and for the establishment of righteousness, purity, and peace.

And if to love what Christ loves be a sign of grace, equally so is it to hate what he hates. Perfect sympathy and oneness with the world's Redeemer ought to be the object of all Christian aspiration. And if this state be attained, we shall enter into the travail of his soul, experience something of his baptism of tears and blood, intensely desire the coming of his kingdom and the destruction of his enemies, taste his agonizing abhorrence of sin, war with him against the Prince of Darkness, share the joy and glory of his successes, and reign with him in his triumphal realm of power and majesty forever.

XXI.

A DRIFT, OR A VOYAGE?

"Thou shalt guide me with thy counsel."—Psa. lxxiii, 24.

WHAT is the nature of our life? What is the significance of our earthly career? Must we wander like children, lost and dazed, seeking vainly to find a path of safety and happiness, or may we grasp an unseen Hand, and have our steps directed by infinite wisdom and love? In a word, is our life a drift or a voyage? Do we float whithersoever we are borne by resistless currents, into balmy or tempestuous seas, underneath serene or stormy skies, to genial or desolate shores, just as our course may be shaped by blind, mysterious forces? or is our life a voyage, having an aim and purpose, battling, if need be, against winds and waves, against tides and tempests, against cyclones and icebergs, welcoming sunny heavens and islands of balm and seas rippling in music, but always bearing steadily on, under all conditions and circumstances, toward a chosen, coveted, and predestined shore? This latter hypothesis is the Christian philosophy of life. Every thing has a meaning. The great object is character and immortality. And the Highest himself is interested, beyond what we are able to conceive, in the processes and issues of the humblest life. Every soul, according to this theory, is a voyager, and that, on the whole, is the most successful voyage which makes the mariner hardy, courageous, and trustful in Providence, and which brings him, at last, to the harbor with the most richly freighted ship, having escaped all perils of founder or wreck, and reached the shore and land and home, which had been the object of his constant desire.

Or, to come back to the figure of the Psalmist, such are the intricacies and dangers of man's career through the world that he needs a guide to direct him in all his ways, and such a guide as is sufficient for his necessities—one who is wise, faithful, constant, and able to go with him to the end. "This God is our God for ever and ever," is the Psalmist's triumphant assurance ; " He will be our guide even unto death." And he alone is competent to be our guide, knowing us thoroughly, discerning the perils and possibilities of the way, loving us with fatherly constancy and fervor, and able to make us always conscious of his presence, and to direct our faltering steps, in light and darkness, over mountains and through valleys, down the steeps of death and up to the golden gates of the New Jerusalem.

If the Lord guide us according to this promise, he will guide us by his counsel, that is, by his Word and by his Holy Spirit. We need not expect to be led in any unusual ways, or by any unusual agencies. The divine presence is most surely found in the old paths, and in the use of the recognized means of grace.

Especially is the unfailing and manifold word a source of instruction and consolation to the saints of

God. "I have lost a world of time," said the learned Salmasius on his death-bed; "if I had one year more I would spend it in reading David's Psalms and Paul's Epistles." And these living Scriptures, constantly inspired of God, are adapted to the exigencies of every soul. They enlighten the mind and comfort the heart. They teach, warn, encourage, inspire, direct, entreat. By precept and by example, by prophecy and by miracle, they show us the way of life and salvation. What Horne says of the Psalms of David is true of the Scriptures generally: "They present religion to us in the most engaging dress; communicating truths which philosophy could never investigate, in a style which poetry can never equal; while history is made the vehicle of prophecy, and creation lends all its charms to paint the glories of redemption. Calculated alike to profit and to please, they inform the understanding, elevate the affections, and entertain the imagination." As the manna which came down from heaven, to use a metaphor from the author just quoted, was adapted to every palate, and fully met all necessities, so these divine Scriptures, the miraculous gift of God, are relished by every devout soul, and completely answer all requirements of our natures and surroundings. "For whatsoever things were written aforetime, were written for our learning, that we through patience and comfort of the Scriptures might have hope."

A few hours before his death, Wilberforce, calling a friend near to him, said: "Let us talk of heaven. Do not weep for me; I am happy. Think of me, and let the thought press you forward. I never knew happiness till I found Christ a Saviour. *Read* the Bible—*read the Bible!* Let no religious book take its place; through all my perplexities and distresses I never read any other book, and I never felt the want of any other. It has been my hourly study; and all my knowledge of the doctrines, and all my acquaintance with the experience and realities of religion, have been drawn from the Bible only. *I think religious people do not read the Bible enough.* Books about the Bible may be useful, but they will not do in the place of the simple truth of the Bible."

The Lord also guides his children by his Holy Spirit, but the impulse and testimony of the Spirit will always be in accordance with the teachings of the written word. The Spirit's influences, moreover, are most likely to be received in connection with the study of the Scriptures, or in pleading its promises at a throne of grace, for the Holy Spirit is "the Spirit of truth," and it is his office to teach, to bring the things which Jesus hath spoken to our remembrance, and to guide us into all truth.

If we would have the Lord for our guide we must choose him for our Captain and Leader, whom we will obediently follow, to whom we will surrender our own wills, and whose constant and unerring and sufficient guidance we will publicly and thankfully acknowledge. Dr. Clarke renders the twenty-fifth verse of Psalm seventy-third as follows: "Who is there to me in the heavens? And with thee, I have desired nothing in the earth." And he adds: "No man can say this who has not taken God for his portion in both worlds." And whoever can use this language may be assured of the divine guidance. He will not be left to wander from the way of holiness, to stumble on the dark mountains of sin and unbelief, and to grope in doubt and fear down to death. "*Thou shalt* guide me"—it is sure. "Thou shalt *guide me*"—it is personal, specific, and full of consolation. He guides the feeblest, most certainly, as a father leads along the roughness of the way, with greatest care and tenderness, a poor decrepit child. How great, how full, how abounding the joy of such divine guidance! "Enough for me," however dark and mysterious the way, attended by whatever loss, trial, or sorrow, leading to whatever disruptions, separations, or alienations—

> "Enough for me to feel and know,
> That HE in whom the cause and end,
> The past and future, meet and blend—
>
> * * * * *
>
> Guards not archangel feet alone,
> But deigns to guide and keep my own;
> Speaks not alone the words of fate,
> Which worlds destroy and worlds create,
> But whispers in my spirit's ear,
> In tones of love or warning fear,
> *A language none besides may hear.*"

Such guidance means success. It is light in darkness, help in need, and sure deliverance. It leads to a realization of the divine purpose in one's life. It secures the largest measure of usefulness. It gives knowledge for ignorance, wisdom for folly, and God's infinite sufficiency for the meagerness of human resources. The clearest faith, the warmest love, and the brightest hope glow, like stars, along this heaven-directed way. "Thou wilt show me the path of life!" is the confident exclamation of the Psalmist; and then he adds appropriately, as revealing the certain consummation of such guidance, " In thy presence is fullness of joy, at thy right hand there are pleasures for evermore." If the Lord guide us by his counsel, he will assuredly bring us, after life's toil and trouble, to the vision of the " excellent glory."

XXII.

THE HOLY SPIRIT THE GIFT OF GOD.

"If thou knewest the gift of God."—JOHN iv, 10.

MANIFOLD are the gifts from the hand of our heavenly Father with which our lives are crowned. He is the great Giver. He overflows incessantly on all his creatures. Impartation, so far as we can discern, is the highest life of God. He pours himself out for the good of his universe. Every moment of our existence proclaims the divine benevolence. In every imaginable way, for our bodies and souls, in view of our present and our future necessities, God showers on us his gifts. But his great, all-comprehensive gift, of unspeakable and inconceivable value, is *the gift of himself*. And this is the only gift which satisfies the hunger of the soul. If the Lord withhold himself from us, nothing besides will suffice. All other gifts are poor, compared with the gift of his Son and his Spirit, which are the gift of himself. The gift of God, that is, the special, pre-eminent, and all-important gift, is *the gift of the Holy Spirit*; for, by the presence and power of the Spirit, God makes himself manifest in the human soul. And this gift is the great promise of the Gospel.

On the day of Pentecost, Peter assured his astonished hearers that, on condition of repentance and faith in Jesus Christ, they should obtain the remission of sins, and receive "the gift of the Holy Ghost." And Simon Magus was blasted with a curse because he thought that "the gift of God," which was transmitted through the laying on of the apostles' hands, could be purchased with money. And it is represented as the peculiar glory of the Gospel dispensation, that on the Gentiles also was poured out the gift of the Holy Ghost.

In his conversation with the woman of Samaria, Jesus describes the Holy Ghost under the metaphor of living water, employing a figure familiar to the prophets, and which aptly presents the freeness, fullness, and life-giving offices of the refreshing and soul-reviving Spirit. By the "living water" is meant the same as by "the gift of God," that is, the Holy Ghost. "The gift of God," we are told, "is eternal life;" the faith by which we are saved is declared to be "the gift of God;" and those who have "tasted of the heavenly gift" are said to be "partakers of the Holy Ghost." In other words, this great gift excites faith, produces a peculiar satisfaction in the soul, and leads, by its transforming power, to the apprehension and enjoyment of eternal life.

It would seem, then, that the Holy Spirit is termed "*the* gift of God," by way of eminence, as being the choicest and best of God's gifts; because other things come to us mediately, but the Holy Spirit directly from God himself; and because the gift of the Holy Ghost is so comprehensive in its character, including the conviction of sin, the regeneration of the heart, the evidence of adoption, the inward and outward work and walk of holiness, unfailing consolations in the conflicts and trials of life, a key to the mysteries of the providence of God, power in prayer and power of usefulness, the certain guidance of unerring wisdom, victory over sin and self and Satan, and everlasting exaltation and felicity in God's eternal kingdom—such is "the gift of God."

The Holy Spirit—the water which Christ gives—allays the thirst of the soul for every thing except God, and is in the heart of every believer "a well of water springing up into everlasting life." Whedon observes: "It is a water of spiritual life, but it jets up into an immortal life; the water of spiritual life as it ascends crystallizes into an eternal life." And this "gift of God," and nothing besides, nor all things else, brings fullness of peace and content to the soul. As the quaint but pious Francis Quarles has sung:

> "Without Thy presence, wealth is bags of cares;
>   Wisdom, but folly; joy, disquiet, sadness;
> Friendship is treason, and delights are snares;
>   Pleasures but pain, and mirth but pleasing madness.
> Without thee, Lord, things be not what they be;
> Nor have they being when compared to thee.
>
> "In having all things, and not thee, what have I?
>   Not having thee, what have my labors got?
> Let me enjoy thee, what further crave I?
>   And having thee alone, what have I not?
> I wish nor sea, nor land; nor would I be
> Possessed of heaven, heaven unpossessed of thee."

This is our unfailing portion, but we must ask for this gift if we would receive it in the fullest measure. And in order to this, we need to appreciate its value.

When this woman of Samaria discerned, though dimly, the spiritual significance of Christ's words, she cried in earnestness of desire, "Give me this water, that I thirst not, neither come hither to draw." And for how many a mammonite, and pleasure-seeker, and panting aspirant for place and fame, would this be an appropriate prayer! This constant thirst drives them to many a deep well, from which they can draw nothing, and to many an illusive fountain, which mocks them with the semblance without the reality of refreshing waters; but only "the gift of God"—the unfailing, up-springing water of life in the soul—will enable them to say, "I thirst no more."

> "Author of faith! to Thee I lift
> My weary, longing eyes:
> O let me now receive that gift,—
> My soul without it dies."

We may reasonably suffer and sacrifice any thing and every thing for "the gift of God." If it required the labor of a life-time; if it were needful to turn from every pleasure; if only the wealth of the Indies could purchase it; if its price were poverty, obscurity, and ignominy; if it could only be found beyond seas, amid perils of malaria and death; if it were surely obtained only in the dungeon or on the scaffold—the outlay, the self-denial, the offering, the sacrifice might be cheerfully made for such riches and glories of God's living, sublimating, and aggrandizing presence in the soul. If a man becomes the temple of God and if his heart is an altar from which a grateful incense always rises to heaven, and if in the inner sanctuary of his being the living Shekinah ever glows possessions and powers and domains of this world are nothing to him. No treasures of art, no wealth of learning, no splendors of genius, no triumphs of oratory, no titles, distinctions or honors, known among men, no sweets of domestic love, no fortune or favor or felicity of any character whatsoever, can compare with the light of God's reconciled countenance, the vision of purity, the recognized beauty of the Lord, the illuminating presence of divinity, and the conscious heirship to an everlasting possession. To such a soul, heaven is already a realization; for he hungers no more, he thirsts no more, and for the Apocalyptic reason, the Lamb which is in the midst of the throne feeds him, and leads him unto living fountains of waters. Such are the experiences of those who receive "the gift of God."

"*If thou knewest* the gift of God!" It is a great blessing to be able to see and understand our opportunities and privileges. Our King, the royal Jesus, cometh, according to the prophecy, "just and having salvation." He has it meritoriously and officially— that is, to bestow on those who know their need and his power and plenitude of love and mercy, and who ask for "the gift of God." And although the Holy Spirit may not be purchased with money, or earned by charities to man, it still remains true that whosoever will may come, draw water out of the wells of salvation, and receive, through rich, abounding grace, "the gift of God."

XXIII.

THE GLORY OF THE GOSPEL DISPENSATION.

"For verily I say unto you, that many prophets and righteous men have desired to see those things which ye see, and have not seen them; and to hear those things which ye hear, and have not heard them."—MATT. xiii, 17.

THIS verse declares the glory of Messiah's kingdom, and the privileges of the Jewish people who lived in the generation in which Christ lived. It was a day which kings and prophets had desired to see, but they had not seen it, except in the dimness of prophetic vision. Devout men, for ages, had desired to hear the glorious utterances of the world's great Teacher; but the exalted privileges of the times of the Messiah they had not been permitted to enjoy. They had not, indeed, dwelt in darkness. No rayless pagan night settled down on them. They were in the twilight of the Gospel day, and some beams of the coming glory illuminated their heavens. But their types and shadows and prophetic voices were dark and doubtful and unsatisfactory, compared with the teachings and miracles and mighty works of the manifested Messiah.

Glorious was the line of the Jewish saints; from Abel, who offered unto God a more excellent sacrifice than Cain, and who obtained witness that he was righteous, to Enoch, who walked with God, and was not because God took him—to Noah, who prepared an ark for the saving of his house, by which he condemned the world, and became heir of the righteousness which is by faith—to Abraham, who sojourned in the land of promise as in a strange country, for he looked for a city which hath foundations, whose builder and maker is God. "These all died in faith, not having received the promises, but having seen them afar off, and were persuaded of them, and embraced them, and confessed that they were strangers and pilgrims on the earth."

And though the prophets did not comprehend "what or what manner of time the spirit of Christ which was in them did signify, when it testified beforehand the sufferings of Christ, and the glory that should follow;" yet they saw and comprehended enough to perceive and understand that the times of the Messiah would be the beginning of a marvelous period in the world's history, fruitful in blessings to the Israel of God. But so far as the prophecies related to the Gentile world, they seemed to have no vision. This mystery of Christ, the mystery of universal redemption, and of a faith and a religion for all peoples, in all lands, in all ages, "that," as the apostle has expressed it, "the Gentiles should be fellow-heirs, and of the same body, and partakers of his promise in Christ by the Gospel," "in other ages was not made known unto the sons of men, as it is now revealed unto the holy apostles and prophets by the Spirit." This full, cloudless revelation, this distinct enunciation of *a Gospel for humanity*, this is the peculiar glory of Messiah's day and reign.

What, then, let us inquire, are some of the peculiar

advantages or privileges of that dispensation of the Gospel which we enjoy?

1. *A Christ manifested is more than a Christ predicted.* We behold the prophecies fulfilled. Ours is not an anticipated Messiah, but an historic Lord. We know that the world's Redeemer has been on the earth; that he has brightened man's pathway with the light of his footsteps; that he has left us an example of perfect holiness and unwearied beneficence; that he has died as a sacrifice for our sins, and that the provisions of his Gospel are abundant for the salvation of our souls.

2. *The kingly presence and power of Jesus is represented by the promised Spirit.*

Jesus comforted his disciples with the assurance that if he went away he would send the Spirit, which by its offices of illumination and guidance and awakening and consolation should more than compensate for his personal absence. We read in one place that "the Holy Ghost was not yet given, because that Jesus was not yet glorified"—not that all who preceded Christ were without the influence of the Spirit, but the day of his dispensation, when he should be to all believers as rivers of living water, had not yet come. But Jesus, glorified, sends the Holy Spirit in mighty power on the Church and the world. This is a peculiar glory of the Gospel dispensation. By the office and work of the Spirit, Christ's presence is made universal. The baptismal Spirit is the soul of Christendom—the life of religion in the world. The gracious anointing of wisdom and power which begun at Pentecost, continues in the Church, and sinners are awakened, penitents are converted, corruption is purged away from the soul, the bonds of sinful habits are broken, mighty consolations are experienced, victories of holiness are realized, the largest beneficence is inspired, and the world is filled with the glories of the Redeemer's kingdom.

3. The growth of civilization is the product of Christianity, and this is one of the advantages which we enjoy under the reign of the Messiah and the dispensation of the Holy Spirit. There are many blessings which seem to lie outside of the Gospel which are yet born of it. Civilization roots in regeneration. A civilized community of unregenerate men would be an impossibility. There must be enough of the power of the Gospel in men's hearts to subdue and shame, if it does not utterly extirpate, selfishness, to create a reverence for justice, to excite some measure of love for man as man, and to make the duty of caring for dependent and unfortunate classes plain and imperative, before there can be a reign of civilization. In other words, the Gospel must so far pervade society as to exert on all its institutions a sanctifying and transforming power, or it cannot be uplifted from barbarism, and saved from anarchy and self-destruction. Christian nations, therefore, have laws, governments, homes, systems of education, and institutions and organizations of beneficence ; and any nation becoming Christian will have these things will increase in its aggregate and in its impartial distribution of individual and social well-being. The general security and happiness of society, and all genuine progress, are to be attributed to Christianity, and these are distinguishing glories of the Messiah's reign.

4. This is a dispensation which is to continue and extend in the earth; and its triumph in all lands, over all opposition, and for man's grandest elevation, will be absolute and forever.

The religion of Jesus cannot encounter any greater opposition in the future than it has in the past. The victories which it has gained are a prophecy of the triumphs which it is destined to achieve. Never before in the world's history did it have such resources at its command—resources of wealth, learning, culture, knowledge of men and things, and of fullest consecration to Christ's cause. Every material improvement, every political advancement, every social reform, every triumph of art, every discovery of science, helps the Gospel. The doors of every nation open to receive the truth, and the language of Christendom is becoming the language of the world.

What, let us inquire in the second place, are the agencies through which these great Gospel successes are realized?

1. The first is holiness, which is at once the strength and glory of the Christian Church. By deliverance from sin, by deadness to the world, by blameless and holy lives, by goodness, mercy, and truth, on the part of Christ's followers, is this religion chiefly commended to the world. Methodism, especially, has from the beginning set forth the doctrine and experience of holiness—the sanctifying power of God in the soul, as an orthodox dogma and a realized fact. And this has been one marked element of its wonderful success. "In 1729," says Mr. John Wesley, "my brother and I read the Bible; saw inward and outward holiness therein, followed after it, and

incited others to do so. In 1737 we saw this holiness comes by faith. In 1738 we saw we must be justified before we are sanctified. But still holiness was our point, inward and outward holiness. God then thrust us out to raise up a holy people." Methodism, since that time, has spread over continents, established institutions, gathered converts by thousands and millions, and sent her ministers and missionaries into every quarter of the globe; but, thank God! holiness is still our point, and, in the future as in the past, will be the secret of our power and prosperity.

And in the journals of the father of American Methodism, Francis Asbury, we find the secret of his success in carrying the Gospel over a continent, and in laying the foundations of an ecclesiastical empire, in such records as these: "I am still sensible of my deep insufficiency, and that mostly with regard to holiness. It is true, God has given me some gifts, but what are they to holiness? It is for holiness my spirit mourns. I wish to walk constantly before God without reproof." And again: "Holiness is the element of my soul. My earnest prayer is that nothing contrary to holiness may live in me." Saintly man! who in his preaching journeys out-traveled Wesley, whose courageous spirit was equal to Luther's when he thundered defiance at the Vatican, and who in labors and sufferings, to preach the Gospel in "the regions beyond," was surpassed only by the great apostle to the Gentiles. The holiness for which he groaned, and which was the element of his soul, he carried, as a flame of fire, from conference to conference, from the Lakes to the Gulf, and from the

Atlantic to the broad, but then sparsely-settled and almost unknown valley of the Mississippi. A great, growing, spiritual people, intent on holiness and the world's salvation, remain as a monument to his faithfulness.

And Methodism still asks of its young preachers, seeking full membership in an annual conference, these searching questions: "Have you faith in Christ? Are you going on to perfection? Do you expect to be made perfect in love in this life? Are you groaning after it? Are you resolved to devote yourself wholly to God and his work?"

Nothing more distinctly or emphatically than these questions could reveal the spirit and purpose of the denomination.

2. The doctrine of justification by faith, and the witness of the Spirit to our adoption, as the common privilege of all believers, must be firmly upheld and persistently urged in order that the glory of this Gospel manifestation may be fully revealed to the children of men.

These are the verities, the certainties of the Christian faith. By these men are grounded and settled in their confidence and hope.

"We are assured," says Froude in a half-skeptical strain, "that if the truth be, as we are told, of vital moment—vital to all alike, wise and foolish, educated and uneducated—the road to it cannot lie through any very profound inquiries. We refuse to believe that every laborer or mechanic must balance arduous historical probabilities and come to a just conclusion under pain of damnation."

Well, the truth *is* vital—vital to the soul's salvation; and, what is more, the road to it does not lie through any difficult path. No truth is so easy to learn, so ready to comprehend, so clearly demonstrated in its own light, as that which pertains to the faith of Christ, and sanctification and eternal life through his merits. And whatever other religious bodies may have done, Methodism certainly has never gone balancing "historical probabilities" to find the place of the sanctuary of the Most High, or asking others to do so, "under pain of damnation." It has chiefly dealt with the fundamental truths—man's ruin by sin, the full provision of mercy in Christ, and the undoubted salvation of every soul who will come to God by him. And a wayfaring man, though a fool, can find this path.

To much better purpose, this distinguished writer has said, in another place, considering the religious characters of Erasmus and Luther: "You will mistake me if you think I represent Erasmus as a man without conscience, or belief in God and goodness. But in Luther that belief was a certainty; in Erasmus it was only a high probability, and the difference between the two is not merely great—it is infinite." Now, in the light of Christ's teachings, and with the office and work of the Holy Spirit, all earnest disciples of the Lord Jesus come to know that they have passed from death unto life, and have been made heirs of eternal salvation. What a source is this of consolation! What a power of resistance against the surging tides of infidelity! What a glory of Messiah's reign!

3. The light and blessedness of this Gospel dispensation, we must also remark, could not be made

known to men without evangelical and missionary zeal and labor. Every Christian, in the very genius and inspiration of his divine life, is a disciple-maker. It is a necessity that he should be a propagandist of his faith. His experience is a constant incentive to missionary activity. He must preach a gospel which burns like fire in his bones. The story of the cross is a story to be told. The love of Jesus is not a love to be hidden from men. As the Son of God came a messenger from the Father to the world, so has he sent forth all his followers to be messengers of the same sufficient grace to the souls of perishing men. And this is the end, and the only legitimate end, of a Church organization—to make Christ manifest to the world.

At one of his early conferences Mr. Wesley inquired, "Have we a right view of our work?" It was answered, "Perhaps not. It is not to take care of this or that society, or to preach so many times, but *to save as many souls as we can*, to bring as many sinners as we can to repentance, and with all our power to build them up in that holiness without which they cannot see the Lord."

And a Church which manifests its living Head and shows forth the superior advantages of the Gospel dispensation will be missionary in its longing and work as well as evangelical. It will covet the ends of the earth for Christ's kingdom, and it will make persistent efforts to attain them. There is not such an aggressive body on earth as the Christian Church, nor one which has such just expectations of conquest and power. The success of Dr. Carey, in India, suggested to the Baptist Missionary Society the motto,

"Attempt great things for God; expect great things from God." They ought to be written over the door of every church, and deeply impressed on the heart of every Christian.

4. Finally, a peculiar glory of the Gospel dispensation is that its light shines into the heart of childhood, and one of its great sources of power is the fact that it includes even babes in its covenant grace, teaches them to lisp the Saviour's praises, and leads them up to manhood in the service of Israel's King. The Church is largely a teaching, conserving, and disciplinary institution, and, as such, children are the most hopeful subjects of its care, training, and watchful labors. And the Church which gives itself most thoroughly to the work of instructing and evangelizing the young will be the most growing, prosperous, and powerful Church in the earth. But it is essential that the children should be converted as well as taught, and when converted exercised and disciplined in Christian holiness and usefulness. This is a fundamental point. The children must be led to experience and know the love of Jesus, and then treated as other Christians, organized and employed in the service of the Master. It is the great, all-comprehensive glory of this Gospel dispensation, and it brings the race, as such, to God, so that whosoever will may be saved.

I have two words in conclusion:

1. The first is admonition. Great light brings great obligations, and the chief obligation is faithfulness. You must endure—must endure to the end. Persevering grace is the crowning grace. It is said that when the ruins of Pompeii were excavated, a few

years ago, the skeletons of its inhabitants were found in the very places in which the lava-flood had buried them. Some were found in their bed-chamber, some were hidden in cellars, and others were in the attitude of running through the streets with their bags of gold. Close by the city gates a Roman sentinel was found, standing at his post, and still grasping his spear. While the deluge of fire, and ashes, and lava was ingulfing him, there he stood, and there he has been standing for a thousand years!

What an example of fidelity and devotion! And when Christ shall come, where will you be found? Standing at your post? Engaged in your Redeemer's work? Or in worldliness, indulgence, and sin? "Blessed are those servants whom the Lord, when he cometh, shall find watching."

2. The second word is consolation. He who has done so much for us will not fail us, but will go with us to the end. When Wallace, the Irish delegate, died at Cincinnati, away from home and friends, and before he had accomplished his mission, he said: "I can leave all my concerns in the hands of Jesus." Blessed confidence! Every Christian may feel it, living or dying, and, resting on this rock, the surging **waves** neither of time nor eternity can move him.

XXIV

THE LONG WAITING FOR GOD.

"Lo, this is our God; we have waited for him, and he will save us."—Isa. xxv, 9.

The splendid picturings of prophecy, the rich provisions of redemption, the divine sufficiency, and the world's necessities, lead us to expect triumphs of Gospel grace among men, and beneficent results of Christian labor, which are not realized. By this apparent failure and certain delay the faith of the Church is greatly tried, while gainsayers mock and infidels revile, saying, "Where is the promise of his coming?"

There is no question in regard to the fact of the long waiting of God to bring salvation. "Providence," says Guizot, "takes one step; ages have elapsed." The Psalmist sighs repeatedly, as he beholds the desolations of Zion and hears the boastings of the heathen, "How long?" How long it was before Christ came to redeem the world! How many centuries have since elapsed, and yet how small a portion of the race is evangelized! How many millions have gone into eternity without ever having heard the name of Jesus! How often is the Church hindered, and communities and generations left in darkness and sin, because, as it would seem, God does not raise up the right instrumentalities—men of wealth, knowledge, piety, high designs, and broad and far-reaching views—to accomplish his work! Dr. Bushnell has published a book on "The Moral Uses of Dark Things;" but of all the dark things which he discusses, nothing is so dark as this providential delay in works of goodness, which the illustrious divine does not so much as mention.

A solution of the problem is difficult, and, perhaps, impossible; but there are two or three considerations which may relieve our minds and comfort our hearts.

"This is our God," who administers the affairs of the universe, in a way, to be sure, which we cannot comprehend, but which is most assuredly in accordance with infinite wisdom and love. Consider, it is God! And he has made us capable of the cognition of himself. Though we do not know him perfectly, yet, so far as we know him at all, we may know him truly. He is not an idol, a myth, an apotheosis, nor an archangel, but the unoriginated, absolute, eternal and all-sufficient God. He is infinite in wisdom, goodness, power, and love, and, therefore, incomprehensible to the loftiest of created intelligences. No marvel that to us his ways, even when glowing in the light of a divine manifestation, are past finding out!

"He is *our* God." This supposes that personal relations with the Highest is the privilege of his redeemed. And the Scripture narratives teach us the same truth. Abraham was the friend of God, as well as the father of the faithful; Enoch walked with God in the close companionship of trust and love; God communed with Moses in the thick cloud which enshrined the glory of the divine Presence; John was the beloved disciple of a Master whom angels worshiped; Paul, who judged himself unworthy to be called an apostle, because he had persecuted the saints of God, was caught up into the third heavens and heard unutterable things; and it is the privilege of every believer to look toward the throne of infinite Majesty, and to say, "My Father"—to contemplate a dying, risen, and interceding Saviour, and to exclaim, in the assurance of an unfailing faith, "Who loved *me* and gave himself for *me!*" And though mysteries remain, dark and inexplicable, even in this confidence of love, and despite all the illumination of the Spirit, yet the assurance that it is "*our* GOD," whose long delay is so trying, and whose administration is so incomprehensible, enables us to trust though we cannot understand, and to wait through the weary years, in joyful confidence that what we know not now we shall know hereafter.

Moreover, it may be said, perhaps, that the aim of Divine Providence in the administration of human affairs is the production of character in man, and that this result will abundantly compensate for any delay, loss, or trial to which the race is subjected. That which we call character, that is, tried and established virtue, is of more value, even in a single human being, than the whole material universe of God; and, indeed, of so great value as to be incapable of estimation except by the infinite Mind. But character is not an ephemeral production; it does not spring up with tropical quickness, and is, moreover, impossible of creation; but it is the result of knowledge, discipline, training, trial, proof; and these require *time*. How our idea of the Supreme, for instance, must grow as we see more of him in his works and ways; and how immensely character is affected by our conception of God! It has been often observed that the principles of morality are the same, and that man's moral nature is the same, in every age; but character is the conformation of manhood to these principles, and by these standards the Almighty tries and proves every generation and every individual of the race. The foulest crimes, without doubt, are the involuntary, which flow from the depraved soul unconsciously, through the power of affection and habit.

Human progress, with its great commanding elements of virtue, knowledge, and industry, can only be realized by growth and time. And law, science, government, civilization, all those things which are most esteemed among men, and which are of greatest value to the race, are, in the very nature of the case, growths. The world has had to wait for them through toilful and burdened years and centuries. Besides, we must not lose from sight the moral unity of the race, and the interest which every generation has in the labors, sufferings, and acquisitions of every preceding generation. "Let it not be grievous to you," said the Puritans in England to the feeble band of colonists which landed from the Mayflower on Plymouth Rock, "that you have been instruments to break the ice for others; the honor shall be yours to the world's end." Not only all the past, but all the future, belongs to man. Of many a hero-martyr it may be said, as Whittier has sung:

> "Thine was the seed-time; God alone
> Beholds the end of what is sown;

> Beyond our vision, weak and dim,
> The harvest-time is hid with him.
> Yet, unforgotten where it lies,
> That seed of generous sacrifice,
> Though seeming on the desert cast,
> Shall rise with bloom and fruit at last."

Our highest satisfaction, moreover, is in those things which come to us as growths. A gradually accumulated fortune; a path of honor, ascended step by step, till the golden, starlit summit is reached; an affection which has come to maturity amid the labors, watchings and burdens of years, like conjugal love in its ripeness and perfection, or a mother's joy in her son grown to a virtuous manhood; of how much more worth are these than a shoddy possession, a sudden splendor, and a career of soft and enervating luxury, with no heroic memories, no tender recollections of sacrifice and forbearance, and no welding of heart-confidences in the fiery furnace of common afflictions! There is said to be such a thing as love at first sight, which flashes out like a meteor on the thick darkness; but a great love is certainly a growth, and by toil and trial and trust it is proved and perfected, till it is set like a star in the heavens, insphered and eternal, or like another sun which illumines the very clouds, and makes the dreariest pathway bright with its rosy beams.

And men may love Jesus when first they see his face and hear his voice; but they will know more about love for Christ when they have followed him for years; met with him the denials, sophisms, and scoffs of Pharisees, infidels, and hypocrites; stood with him on Tabor's illuminated summit, and felt the joy of a divine communion; gone with him into the judgment-hall of Pilate; fainted with him under the fearful burden of the cross; combated with him the powers of death and hell; cried out with him, in the utter agony of earthly desolation, "My God, my God, why hast thou forsaken me?" and rejoiced and triumphed with him, in perfect submission to the Father's will, and in the calm assurance of an everlasting kingdom, and an eternity of exaltation and happiness.

The highest glory of the divine character is forbearance—the infinite patience of love—and this is also the crowning Christian grace: "Let patience have her perfect work, that ye may be perfect and entire, wanting nothing." But patience supposes trial and contradiction, and involves the necessity of waiting and suffering. It is the power of cheerful endurance. It is thus that Christians become partakers of Christ's suffering and glory.

Then let us wait and watch with patience and hope. "Lo, this is our God; we have waited for him, and *he will save us!*" He *will;* he has promised, and his word cannot fail. He will *save* us; we shall find complete deliverance, assurance, exaltation, honor, and glory through his matchless grace. Then let us cling to the promise, and trust, and not be afraid; for "His going forth is prepared as the morning, and he shall come unto us as the rain, as the latter and former rain unto the earth."

XXV.

THE PRIVILEGES OF THE SONS OF GOD.

"To them gave he power [privilege] to become the sons of God."
JOHN i, 12.

THIS Christmas season, reminding us all of the incarnation of the world's Redeemer, is an appropriate time for considering the privileges of the sons of God; for it is only because of the manifestation, expiatory sufferings, and living intercessions of that Divine Jesus who was proclaimed by the prophets, foreshadowed by types and sacrifices, heralded by angels, and "declared to be the Son of God with power, according to the Spirit of holiness, by the resurrection from the dead," that any of us are able to attain adoption and heirship to eternal life.

What a view this passage gives us of the dignity, majesty, and kingly authority of the Son of God! He has the exalted privileges of the sons of God to bestow. He can bring men into this high and ennobling relation. He can enrich the sons of men with all the advantages which follow adoption into the household of faith, And he who can thus uplift, purify, transform, aggrandize, and superbly endow our poor, sinful, degraded humanity, must stand at the head of the universe, and possess a nature which is incomprehensible to finite minds.

And what is this gift which the Son of God has to bestow? It is the *right, power, privilege* to become the sons of God. It takes these three italicised words to express the meaning of the original Greek. Bengel defines it as "the *capability, the inner-enabling;* for," he reasons, "by being sons of God, John means *an actual partaking of the divine nature.*" Unquestionably the adoption of sons is of such value and importance as only celestial intelligences can properly estimate; and in the relation certain rights or privileges inhere, as possessions or prerogatives, which are the princely endowments of the accepted children of the Most High. Let us consider these privileges of the sons of God.

Entire deliverance from sin and all its disabilities must of course be realized. It is sin which makes men aliens and strangers to the commonwealth of Israel, and to the God and Father of all grace. Sin, therefore, must be destroyed; its guilt must be pardoned, its pollution purged, its bondage broken, and its punishment averted. For this marvelous deliverance the Gospel scheme provides as an immediate result. But there are consequences of sin, such as physical disorder, the general derangements, and ofttimes serious sufferings, growing out of the fallen condition of the world and inexorable law of mortality to which all are subject, from which there can be no immediate release. But of ultimate deliverance the sons of God are assured, It is part of their inheritance. Even death will be counter-worked and overcome by a glorious resurrection to an immortal life. Every disability produced by transgression will be removed as soon as the scheme of the divine government will permit. That scheme is beneficent, though it does not exclude sorrow, temptation, and trial, but uses them as forces for purification and ennoblement. The believer, therefore, finds his advantage in the delay, and when the full deliverance comes it will be all the more joyful and glorious.

Access to God, communion with him, a divine fellowship in Christ, the conscious indwelling and leading of the Holy Ghost, with the exaltation and happiness certain to follow, are the manifest privileges of the sons of God. This is Christian syntheism; and those who experience its reality constitute the only genuine order of nobility on the face of the earth. They can come to the Highest, at all times, with the greatest freedom and the fullest confidence, presenting every interest of their souls at the throne of heavenly grace, and committing their future for both worlds, with unquestioning assurance, into the hands of their reconciled and loving Father and God. The power of faith and prayer is sufficient to lift the soul into a new plane of life and experience. And those who are accustomed thus to approach their heavenly Father become convinced of his interest in the least things which concern his children, and of his desire that they may be, to use Bloomfield's words, "as happy in this world and the next as infinite goodness, under the guidance of infinite wisdom, can make them." "Behold," therefore, "what manner of love the Father hath bestowed upon us, that we should be called the sons of God!"

In regard to the great future, the doctrine of the Scriptures is clear and determinate: "For as many as are led by the Spirit of God, they are the sons of God." "And if children, then heirs; heirs of God, and joint-heirs with Christ." The believer, then, is a joint-heir with Jesus, the only-begotten and eternal Son. Why a joint-heir? Because an heir. Why an heir? Because, by adoption, a son. How does he know that he is a son? Because he is led by the spirit of God. The logical connection is complete from the leading of the Spirit to co-heirship with the Lord Jesus—the Prince of Life. And this shows how great, how magnificent, how imperishable the inheritance of the saints! How inestimable the privilege of becoming co-inheritor with the Son of God to his kingdom, throne, dominion, happiness, and glory! And this exaltation, honor, and felicity are within our reach—the present assurance of an everlasting possession. "Wherefore come out from among them, and be ye separate, saith the Lord, and touch not the unclean thing; and I will receive you, and will be a Father unto you, and ye shall be my sons and daughters, saith the Lord Almighty" Such are the rights, privileges, immunities, of the sons of God.

But these privileges are gracious—the bestowment of infinite goodness and love. They are obtained only through faith in Christ. They belong "to them that believe on his name," that is, in Jesus himself as the way, and the only way, of life and salvation; for the words, "*His name*," as Whedon affirms, "stand for all that his name comprehends. Our faith must embrace Christ in his fullness. And with how transcendent a fullness does the evangelist's description endow him! To receive him is faith in *act*. It is not, as Olshausen says, a mere *susceptibility*, but an *activity*, an appropriation of Christ by a free putting forth of the *will*." Faith in Christ, therefore, as the Son of God, having power and authority to bestow the privilege of sonship on those who are regenerated to a new life by his Holy Spirit, is the means of all the right, acceptance, endowment, dignity, exaltation, happiness, glory which we obtain under the Gospel. "For ye are all the children of God, by faith in Christ Jesus."

"Sons of God!" How distinguished and transcendent the honor! And yet it is to strangers and enemies that this gracious immunity is proffered! How infinite the mercy of the Gospel!

"Sons of God!" How much is implied in being the children of such a Father! What more can we desire if we have God for our Father? He knows what things we need. He is mindful of our slightest necessities. And he is able to fill our being's largest capacities with his own infinite fullness.

"Sons of God!" How carefully ought we to walk, in what ways of holiness, with what love and charity toward men, who claim to be the children of the Highest!

"Sons of God!" If we are truly such, we shall come, one day, to our Father's house and bosom, safe sheltered from the storms of time, for the endless repose and bliss of heaven.

XXVI.

CHRISTIAN WOMEN, GOSPEL HELPERS.

"Help those women which labored with me in the Gospel."—
PHIL. iv, 3.

THE elevation of woman marks the progress of Christian civilization. The Gospel is for all classes and conditions, but especially for the poor, weak, dependent classes. To woman, therefore, it has been an evangel of light and joy. Its principles have been her defense, and its triumph has been her deliverance, exaltation, and happiness. The Gospel asserts the absolute equality of woman with the other sex in the provisions of the atonement, guards the sanctity of her person and home, gives her perfect freedom of access to the altars of God, makes her the anointed priestess of childhood, and calls her to activities in the Church of Christ in which she may usefully and happily employ her noblest powers.

I consider the New Testament recognition of woman, in view of the time of its composition, and the ideas which then prevailed, and do still prevail, in Oriental countries in respect to women, as one of the proofs of its divine origin.

Jesus, born of a woman, was ministered unto by devoted members of the sex in all his life and labors. When he hung on the cross, "many women were there beholding afar off;" and "certain women," who "were early at the sepulcher," greatly "astonished" the apostles by a report of a "vision of angels," and celestial testimony to the fact of the resurrection of the Son of God from the dead. "Last at the cross and first at the sepulcher," is not more a tribute to the faithfulness of woman than it is a revelation of the genius of the Gospel. One of the most important of our Lord's discourses was delivered to a single auditor, and that a Samaritan woman. When the disciples came they "marveled that he talked with the woman," a thing which no Jewish doctor would have done in a public place. But Jesus, while he denounced the sins, also defied the prejudices of his countrymen. The tender regard of the world's Redeemer for the family at Bethany can never be forgotten, nor the fact that this household was two thirds of the gentler sex. The record is: "Now Jesus loved Martha, and her sister, and Lazarus." And did the Lord of life ever pronounce a higher eulogy on any human being than on that woman of whom he said, "She hath done what she could?"

The historic period covered by the Acts of the Apostles is also rich in its testimony touching the relation of woman to the Church. "The women" are specially mentioned as included in the first prayer-meeting which was protracted into Pentecost. The divinely inspired account of the introduction of the Gospel into Philippi, "the chief city of that part of Macedonia and a colony," is in these words: "And on the Sabbath we went out of the city by a riverside, where prayer was wont to be made; and we sat down, and spake unto the women which resorted thither. And a certain woman named Lydia, a seller of purple, of the city of Thyatira, which worshiped God, heard us: whose heart the Lord opened, that she attended unto the things which were spoken of Paul. And when she was baptized, and her household, she besought us, saying, If ye have judged me to be faithful to the Lord, come into my house, and abide there. And she constrained us."

It was, then, a company of women which was addressed; one of these, Lydia, was converted and baptized, and her house became at once the home of the messengers of salvation. "Chief women" and "honorable women" are frequently mentioned as having believed, and engaged in the work of spreading the Gospel.

Whether in the constitution of the Christian Church, in the time of the apostles, women were designated for important offices; whether the deaconess and the female presbyter or elder were creations of the apostolic or of a somewhat later period, is a question which I shall not presume to decide. There are some passages which seem to indicate that women were ordained, by the apostles, for the instruction of their own sex, for the visitation of the poor, and to labor in the Gospel; but the interpretations of the ablest critics do not harmonize, and there is great weight of learning and authority on both sides.

There can be no doubt, however, that the baptism of the Spirit and the life of God in the soul moved women as well as men to put forth earnest endeavors to propagate the Gospel faith; and it was, moreover, a necessity, especially in the Grecian and Asiatic countries visited by the apostles, to employ largely the agency of devout women to teach those of their own sex, and to visit, relieve, and comfort them in their distresses, for the reason that the apostles, because of the social customs which prevailed, could have scarcely any access to the women of these sections. It is certain that the order of "deaconess" existed in the early Church, and it has been argued, with great plausibility, that the germ of it must have existed in the Apostolic Church itself. The duties of those who held this position, according to Tertullian, were not to teach, nor baptize, nor administer the sacrament, nor arrogate to themselves any manly function or priestly office; but their work seems to have been the visitation of the sick and poor and those who were in prison, especially of their own sex, and to exercise a general oversight over the female members of the Church, making occasional reports to the bishops and presbyters.

"Help those women," says the apostle, "who," as Macknight renders, "for the Gospel have combated together with me"—that is, like those engaged in the Isthmian games, have wrestled, or contended, with me, for the faith of Christ. "The word does not imply," says Benson, "preaching, or any thing of that kind, but opposition, danger, and toil endured for the sake of the Gospel."

The personal salutations, in the sixteenth of Romans, honorably mention a number of tireless, self-sacrificing, and heroic women who labored much in the Lord, who "laid down their own necks" to preserve the life of the great apostle to the Gentiles, and who were chosen, beloved, and sainted. Of Phœbe, the most eminent of these women-workers, the servant, or *deaconess*, of the Church at Cenchrea, and the succorer, or *patroness* of many, including Paul himself, and who carried this epistle from Corinth to the Romans, Whedon says : " The ability and eminence of Phœbe appears from the apostle's earnest commendation, from these her titles, from her travel and business, and, as Renan, in his flippant style, expresses it, 'she bore in the folds of her robe the whole future of the Christian theology—the writing which was to regulate the fate of the world.'"

It is plain, therefore, that Christianity has, from the first, honored woman, recognized her power of usefulness, incited her to genial labors of charity and beneficence, commended her diligence in the service of her divine Master, and carried her forward and upward, with the advancing conquests of a Christian civilization, to a purer life, a higher culture, and a grander destiny.

If, then, Christian women are Gospel helpers, and have a great work to do for the furtherance and triumph of the Messiah's kingdom, how, we may ask, can they best employ their faculties and improve their opportunities in the fulfillment of their sublime mission ?

In order to their widest usefulness there are some things that ought to be avoided, of which two only shall be mentioned.

1. The first is extravagance in dress.

It may not be true that vanity and love of admiration are besetting sins of the sex, but it does seem unquestionable that a disposition to adorn her person is deeply imbedded in woman's nature. And many of the sins, whether of men or women, are because of excess in such things as within legitimate bounds are right and proper. It is certain, also, that the Scriptures admonish women to "adorn themselves in modest apparel, with shamefacedness and sobriety; not with braided hair, or gold, or pearls, or costly array; but, which becometh women professing godliness, with good works."

Especially should Christian women dress plainly at church, and in the visitation of the poor. A style of dress calculated to attract attention, to excite envy, to humiliate the poor by striking contrasts with their own meager wardrobes, to gratify vanity by display, and pride by ostentation, and to distract the minds of the worshipers, is certainly wholly out of place in the sanctuary of God. And a wealthy woman who cannot consent to wear the plainest garments in the visitation of the poor at their own houses had better abandon at once her mission of assumed beneficence. The reasons are obvious to any thoughtful mind.

I think a great deal of the alleged extravagance of women is imposed on them by husbands and fathers, who desire in this way to proclaim their own wealth and social consequence, and who use their wives and daughters for this purpose precisely as the dry-goods' dealer uses his dummies for the display of his fabrics. It must be said, however, that this is a species of tyranny to which most women submit with a remarkable degree of resignation. But the Christian woman who desires to do the most for her Master will not be inconsiderate to so small a matter as that of dress, and will deny herself in this, as in other directions, that she may win souls to Christ, and accomplish the greatest possible good for the cause of God.

2. In the second place, it should be observed that any woman who neglects home duties for the sake of public activity in any direction, however noble, beneficent, and Christian, rather hinders than helps the advancement of Christ's kingdom in the world. "Let them learn first to show piety at home" is a rule of universal application. To bring up children, to lodge strangers, to wash the saints' feet and to relieve the afflicted, are as honorable now as in the days of the apostle. The divine requirement of all women who would be active in the Church is such "behavior as becometh holiness"—that they be "discreet, chaste, keepers at home, good, obedient to their own husbands, that the word of God be not blasphemed." The Church has many effective workers, in the ranks of her noble women, whose light shines brightest by their own hearth-stones, whose ministrations of love are most hallowed and heavenly at their own home altars, and whose own children, as well as the inmates of orphan asylums, will rise up and call them blessed.

There are many things which a Christian woman can do, without any neglect of home duties, for the advancement of Christ's cause in the earth. Let us briefly enumerate:

1. She can, by her personal exertions, increase the congregations in all our churches; and it is no small matter to bring careless souls to hear the word of God.

2. She can give a healthy tone to society. She can exert her influence in favor of temperance, social

reform, purity of morals, honest industry, and real worth. She can show that she thinks more of a man than his clothes—that she is not ashamed to take an upright laborer by the hand, but does shrink from the touch of a libertine despite his wealth and distinctions. She can honor her own sex, and promote its culture, education, and influence, saving society. at once, from what is frivolous and what is impure. She can carry the religion of Jesus into any circle, for no skeptic dare sneer at *her*. She is the prophetess of God, chosen and anointed for the sanctification of society, if not for the salvation of the world.

3. Christian women, are ministering angels for the sick and poor. It has often been told that the English soldiers in the Crimean hospitals used to kiss the shadow of Florence Nightingale as it fell on their pillows. Many noble American women greatly honored Christ and served humanity in our hospitals during the recent fratricidal strife. Women have access to the sick and poor, especially of their own sex, in every community, which no man, not even a minister of the Gospel, can secure ; and they come with a gentler step, a softer touch, and a kindlier tone, which makes them doubly welcome.

"Christianity does not so much exalt woman," a woman has said, "as exalt service ; by making of those lowly offices it is the lot of woman to exercise a work as high as Gabriel's—' doing the pleasure of God '—the Gospel does not emancipate woman, but makes service free."

4. That women, as well as men, can do much for the promotion of the material, as well as the spiritual, interests of the Church, the whole history of Chris-

tianity proves. The finishing of the Tabernacle was accomplished on this wise:

"And they came, both men and women, as many as were willing-hearted, and brought bracelets, and ear-rings, and rings, and tablets, all jewels of gold and every man that offered, offered an offering of gold unto the Lord. And all the women that were wise-hearted did spin with their hands, and brought that which they had spun, both of blue, and of purple, and of scarlet, and of fine linen." It requires the labors, sacrifices, tears, and offerings of both men and women to build the temple of God in this world.

The grandest opportunities are presented for such labors and contributions and noble achievements to the women of the Methodist Episcopal Church, not only in the ordinary duties and privileges of the Church, but in the operations of the "Woman's Foreign Missionary Society" and of the "Ladies' and Pastors' Christian Union," both of which truly beneficent and Christian organizations have been recognized and indorsed by the General Conference, and commended to the sympathy and support of the Church. Devout women cannot, any more than consecrated pastors, disregard or neglect these mighty agencies for extending the kingdom and hastening the coming of the Son of God.

I remark, finally, that women need these exercises, which Christianity imposes as duty and reveals as privilege, in order to health, mental growth, and spiritual progress.

1. They need them for *health*. Dr. Bushnell says of our New England mothers: "If they were some-

times *drudged* by their over-intense labor, still they were kept by it in a generally rugged state both of body and mind. They kept a good digestion, which is itself no small part of a character. The mothers spent their nervous impulse on their muscles, and had so much less need of keeping down the excess, or calming the unspent lightning, by doses of anodyne. In the play of the wheel they spun fiber too within, and in the weaving wove it close and firm."

Invention, art, and the progress of physical science, have emancipated woman from the loom and the wheel, and many other forms of domestic servitude, and for health, muscle, and physical vigor she now needs intenser occupations in the way of Christian beneficence. Thus only can she be saved from a life of fashion, folly, and physical decay.

2. For *mental growth*. Increase of faculty and intellectual power cannot be secured by any human being without thought, activity, and collision of mind with mind. The brain, to be kept growing and vigorous, must be fed with the truths of nature and God. And if women would be the companions of men, they must have corresponding culture and development. They must not permit their husbands and brothers to outgrow them. Not only by reading and study, but also by active contact with great interests, by endeavoring to comprehend and settle great questions, are men educated. For mental growth, women must seize and try to handle even such gigantic problems as the world's redemption.

3. And also for *spiritual progress*. How can a woman, any more than a man, grow in grace without activity, energy, and zeal? The Gospel is spiritual

life, and, on its highest plane, deals with us not as men and women, but as rational and immortal souls. And the souls, whether of men or women, receiving most of Christ's image, and doing most of Christ's work in the earth, will shine the brightest in the everlasting kingdom.

XXVII.

THE CHILD'S GROWTH IN CHRISTIAN CHARACTER.

"Bring them up in the nurture and admonition of the Lord."
EPH. vi. 4.

How to secure a child's most rapid growth in Christian character is a question of more than ordinary importance. It is a question which greatly concerns the child itself, as well as his parents, his religious teachers, the Church, and the world. The question supposes that the child *has* a Christian character—that he has become a Christian, and has, in some measure, that strength of principle, power of resistance, purity of affection, and beneficence of disposition which, in the best sense of the word, constitute character. The capacity for growth is also assumed, so that we have neither of these points to argue, enforce, or illustrate. The only question is, How can this growth in Christian character be secured?

In the first place, let it be observed that God is the great worker on character. To perfect sentient beings, possessed of intelligence and free volition, in those moral dispositions which are the crowning glory of his own nature, would seem to be the grand purpose of the Supreme Governor in the administration of the affairs of the universe. To our fallen world God has given, for the accomplishment of this object, the Church, the Civil Government, and the Family. This is the trinity of divine institutions, closely related to each other, and neither of them existing in perfection without the other, through which our Lord and King seeks to bring in everlasting righteousness. The family is especially for the child—for his care, nurture, growth, and establishment in manly and Christian character. To maintain the household, then, to guard its purity, to place on it the divine sanction, to reconvert it into its original Eden, to kindle on its altars the fires of Christian love, and to recognize and uphold it as a divine institution of unimpairable authority, is a matter of primal consequence for the growth of the child in Christian character. The Sabbath-school is, at the most, but an expediency of usefulness, of great value, to be sure, but by no means indispensable. Like the love-feast, it is a means of grace; like the missionary society, it is a mode of evangelism; like the godly family, it is a Christian home for childhood; like the Church, it is a sanctuary for perishing souls. But it cannot be substituted either for the Church or family, and if it were swept out of existence the cause of God would not perish from the earth. For many centuries the Church did its work successfully without the Sunday-school, and could do it again if it were necessary. It never disregarded, however, its solemn obligation to provide Christian nurture for the young, and it never can be oblivious to this duty and build up Christ's kingdom in the world. The roots of Christian nurture are in Christian households. God, by divine ordinance, has made the family the unit of society. Households, and not individuals, constitute society. When there shall be no family there will be no State and no Church. Civilization, human progress, and all our hopes for the future of the race, will perish on dishonored hearthstones. When our households are engulfed in worldliness and infidelity, every thing we hold dear—all material good, all moral achievement, all spiritual realization—will be drawn into the same bewildering maelstrom of death and hell.

We must not, therefore, for a moment, permit the thought a place in our minds that the Sabbath-school can, in any way, be a substitute for the training and culture of Christian homes. It may be a great help to godly parents, and it may be a missionary institution for impenitent parents, and the youngest child in the household may be God's messenger of light. And the Sabbath-school accomplishes its greatest work when it adds a new charm of sanctity to a home already Christian, or when it sends the blessed Jesus, fondled to the bosom of a child, into a home darkened by misery and sin.

If we would promote the child's growth in character, we must consider that character itself is a growth. And because it is a growth, it has no external source, but roots within. Character is purity of motive and desire. It is not what others esteem us to be, but what we are in the sight of God. It is acting habitually from the highest considerations. The Psalmist expressed it when he said of God, "Thou desirest truth in the inward parts;" and he has character, in its purity and power, who, "in the hidden" recesses of his being, has been made "to know wisdom." Character is not, therefore, a thing which we can put on to a child, as we put on its clothes. We must inspire in him the elements of a pure and noble life. It is not sufficient to choose the right thing for him; he must be led to choose the right thing for himself. The heart-hunger for God must be awakened in him, and directed to its proper object. He must, in some way, be induced to see vice as it is, and loathe it; to see virtue as it is, and love it. A power of resistance to low and mean solicitations must be aroused in him, and a strength of devotion to what is worthy, noble, and Christian. He must be enabled to discern how grand and glorious it is to be pure in his own eyes, to be good when no commendation will follow, to be honest when his defalcation could not possibly be detected, to be self-denying, generous, and magnanimous when only angel eyes can read the inspiring record, and to consider it more an object to please God, and have his favor and love, than to possess the riches and honors of kings. This is character, and this is the only true greatness possible to man.

It is sometimes said that the child's mind is like a blank sheet of paper, and that you can write on it what you please. Well, it may be that the child's mind is like a blank sheet of paper, but nobody can write on it but the child himself. And when we set up as writing-masters for a child, we must remember that the world and Satan attempt the same office, and, from the perversity of the child's fallen nature, he is more inclined to follow their copies than ours. And sometimes Christian parents are startled and grieved when they behold what is written, and they say, "Where did the child learn the thing?" Where? Earth and heaven are full of revelations to the heart of a child. It is not only true, as Wordsworth has conceived, that "Heaven lies about us in our infancy," but it is also true that the subtle spirits of evil throng the rosy paths of childhood, eager to poison their unsuspecting souls. As early as possible, therefore, the child should be taught the doctrine of selfhood, should be shown the importance of his free activities, and should be inspired with hatred of sin, and genuine love for whatsoever things are just, honest, true, and of good report, so that he will be constantly drawn to write on his soul's tablets the words of wisdom and the lessons of salvation.

Whoever makes a Sunday-school speech is expected to refer to Michael Angelo, beholding the beautiful statue imprisoned in the shapeless marble, and forthwith going to work, with the sculptor's skill and the inspiration of genius, to find the realization of his thought, and disclose it to the admiring eyes of men. But if any Christian parent or Sunday-school teacher supposes that the living child which he has to train for Christ and bring to a virtuous manhood is at all like this marble statue, he will be very much mistaken. There is in this child the throb and quiver of an immortal life. There is a certain spice of the devil in him. There is an irrepressible disposition to have a hand in carving out his own character and destiny. Depend upon it he will use the chisel for himself, and oftentimes in the most absurd, grotesque, and calamitous ways. Michael Angelo never had a problem like this. There is no other way for us but to lead this little sculptor to some faint appreciation of the value of the material on which he works We must show him how he is chiseling out destiny for both worlds, and how much he needs the inspiration and guidance of the one great artistic Mind of the universe. We shall be of value to him, and shape his being and future, just as we lead him to earnest efforts of his own to find God's grand ideal in his life, and to grow up, in all things, into Christ Jesus, his living and fruitful Head. If we would fill our gardens with beauty and bloom we must bring our rose-trees into a healthful and vigorous state, not tie dead roses on their barren branches. In other words, we must do like the wise physician, who, when he would restore his patient to health, depends chiefly on the vital forces, and applies his energies to strengthen and develop those forces. In the case of the child, the *vis vitæ* itself is impaired; but the blood of Jesus is a healing fountain, and where sin has abounded grace has much more abounded. We may, therefore, expect the happiest results, if we only have wisdom to employ right methods. And we proceed to inquire, What are some of those practical agencies which will certainly secure the child's most rapid growth in Christian character?

1. I mention, in the first place, an atmosphere of piety in the home and in the school. What we breathe in, every moment, is the principal thing with us, either as physical or spiritual beings. Before the question of food, even, comes the question of atmosphere. What matters it that the earth be fertile and the heavens genial, if, with every pulsation, we inhale malaria and death? A healthful breeze is worth all the sanitary regulations ever devised, because it sweeps away the foulness which breeds pesti-

lence, and inspires with recuperative energy every function of our natures. In like manner, the soul's first necessity is an atmosphere healthful as heaven; and not only healthful, but invigorating and productive of growth. I noticed on Cape Cod that the apple-trees clung to the earth as if stunted by the hard winters, or as if afraid of being blown into the sea by some furious ocean blast. They evidenced the temperature which prevailed. In like manner, the children in many a household bear silent but impressive testimony not only to the spiritual coldness of their parents, but even to the fierce gales which sometimes beat around the hearth-stones. Roses bloom in a hot-house even when the air without is chill with March winds; not because the soil is richer, but because the air is blander and the mercury stands uniformly high. And if the mercury of piety shall go up ten degrees, or twenty degrees, in a family or Sabbath-school, what, think you, will be the result? The order of the family may be undisturbed, the officers and management of the school may remain unchanged, but every child feels the difference, though he cannot explain it; little buds of promise begin to open in the genial sunshine, and the air is redolent with the breath of flowers; icy indifference and frost-bound prejudices melt away and disappear; the heavens glow with strange beauty, and the gladness of spring-time steals like a melody into every heart. The child's most rapid growth in Christian character will certainly be realized in such an atmosphere. And no impressive forms of worship, no machinery of religion, no intensity of orthodoxy, no beautiful Sunday-school order, in which every thing shall move with military exactness and precision, can by any possibility atone for a deficiency in this regard. That fervor of piety, that genuine Christ-love for a human soul, that earnest solicitude for the child's conversion, which he feels even when it is not told to him, and which somehow finds a lodgment in the sanctuary of his being, and ever after mingles with his tenderest memories and is the source of his purest inspirations—that is the indispensable thing in both household and Sabbath-school. Happy child, who makes weekly visits to a Sabbath-school which is not only the vestibule of the Church, but also the gate of heaven! Happier child, most favored of earth, whose daily home-altars glow with celestial fires, who breathes perpetually the atmosphere of the skies, and who learns to associate the most cherished words of human endearment with the name of Jesus and the hope of immortality!

2. In the second place, the child must be well and judiciously fed in order to secure growth. It requires bread and beef to make blood and muscle and bone. The truth of God, revealed in his inspired word, is the *pabulum* of souls. This is the corn of heaven, the bread of eternal life. Nothing can take the place, in family or Sunday-school, of the Holy Scriptures. These must be diligently, systematically, and thoroughly taught. To teach them in such a way as to make them interesting and attractive, so that the child shall be drawn to them, find in them the sincere milk of the word, and be able to grow thereby, and learn to look on them, not as a dry book of theology, but as the kind utterances of a loving Father, is the great problem of parents and teach-

ers. And surely the Bible can be invested with these charms if any book can under heaven. Here is history, narrative, eloquence, poetry, proverb—every thing which is calculated to win the heart of a child. Let the Scriptures be always reverently read at family worship, let the Sabbath-school lesson be thus always reverently read, let the authority of God's word be always invoked in the practical direction of life, let every child have a Bible of his own, neatly printed and bound, and lettered with his name, and above all, let him be encouraged to commit, every week, some portion of Scripture to memory, and, by and by, this precious truth will be in his heart, like honey in the cells of the honey-comb, a source of strength and refreshment in his time of need.

3. The child must be subjected to the training of Christian discipline—to wholesome restraint, guidance, and authority—in order to its most rapid advancement in the elements of the spiritual life, and the speediest attainment of the crowning graces of a matured character. The Scripture requirements, in this regard, are explicit and unmistakable: "And the Lord said, Shall I hide from Abraham that thing which I do? for I know him, that he will command his children and his household after him and they shall keep the way of the Lord, to do justice and judgment." "And these words, which I command thee this day, shall be in thine heart; and thou shalt teach them diligently unto thy children, and shall talk of them when thou sittest in thine house, and when thou walkest by the way, and when thou liest down, and when thou risest up." "And ye fathers, provoke not your children to wrath; but bring

them up in the nurture and admonition of the Lord."

Dr. Bushnell describes a certain kind of parental nurture as "the ostrich nurture," or the nurture of neglect, indifference, and forgetfulness. "It is just now beginning to be asserted by some," he says, "that the true principle of training for children is exactly that of the ostrich, namely, no training at all; the best government, no government." Certainly, this view has no warrant in the passages which I have quoted; but, on the contrary, the parent is required to exercise authority, to furnish example, to teach religious truth customarily and persistently; to govern himself, that he may be able to govern his children, and to nurture and admonish them in the Lord. Macknight renders Eph. vi, 4, as follows: "Now, fathers, do not provoke your children to wrath; but bring them up in the correction and instruction of the Lord." Bloomfield renders the Greek, not "nurture and admonition," but "education and discipline," and adds: "The former term seems to regard the instructory part of education, and the latter the corrective part, by forming their morals." He also quotes Doddridge approvingly, who says that parents are herein taught to give their children "such a course of discipline and instruction as properly belongs to a religious education, which ought to be employed in forming them for the Lord, by laying a restraint upon the first appearance of every vicious passion, and nourishing them up in the words of faith and good doctrine." "Train up a child," it is said, "in the way he should go, and when he is old he will not depart from it." But what does the word "train" signify? There are those who teach children morals as they teach them manners, by precept and repetition and a kind of mechanical process which is chiefly effectual in producing external results. In precisely the same way a dog is taught to stand on his hind feet, and a colt to lead by the halter. The margin renders the Hebrew verb by "catechize," which lifts our minds to a demand for a higher order of training. Give this child, is the requirement, thorough disciplinary instruction. Get the truth of God into his soul, so that it shall govern him. Train him to employ his own faculties in the service of Christ. "Bring them up"—that is, *nourish, strengthen, educate* them—" in the nurture and admonition of the Lord," is the injunction of the apostle. The more wisely, lovingly, and thoroughly the children of our households and Sunday-schools are thus trained and educated for Jesus, the more rapid, harmonious, and beautiful will be their growth in Christian character.

4. Every child is entitled to an *example* of Christian integrity and purity on the part of those who are called to be his parents and teachers.

History, it has been said, is philosophy teaching by example; but nothing teaches by example like the Gospel of Jesus, and children are susceptible of being more powerfully influenced in this way than any other class of persons in the world. There is a ceaseless charm in pictorial teaching, especially for children. They are most influenced by what they see, particularly in those whom they love and in whom they confide. Parents and teachers who would effectually lead the young in the way of the most rapid advancement in Christian character must themselves walk in the paths of holiness, and show forth the loveliness of a consecrated and beneficent life. It has been well said that "there is no cheap way of making Christians of our children ; nothing but to practically live for it makes it sure." If they discern in us a worldly mind ; if they see that we are formal rather than spiritual ; if they notice that our words, aims, purposes, enjoyments, and associations are of the earth, earthy, and especially if they discover inconsistencies and contradictions in our Christian life, how can we expect them to be so influenced by our teachings as to overcome the counteractive argument of our example, and engage in the service of our Lord and Christ? But if, on the contrary, it shall be manifest that we have a life which is not of this world, an informing and comforting presence, a peace and assurance which are heavenly in their origin, a communion with God as a Father and friend which is elevating, transporting and satisfying, how greatly, even though our words of counsel may be disregarded, will such a fact influence and mold the being and ways of the children we love and teach. It will be, with them, the heart's most precious memory ; it will be such a demonstration of the reality of experimental religion as no infidel argument, however subtle and powerful, can ever shake ; and it will create, by our firesides and in our school-rooms, an atmosphere of piety, an inspiration of love, and a power of spiritual nurture, in which the children of the Church will find their most rapid growth in all the elements of Christian character.

XXVIII.

THE ARMED SUPPLIANT.

"Praying always with all prayer."—EPH. vi, 18.

In the context the apostle clothes the Christian soldier with a complete armor for his defense, and places in his hand withal the sword of the Spirit, to make battle against his foes. He is protected in every vulnerable part. He has the helmet of salvation, the breastplate of righteousness, and the shield of faith. He is to withstand and, having done all—conquered all—still to stand as a triumphant hero on the field of conflict. Moreover, he must thrust his enemy with the sword of truth, and drive him from the field. This looks very much like salvation by works; but the apostle adds, "Praying always with all prayer." This drives him to God, in appeal and supplication, with a sense of need and dependence, for help and deliverance. The man who truly prays will earnestly contend for the faith of the Gospel. And he who bears the Christian armor, fights the good fight of faith, confronts Apollyon and all the enemies of Christ, and persistently wages his warfare for the final victory, will feel the need of prayer, will learn that all his strength is in God, and always, and by every sort or species of supplication, will seek the mysterious power of the divine Presence. This mailed and plumed warrior will lowly bow at a throne of grace for the holy chrism, the spiritual anointing, the unction from our sacerdotal King, in which is strength and victory.

But "how absurd to pray," says the skeptic. "Prayer has nothing to do with morality, and could not a wise God supply our wants without prayer?"

The objection, however, is false in fact. Prayer *has* something to do with morality. There is no genuine prayer without repentance; which implies the renunciation of sin; and the renunciation of sin is a chief fact in morality. The constant tendency of prayer is to arrest the tide of sinful conduct. Prayer is aspiration for goodness, for an experience of purity, and for a life of practical beneficence like that of the Son of God. Are not such aspirations seeds of moral excellence? Prayer, moreover, seeks blessings, not only for ourselves, but also for others. It is, therefore, an unselfish and benevolent spirit, in harmony with the noblest aims of morality. Did we know, in a word, that any man possessed constantly the spirit of prayer, could we distrust either his integrity or his purity? Again, prayer brings a man into contemplation of, and communion with, the highest and holiest Being in the universe—a Being in whom infinite wisdom is united with infinite purity. There is more in God than in his works—more than in all finite powers; infinitely more; and this Being *hates sin* with an infinite abhorrence. How is it possible that one should contemplate his character, habitually dwell in his presence and feast on the riches of his goodness and love, and not learn to hate sin also? And what interest has morality so great as that men should learn to loathe sin? As matter of fact, when you take the praying men out of a community morality dies out of that community. And this is only another form of saying that morality roots in spirituality, and that spirituality cannot be maintained without prayer. Thus prayer furnishes the highest motive to morality, and is its grandest inspiration. The praying man does what is just and right in his intercourse with his fellows, that he may please God, maintain the spiritual life, and rejoice in the hope and expectation of a heavenly reward. This is a motive which never fails to be operative, sufficient, and inspiring. It follows, therefore, that prayer is the *alma mater* of a pure and ennobling morality.

The other part of this objection is, that God could supply our wants without prayer. It is granted. He could also give us the fruits of industry without toil, knowledge without study, and character, perhaps, without temptation and trial. Does he? or would it be best for us if he should? It is enough to say that such is not the economy of the universe; and if this objector is not satisfied with the economy of God's universe, perhaps he had better construct a universe of his own. One might easily imagine the Almighty saying to such a skeptic: "Where wast thou when I laid the foundations of the earth? when the morning stars sang together, and all the sons of God shouted for joy? Declare if thou hast understanding. Hast thou commanded the morning since thy days, and caused the day-spring to know his place? Hast thou perceived the breadth of the earth? Declare if thou knowest it all. Knowest thou it because thou wast then born? or because the number of thy days is great? Canst thou bind the sweet influences of Pleiades, or loose the bands of Orion? Canst thou bring forth Mazzaroth in his season, or canst thou guide Arcturus with his sons? Shall he that contendeth with the Almighty instruct him? He that reproveth God, let him answer it."

Again, it is objected that "as God is omniscient he knows what we need before we ask him, and that, therefore, we have no occasion to ask him."

I answer:

1. This a *non sequitur;* the conclusion does not follow from the premise.

2. The objection assumes that the sole office of prayer is to inform God of our wants. But this is not the sole office of prayer, nor the chief office of prayer, nor any part of its office whatever. No intelligent Christian supposes for a moment that he adds any thing, when he prays, to the stores of divine knowledge. It is in the *popular* and not in the *philosophical* sense that men are said to make their wants known unto God.

3. Such a presentation of our necessities to our heavenly Father, as is implied in prayer, has many advantages, especially as it makes our dependence manifest, and enables our faith to grasp the divine promise of salvation.

4. The President of the United States might know the wants of all the citizens of this Republic, and have the means of supplying them, and yet the Constitution of the country make it necessary for those wants to be presented to him antecedent

to, and as a condition of, his executive interposition.

A father may know, and often does, the unuttered needs of his children; and may know also that *their greatest necessity is to come to him* for the supply of their wants, and that this constitution of things is best for them, for the family as a whole, for the community, and for the near and remote future.

Whoever complains of these things complains of that constitution of the universe which God in his infinite wisdom has established.

The objection to prayer, based on "man's insignificance and God's greatness and infinity," has been so often answered that it scarcely need be noticed.

Admit man's insignificance—what then? A great God might overlook him, but an infinite God cannot. An infinite God does not need the revelations of the microscope any more than of the telescope to find out his universe. The highest finite intelligence has climbed no nearer to his infinite height than the lowest. An infinite God is infinite in goodness and love as well as in wisdom and power, and is as actually, as graciously, as mercifully present with the least as with the greatest of his creatures. He hears the widow's moan, and sees the little child who bows his bare knees in prayer as distinctly as he hears the songs of the glorified, and sees the arch-angelic crowns cast glittering at his feet.

I know a mother who sleeps so soundly at night that though you might gather beneath her window a score of sweetly attuned voices, and, with stringed instruments, make such melody as would arrest the stars in their courses, yet she would remain unstirred;

but the faintest moan from the fevered lips of a sick child will arouse her in a moment, and direct all her energies to its relief. In this regard she has sometimes reminded me of Jesus himself, who slept soundly on the hard bottom of the fisherman's boat, with the spray dashing in his face, undisturbed by the noise of the tempest or the alarming outcries of the men, but who was reached in his inner consciousness, and aroused in a moment, at the first cry of distress: "Master, carest not thou that we perish?"

But in what respect is man insignificant? It is true that his powers are feeble, his knowledge small, and his years few; that his researches often lead to contradictory results; that the labors of one age are largely employed in correcting the mistakes of a preceding one, and that his progress is slow, difficult, and frequently arrested; but, despite all these things, he may be a being of great and growing importance.

Man's body, to be sure, is insignificant as a physical force, but this does not furnish any presumption against prayer; for, despite physical weakness, there may be mental vigor, moral activity, and spiritual apprehension.

The mind, however feeble, cannot be termed insignificant if capable of mental functions and intellectual acquisitions.

That the soul of man is not insignificant is proved by its creation in the image of God, by the fact that it is capable of knowing and loving God, by its redemption through the offering of the Son of God, by the gift of the Holy Spirit, making it the temple of God, and, not to mention other points, by its immortality. Admit growth and immortality, and the whole domain of God, this side of the infinite, is the possible possession of the soul.

Again, it is said that "prayer is a healthful and salutary exercise of the mental and spiritual faculties, but that it is folly to suppose that any thing is really received in answer to prayer."

1. But as the stream can rise no higher than its fountain, it is difficult to see, on this hypothesis, how any moral or spiritual advantage can result; for what the sinner needs is not the exercise of his depraved powers, or any reflex advantage which may result therefrom, but help, deliverance, salvation. Luther goes to Rome distressed in regard to his spiritual condition, and agitated with the great question—the question which has burdened ages—how a guilty soul may come acceptably into the presence of a holy God. In Rome he found antiquity; but what is antiquity, as the historian inquires, to a man seeking to be justified from his sins? What to him were venerable forms? What was art, culture, tradition, authority, sacraments, any thing, every thing, which did not show him the way to the reconciled countenance of his heavenly Father. If prayer be not answered, the soul must remain in its moral pollution and unrelieved misery.

2. This makes prayer for others useless; and our lives are bound up with the lives of others, and we crave blessings for those we love as for our own souls. Of how much value would prayer be to any parent if it did not prevail for his child?

3. Prayer, considered as a duty or a privilege, is a matter of revelation, and God's word is, "Ask, and

it shall be given you; seek, and ye shall find; knock, and it shall be opened unto you; for every one that asketh receiveth; and he that seeketh findeth; and to him that knocketh it shall be opened." These words certainly teach that something will be done for us in answer to prayer.

4. The example of the great apostle to the Gentiles is instructive. He frequently asks prayers for himself. He writes from Rome to Colosse, from Athens to Thessalonica, saying, "Pray for us." He evidently expected that such prayers would be a benefit, not only to those who offered them, but also to himself and his fellow-laborers.

We ought to learn to regard prayer as a power—as a successful agency for the accomplishment of results. The philosophy, the connection between the prayer and the end realized is inexplicable, but there is no mistake in regard to the fact. Congress has incorporated Dr. Loomis's Ærial Telegraph Company, which proposes to form its circuit, not by means of the earth, but by means of a supposed current of electricity in the heavens. I do not know that this supposition will be sustained by the facts, but I do know that the eternal spaces of the universe are filled with the love of God, for he is every-where present; and by prayer we make our connection with a battery of infinite grace and power. The philosophy of prayer is no more incomprehensible than the philosophy of natural facts—no more unsolvable than the great historic problems of the ages. Who can tell why light is essential to growth? or, indeed, what growth is? Who can tell why elements must combine in certain proportions to make known substances? Who can account for the weary ages of the world's history? Who can explain the miseries which millions suffer under the government of a wise and good God? Moreover, as prayer brings us into the plane of spiritual things, where the invisible is revealed, is it a strange thing that we find ourselves dazed by excessive light?

It is also said that our "prayers may be mistakes," that "prayer-unions for specific objects are an impudent assumption of power, by combination and persistence, to change the purposes of an immutable God, and that, as matter of fact, prayer does not prevail, for the world is not converted."

1. "Good prayers," says an old English divine, "never come weeping home. I am sure I shall receive either what I ask, or what I should ask." God does not give according to our measure, but according to his own. A Pope of Rome, pleased with a boy, opened a drawer filled with small coin and bade him take a handful. "Holy Father," said the boy, "take it out for me; *your haud is larger than mine.*" And such is the practical wisdom of the child of grace. The underlying petition of every prayer is that of the Psalmist: "Lord, choose thou mine inheritance for me." His paramount desire, no matter what may be the specific request, is that the wise, good, and supremely excellent will of his heavenly Father may be done always and in all things.

2. Union and persistence in prayer have the divine warrant, and are attended by gracious results.

3. It does not follow that prayer is vain because the world is not converted. In answer to prayer, light and influence are given, forbearance is shown,

life is prolonged, and multiplied agencies combine for the sinner's salvation. But the offender against God's law is a power, not a thing, and has to be dealt with as a free moral agent. It requires the concurrence of divine and human forces to secure the conversion of a soul. The sinner must choose, determine, and act. The most that can be done for him, in answer to prayer, is to enlighten his understanding, quicken his conscience, stir his affections, excite his hopes and fears, and address to his will, where the free soul reigns supreme, the grand, unanswerable argument for a holy life.

Prayer, then, is privilege and consolation. It is the way to obtain help from God, and help according to the measure of his infinite wisdom and love. It is a common privilege—an every-day privilege. It is not limited in time or place, like the opening of the Porta Santa, in St. Peter's in Rome, by the Pope and his Cardinals, on Christmas eve, *four times in a century!* The gates of Gospel grace stand open night and day.

> "O when the heart is full, when bitter thoughts
> Come crowding thickly up for utterance,
> And the poor common words of courtesy
> Are such an empty mockery, *how much*
> *The bursting heart may pour itself in prayer!*"

XXIX.

LIFE, CAPITAL FOR IMMORTALITY.

―――♦―――

"And he saith unto him, Out of thine own mouth will I judge thee, thou wicked servant. Thou knewest that I was an austere man, taking up that I laid not down, and reaping that I did not sow: wherefore then gavest not thou my money into the bank, that at my coming I might have required mine own with usury?"—LUKE xix, 22, 23.

You will of course recollect the context. It is parallel to the parable of the servant in the twenty-fifth chapter of Matthew, which I have read for our lesson this morning. The language of this text is strongly ironical: "Thou knewest that I was an austere man, taking up that I laid not down, and reaping that I did not sow." Indeed! "wherefore then," that is, upon thine own supposition, "gavest thou not my money into the bank, that at my coming I might have required mine own with usury?" with produce. The word rendered "usury" has no bad sense, as, perhaps, the word usury itself had no bad sense at the time this translation was made. The gist of the inquiry was this: "Thou regardest me as a hard man, a severe master; why, then, wast thou not attentive to my interests? Why was not the pound which I had intrusted to thee faithfully used? Why was it not placed in the bank? How is it that at my coming I am not able, to obtain mine own? Why do I not receive the pound, and with it the produce which is, at the same time, as much mine as the original pound intrusted to thee?" Passing away from the mere technicalities of the text—for these preliminary remarks will lead to its clear comprehension—it seems to me that the doctrine taught, the great truth underlying these words, in this whole parable and the kindred teachings of our Lord, is this: *Life, with all its powers and faculties, is to be regarded as a sum of money to be laid out for God.* In other words, pressing the thought into a brighter compass, the theme is, *Life, Capital for Immortality.*

It may appear to you that this is a very commercial rendering of this passage; but if you will reflect for a moment, it will occur to you that the whole transaction is a commercial one, and is to be viewed in the light of commercial affairs and commercial interests, and our Lord chose thus to explain the relation which men sustain to their Maker, so that every man, in the light of this truth, must say of his capacities, as if they were a sum of money which he could hold in his hand: "My life, intellect, affections, power of usefulness, and all favorable gifts and surroundings in the world, intrusted to me by my Lord and Master, are to be used for the advancement of his cause and the promotion of the interests of his kingdom in the earth." This is the one grand thought of life, its relations and its responsibilities. Could the matter be more simplified, could it be brought more completely within the range of our thought, that, simply as a sum of money, intrusted to us by another, to be expended for him, and in accordance with his will, his affections, the modes and purposes which govern him, so we are to regard life with all its opportunities?

Now, in the first place, it is of immense consequence for the ordering and government of a man's life that he should have true conceptions of his position, and of his relations, and of the significance of life itself. He may regard his life as an opportunity for enjoyment, as an opportunity for the transaction of business, or for the furtherance of selfish matters and purposes. He may employ all life's powers and all its resources for the promotion of his pleasure, and the advancement of his honors, and the increase of himself in distinctions among men. Such a life will prove a failure. If it be a success in a worldly sense, yet, in a higher sense, it is a failure. The probability is that in a worldly sense also it will be a failure. There is a kind of perverseness in selfishness which leads it constantly to defeat its own ends. It turns back upon itself. There is no consistency in it—no certainty of results. There is in it such crookedness, such narrowness, such poverty, or bankruptcy, and there follows such dissatisfaction and wretchedness, that the selfish man can hardly seek the fulfillment of his own selfish ends in any constant and harmonious way, unless it be that he comes under the influence of some master passion of evil which impels him to make his life such that, in order to attain the gratification of this passion, he is ready to sacrifice every thing else, even that which is of a selfish character, for the promotion of the one darling selfish aim of his life. But as man stands related to God, governed by an infinitely wise and holy Being, such a selfish life must end in bankruptcy and ruin.

What, then, is the Gospel idea of life? It is that substantially presented in this passage: "Wherefore gavest thou not my money into the bank, that at my coming I might have required mine own with the legitimate produce of mine own?" That is the Gospel idea. It reveals God as the owner and master, and man as the property and servant. So that the man that has this conception of life must say in reference to himself, "I am not my own, I do not belong to myself. This body is not mine, but the gift of God, this mind is not mine, this intellect is not mine, this heart, blossoming with immortal affections, is not mine, but they are an expression of my Father's love; and these powers of usefulness, these opportunities in the world for influence, are not mine, I could not produce one of them, they are God's gift. I am simply a recipient of these gifts. They come flowing to me as so many exhaustless streams from the fountain of infinite goodness and love. I receive them. I owe every thing to God himself; all my powers, all my belongings, all my capacities for doing and suffering. This is the first great object for which my life is given, and it is to be borne constantly in mind in the enjoyment of every particular thing, and in every relation which I sustain in the world, that I belong to Christ, that I must live for Christ, that I must find the great end of my being in Christ, that I must seek the joy of my heart in Christ, and that my success, my crowning honor, my everlasting felicity, my glory, will be in Christ, and as the fruit of the work which I shall have accomplished for him."

It is hardly a step in advance of this to say that

these Gospel demands of necessity govern every thing. I say, *of necessity*, because we have gone to the root of the matter already. Hence, power of body, of social position, culture, reputation, means of usefulness, whatever we may have or know, which can be employed in the advancement of Christ's cause and kingdom, all these things are to be regarded not as our own, but as so many munitions of war, gathered together by the great Master of the battle-field, to be employed for the furtherance of his cause and the establishment of his kingdom in the earth.

The Christian sense of this word *talents* has come to be the popular sense. Of course the word means a sum of money. But then it is used in the Scriptures to convey the idea of our Lord in a broader sense—in the sense of every thing which money can purchase, in the sense of every thing which can be employed for usefulness as money can, in the sense of all resources, of all competency, and of all power of execution whatsoever. We have come in general to extend the meaning of the word, so that we speak of a man's talents, not with reference to his wealth, but with reference to his powers; and, in Christian usage, whatsoever a man is, or whatsoever a man has, which can be consecrated upon the altar of Christ's service, is included in this inventory of his powers or "talents." The Gospel purpose is that we must all go forth in our Redeemer's name, and labor, wherever and however we can, for the interests of his cause.

If we turn this subject over and look at it on another side, it may be observed that the kingdom of Christ is very extended, and includes every lawful and honorable position in life. This has been true of every age of the Christian Church. What a variety of talents and powers in the Apostolic College! What a difference of temperaments there was in Paul, Peter, and Andrew! How different their spheres of influence! In the Reformation, you see the same difference in Melanchthon, Calvin, and Martin Luther. In the Wesleyan Reformation there is likewise a cluster of great and distinguished names—a variety of talents and powers. Wesley himself, a logician, a theologian, with a mastering ability for organization and government, an orator, a statesman of the broadest and most comprehensive views; how little could he have accomplished, after all, without the aid of his brother Charles and the wonderful songs he sung and taught all the Methodists to sing; without the saintly Fletcher to defend his doctrines with a logic like that of Paul, and with a sweetness of spirit reminding us of the beloved apostle! How little would he have accomplished if Whitefield had not gone before him, turning the thoughts of men toward religious subjects! Wesley said of Coke that he was "a right hand to him." These men were like a cluster of stars of the first magnitude in the religious firmament of that time. This remark will apply also to the devoted laborers in the humbler ranks of Methodism, in every sphere of life, where the cause of Christ may be advanced. So indeed is it in every Church and place. While, on the one hand, you may see the divine will directing every order of culture, power, and talent for this service, if you choose, on the other hand, to study that service, and to study its necessities, you will see that it needs not only the wisdom of the wise, not only the labors of the great, not only the resources of the learned, but that it needs every talent, of every order, in every condition of society, from the lowest to the highest, through all the relations, however manifold, which good men sustain in the world. Thus God's cause is advanced in the earth by all classes of agencies which can be brought from any of the resources of his people and consecrated to his work. What is chiefly necessary is that thoughts of Christ and of his service should be in every man's mind. Now every man may say: "The demand of the Head of the Church upon me is that I shall use all my powers and resources in his service. I must think and feel, pray and speak and testify, and transact my business, and do my work in the world, and conduct myself in my household, and in my relations with men in the world with constant reference to this fact, that I am just as truly a minister and embassador of Jesus Christ in the world as was Wesley, or Calvin, or Luther. I am just as truly an instrument in building up the temple of God's power in the earth as the most illustrious laborer who has worked thereon. The power and resources which Christ has given me have been given me for this purpose. With such resources as I have at my command, I am to labor for the advancement of his cause."

You will find your work, if you will obey God's command, not in some distant portion of the earth, but by your own hearth-stone, it may be, in the very block in which you live, on the very street where you reside, among the companions with whom you are most intimately brought into contact, with your brother-clerk in the counting-room, with the man who stands nearest to you in society. Ah, Carlyle's utterance was half inspired when he said, "Do the duty which lies nearest thee, and the second duty will already have become plainer."

The last hours of Charles Goodyear were spent in perfecting inventions for saving life in water. His one great invention of vulcanizing rubber was enough to secure his fame and the resources of fortune, and he might have retired and lived in his old age in peace and comfort. But Charles Goodyear was an eminently Christian man; he was a philanthropist. His ideas of life were expressed when he said to a missionary who was about sailing to a foreign land: "I am as much a missionary of the Lord Jesus Christ as you are." And it was with a thought like this in his mind that he labored at his great invention of vulcanizing rubber, and in his advanced years he strove from this vulcanization of rubber to secure some invention by which to save the multitudes perishing by shipwreck at sea. His wife asked him the cause of his continued sleeplessness, she having been disturbed by his hours of restlessness. He replied: "How can I sleep when so many of my fellow-creatures are passing into eternity every day, and I feel that I am the man to prevent it!" I think that every man who has attained to a truly Christian idea of himself, of Christ, and of the world to come, feels the stirring influence of the Holy Spirit in him, forcing him to say, "There is some evil in the world which I can and must prevent. There is some portion of God's love put in my heart for a purpose. There is some object which I am able to realize in the world. There are some who can be turned back from sin and ruin through my agency and instrumentality. There is some cheer and encouragement for God's servants which I can give. There is profanity, and I am the man that can prevent it. There is intemperance, with its desolation sweeping over the land, and I can do something to prevent it. There is Sabbath desecration, there is ignorance of the ways of God, there are necessities of the Church and of perishing souls, and I can do something to prevent this want and waste and ruin." All these evils are a burden on the heart of Jesus, and it is the business of his servants to prevent these evils in their ravage and waste in the world, and some power, some resource, has been given to every one for that purpose. Don't say, "I have no influence." You might as well say, "I am nobody." Write, instead of your name, "Nothing," if you have no influence. As well say, "I am a cipher, and not a significant figure at all." Signify something, if it be but a fraction. As Carlyle says: "Be no longer a chaos, but a world, or even worldkin. Produce! produce! Were it but the pitifulest infinitesimal fraction of a product, produce it in God's name! 'Tis the utmost thou hast in thee; out with it then! Up! up! Whatsoever thy hand findeth to do, do it with thy whole might. Work while it is called to-day, for the night cometh wherein no man can work."

Indeed, a man possessed of this spirit and purpose will not give up, saying, "I can do but little." It is not so much his business whether he can do little or much. It always augurs a spirit of false humility when one is ready to exclaim, "I can do but little," as if he expected some one to say to him, "O yes, brother, you can do a great deal." What a meanness it is if you will not do something! If the little which you can do is not done, what excuse will you have when you stand before the Judge? If you can do but little, you may be certain Christ never expected you to do more. But ah, when you rise to a higher range of thought, what is "little?" It was a very little thing when Andrew, with his face glowing with a new light of love, went and found his own brother Simon and brought him to Jesus. Almost any body could have done so little as that. But hardly any act more important is recorded, and Simon Peter stands, and will stand for all ages, as the representative of that one act before the world. And when Peter stands in heaven before the eternal throne, where will be Andrew's position, who took him by the hand and led him to Jesus? It was a very little thing when a faithful Sabbath-school teacher taught Edmund S. Janes the way to life; but that apostolic Bishop goes through the earth proclaiming the riches of Jesus' love, a representative man before the world of the faithfulness of that teacher and of the great work he has accomplished. It is insolent in us to call any thing little, or any thing great, as if we could see the end, as if we could measure results. Why! can we measure magnitude at a point? The results of an act stretch beyond us in an infinite line; who shall tell what is their magnitude? A word spoken, a tear shed, a tremble of the lip, the earnestness of a tone, may change the destiny of an immortal soul. What is a little thing? Do what you can.

Penetrated with this idea, that I am not my own, that I have received my life and every thing which belongs to it, as a sum of money placed in my hand to be laid out for God, I go into the world's market-place, not inquiring what this will bring, how much value will the world place on this talent intrusted to me, but how shall I expend it most wisely for him who hath sent me. I go forth not inquiring whether I shall gain the world's approbation, but what reception shall I receive from the great Teacher and Master when I come back from my life-work. I ought only to inquire, "What will *he* say of my work, and of the fruits of my labors?" A man inspired with such a purpose will not choose; to use Bacon's words, "a goodness solitary and particular, rather than generative and seminal?" It is not enough for him that he dwells in his closet in conscious enjoyment of the divine favor, reveling in the manifestations of his Lord's regard, enchanted with beautiful visions of an open paradise, feasting in the solitude of his soul on the manna which falls to him from heaven; but his goodness is of an active kind; it is goodness generative, which seeks to raise, in every sphere of usefulness, means of multiplying the active powers of the human soul, to be used in laboring for our Lord and Master. So a man who has passed from earth may still be said to live. Paul still preaches up and down the earth; Luther still blows the iron trump of his mother-tongue, whose blast once shook the nations from Rome to the Orkneys. Whitefield and Wesley still go forth on their errands of life and love, and the songs of the Church, born out of devoted and loving hearts, wing their way, like summer birds, from sphere to sphere, still remaining melodious in the souls of the redeemed. Possessed with this idea, a man will faithfully use all the means of grace that God has given him. God has sent him forth, *as an agent*, and expects, as in affairs of life, that he will avail himself to the utmost of his opportunities for activity and usefulness.

You go to New Orleans, New York, or any other place, for illustration, to represent me in business. I expect you to avail yourself of all the means of knowledge which you possess or can acquire, for the advancement of the interests intrusted to your hands; you are to find out all you can; you are to make yourself as competent as possible to perform the work you have undertaken.

The Christian man having this sense of service and responsibility will say, "I must study God's word, I must be often in my closet; I must hear the voices of my brethren in prayer; I must maintain religious worship in my family, I must go to God's house where he specially dispenses the blessings of his kingdom; I must make myself as wise and strong and well-furnished as possible for the great work which I have to do in the earth." And no other interest will be permitted to fall, like a shadow, across this path of life. I read the other day of a little girl asking her mamma about heaven. She said, "Mamma, you will be there?" "Yes." "And Aunt Laura will be there?" "Yes." "What a nice time we will have in heaven, wont we?" And her mother, thinking she had overlooked one object of her affection, said, "Papa will be there too, wont he, dear?" "No," said the little girl, "papa will not be there." "Why not?" said the mother. "Because," said the little girl, "papa *can't leave the store.*" That, it seems, was a matter distinctly understood in the household: for religious worship, for the prayer-meeting, for the demands of beneficence, papa could not leave the store. His business was first and imperative. The child's logic, like children's logic always, was conclusive, and leaped at once to the sequence of the argument, that papa had no time or place for labor or enjoyment in the heavenly world. The truth is that business, social relations, affairs of life, and every thing connected with a man's operations in the world, will be made tributary to his chief object and work. His chief aim in life rules him, whether it be selfish or otherwise. If he be truly a Christly man, his whole object is to use his life, his talents, and his opportunities for the Head of the Church. He will question only how he may do his work most wisely and most effectually for his Master.

It is said that Howard, that most eminent philanthropist, had a wife who was worthy of him. At one time when they had received unexpectedly quite a legacy, in addition to their fortune, he said to her, "Now we can gratify our long-cherished desire to spend a season at the Springs." After a moment she replied, "But what a fine row of cottages that sum of money would build for our poor." Nothing more was said; but the jaunt to the Springs was not taken, and the row of cottages was built. Many a woman thus, by a word, has changed the whole tenor of a man's life. I hardly need say that when a man has this one great thought of Jesus in his mind, that his life is as a sum of money intrusted to him, to be laid out for God's service, he will become divinely in earnest. There are some men in the world who have no earnestness in their lives. They are like oysters and clams in the mud. Their lives are cold and uncertain, now up and now down. Men do not attain any great object in the world until they become indomitably in earnest. A Christian man has earnestness of soul, and from the moment he becomes a Christian all his powers are engrossed for God.

There is no such thing as sluggish Christianity. There is no such thing as dormant Christian manhood—no such thing as lazy grace. Grace always generates grit. If a man has the warm love of God in his heart, it takes the flabbiness out of his muscle. There is some hardness in his bone; there is some life in his marrow; there is some firmness to his heart, some constancy to his purpose. He means something. He knows something for himself. How many things the Christian man knows! He knows there is a God in heaven; he knows that Jesus Christ is the world's Redeemer; he knows he has an immortal soul; he knows that he has been ransomed with precious blood, and regenerated by the power of the Holy Ghost; he knows he was blind and foolish, that he has been redeemed, and that now he is fixed in purpose to use the strength and vigor of his manhood in his Master's service.

I heard a brother once say in a love-feast that he hoped to obtain some poor seat in heaven. Another brother interrupted him and said: "Brother, you will be disappointed; there is no such place there." He was right. There is no poor seat in heaven; there is nothing less than a throne there. Whoever finds his place there will sit on the throne with Jesus. Whoever has an ambition for a poor place there will not get there. *That is not the way to heaven.*

When he who has striven to obtain a high place in heaven, by devoted service to his Master, is taken up among the ranks of the redeemed—redeemed from sin, redeemed from an eternal hell by the precious blood of Jesus, and clothed in heavenly robes—all the crowned angels will gather around him, and ask him the story of his ransomed and consecrated life.

Now, my hearer, suppose yourself in such a place, searched by such questions. After you were converted, what did you do for Jesus? what did you testify? what work did you perform? what burdens did you cheerfully bear for his name's sake?

There are many who are not willing to do any thing for Jesus, but they aim to get to heaven. Such would not become the place. It would be no heaven to them; for they have rendered no service for which they can be crowned. Reward comes after labor. They who have suffered with him shall also reign with him. No Christian man having this conception of life and God will be satisfied without doing something for Christ.

I must say a few words of the results which will flow from such a life of service to Christ—such an expenditure of life as a sum of money for the Lord and Master.

1. There is an immediate result on character.

Nothing so much concerns a man as self-hood. What he is, is the matter of chief concern. And a man's life is every way richer for having given it to Jesus. Character is ennobled and beautified by this process.

What power there is in a thorough awakening of

the dormant faculties, and a gathering up and concentration of all our resources in the work of Jesus! This is the royal road to greatness. It is certain a man becomes more like Jesus as he studies his character and attempts to reproduce it. Looking at the likeness of the Son of God, he is changed from glory to glory as by the Spirit of the Lord.

2. A life of sin and selfishness, on the other hand, is always a mistake and a crime.

Why, there are men in this city, prosperous in the world, who are universally commiserated. Men do not envy them as they see them on the streets, or as they roll by in their carriages. They rather pity them. There are able men, that is men of great power and culture, intellectually, who are universally despised. They are contemptible as they are powerful. There are cultivated men who are fools; creatures of fashion, gay as the butterfly, and signifying just about as much. Who envies them? Nothing is ever gained by sin. It is an impeachment of God Almighty's character for us to suppose that any good can come to any creature in his universe from transgression. Never. As he is a just, a righteous, and a holy God, he permits no prosperous, gainful sin in his domain. A soul without God, a soul bankrupt of its immortality, may have the honors, the pleasures, and the distinctions of the world, but it can find no compensation for the loss and ruin.

3. In respect to the future.

Whedon's remark is significant: "For every hath there is a richer hath, and in every hath not, there is a deeper, poorer hath not." "From him that hath not shall be taken away even that which he hath," that is, the original pound intrusted to him. And that is just and fair. You would not loan your money to a man who did not intend to pay you interest. You would not submit to it. That is the very idea in this passage. The man hath not the produce or return which he should have brought, therefore take from him that which he hath—the original pound intrusted to him. But if he hath, if he brings an increase, if he can say, " Lord, thy pound hath gained another pound ; " " Lord, thy pound hath gained five pounds besides ; " if he hath, in other words, made the most of life and its opportunities in the advancement of his Redeemer's cause, there is for him a "richer hath," and a more abundant and glorious possession.

Let us then devote all the resources of our strength and life to this cause, remembering that service is richly rewarded, and that neglect brings failure and loss. For " to him that hath shall be given, and from him that hath not shall be taken even that which he hath." Our lives are to be regarded as a sum of money to be laid out for God ; and when the Master cometh to us may he say : " Well done, good and faithful servant, enter into the joy of thy Lord."

Leighton's words on entering into the joy of our Lord, are beautiful and appropriate : " It is but little we can receive here, some drops of joy that enter into *us*, but there *we* shall enter into joy, as ships put into a sea of happiness." But let it not be forgotten that it is only through the service of Christ and through the fellowship of his sufferings that we learn how to enter into his joy, and to share in the glories of his heavenly kingdom.

In conclusion, mark these four things, which I trust you will bear away with you:

1. The essential dishonesty of sin. The sinner says, "*my* money," "*my own*," when he has nothing, except what he holds in trust. Sin is robbery, and robbery of the Almighty.

2. "Out of thine own mouth will I judge thee." The sinner will be condemned by principles which he has always acknowledged. When he lent to others he demanded produce. God lent to him life's grand opportunity, and he will require a return. If he has not used his pound for his Lord, it will be justly taken from him.

3. Our faithfulness is in a *very little*, but the reward is *great*. "He that reapeth receiveth wages and gathereth fruit unto everlasting life." What wages God pays! What a reward it will be to shout the harvest-home! What dignity and honor to rule among the powers and hierarchies of heaven!

4. Consider the importance of beginning early to serve God, of loving him with the whole heart, and of making the most of life for eternity. If you can say in that day, "I have given my whole life to Jesus; I have loved him with all my heart; I have made the most of my opportunities, and devoted time, talents, influence, possessions, all things, to the furtherance of his kingdom; *I have given my life as a sum of money to him*"—then great will be your reward, exultant your joy, and resplendent your crown, in the eternal world.

XXX.

"STRENGTHEN THE THINGS WHICH REMAIN."

"Strengthen the things which remain, that are ready to die."
REV. iii. 2.

UNQUESTIONABLY, there are many in the Christian Church who have a name to live while they are dead. There are many more, however, who have the Christian life in such small proportions, with such feeble impulses, characterized by such inconsistencies, involved in such contradictions, and bewildered in such labyrinthine doubts, that a happy termination of their probationary career can hardly be anticipated. It is true that these persons have the knowledge of the law, conviction of duty, desire for spirituality, and a care for the forms and decencies of religion. They are upright, amiable, moral, and excellent in the judgment of their fellows. Nor have they by any means ceased to be religious. They have not given up their hope of heaven. The name of Jesus still charms their ears. The story of the cross still ravishes their souls. But *they are not satisfied.* There is an emptiness within, a meagerness in the life, a shallowness in their experience, a narrowness in the performance of Christian duty, which, when contemplated, sicken and appall. The craving soul is not satisfied with the bread of God. Deep draughts are not taken from the wells of salvation. The dews of heavenly grace seem not to fall, and the virtues of the Christian character, which did spring up as the tender grass, and expand as the opening blossoms of Spring, are now, although living at the root, blanched, withered, and dry. There is no fullness in the spiritual life, no exhilarating enjoyment of the things of God, no undimmed hopes of a radiant immortality The soul is consciously insufficient for duty and trial, and has no immediate preparation for death, judgment, and eternity. Alas, how many experiences do these words describe! And yet a sadder truth rises on the horizon of our vision: *These things which remain will also perish, except they be strengthened.* This will follow in the very nature of things. The feeble man is likely to die, the small fortune is easily spent, and little religion soon becomes no religion. The form without the power is burdensome, and the dogma of faith must be discarded when the conduct can no longer vindicate itself to the understanding. Orthodox beliefs and salutary forms of godliness simultaneously disappear when they become the constant rebuke of a faithless and disorderly life. Imperfect works cannot be productive of a finished character; and the lack of completeness and proportion is the source of defection, decay, and irretrievable disaster.

Does any one say, "This is my condition," and at the same time despairingly ask, "What can I do?" I answer:

1. Consider that you are in peril; that so long as any sin remains in your heart it is in the nature of a temptation; that you must be strong to overcome the world, and that there can be no compensation for the

loss of the soul. Such reflections will make you watchful and earnest.

2. Remember the past miracles of grace in your experience, the way in which the Lord led you, the goodness, love, and infinite patience shown you, and the joys which once bubbled up like a living spring in your soul. Can you think on these things with eyes unmoistened or with heart unmoved? And Jesus has not changed, while your affections have cooled. His heart is still a flame of love.

3. Cherish the grace you have. Hold fast, with a life-and-death grip, to what remains to you of the Christian life. Satan may say, "You have so little religion, and serve God so imperfectly, you might as well give it all up." Beware! this is the crowning temptation, designed to work your utter ruin. *A little religion is infinitely better than no religion.* A little religion has immeasurable possibilities in it; but no religion means darkness and despair. The flickering light may be restored to steadiness and strength; but *if it go out* the case is past remedy. That waning life may be won back to hope and promise, but no roses bloom under the pall of death. The parent gives to his child tenderest care and unwearied attention while the pulse beats and the heart throbs, *be it ever so faintly*, but when death comes love sinks hopeless into the silent grave. And our tender, loving Saviour doth not quench the smoking flax, doth not willingly see us perish, and doth not cease to feed, with the oil of his grace, the feeble flame of spiritual affection in our hearts. Jesus recognizes any measure of good, wherever found. He is not unmindful of our tears, our struggles, our aspi-

rations for a higher life. Be encouraged, therefore, and let not your heart fail you through fear; for *if you hold fast to Christ, he will hold fast to you;* and herein is your hope of final salvation.

4. Confession confirms faith. "If thou shalt confess with thy mouth the Lord Jesus, and shalt believe in thy heart that God hath raised him from the dead, thou shalt be saved ; for with the heart man believeth unto righteousness, and with the mouth confession is made unto salvation." And to increase and confirm faith is to strengthen the things which remain of the spiritual life at the very root, and in their most vital elements; for faith is the golden link which binds us to the unseen, the spiritual, and the eternal. It is the substance of things hoped for, the evidence of things not seen. It is the power which enables us to endure as seeing Him who is invisible. It is only through faith that we come into the place in which God is discerned. Without faith we are cut off from the spiritual and shut up to the material. Nothing, therefore, can be more important to us, as spiritual and immortal beings, than faith. Without it we cannot please God, for we are earth-bound, and have no capacity to apprehend the divine. Faith is the sense with which the soul sees God. It opens to us the realm of invisible things, and brings us into intercourse with the highest. Faith may be cultivated, increased, strengthened. It is the duty of every Christian to grow in this matchless grace. Every other Christian virtue blooms in the sun of its prosperity. Now, it is said, faith is confirmed by confession. There can be no doubt of the truth of this statement. The reason, the philosophy, is not so

manifest. A thought needs, perhaps, to be uttered in order to be fully thought. The mental process does not seem to be complete without speech. When we project the idea forth from the mind, and look at it as an external thing, a child born of us, we see its proportions, importance, truthfulness, beauty, and power. When we proclaim our faith in Jesus, we discover what it is to have faith in Jesus. Perhaps the faith, for its maturity, requires expression. Certainly confession increases and confirms the faith which was needful in order to confession. "I believe in Jesus Christ," were the words with which a good man used to baffle his spiritual foes. "I believe in Jesus Christ" has sustained many a drooping spirit, given the victory in many a doubtful struggle, turned the scale for rectitude and purity in many a trying temptation, and softened for many an aching head the dying pillow.

It is worthy of remembrance that Jesus thus tested and developed the faith of those who came to him for works of healing and miraculous power. "Believe ye that I am able to do this?" were words which searched the doubting heart and gave opportunity for the heroic confession. "According to your faith," he said, on one occasion, "be it unto you." It is still the rule of the divine dispensation. Faith still subdues kingdoms, obtains promises, stops the mouths of lions, and puts to flight the armies of the aliens. With the heart man believeth unto righteousness, and with the mouth confession is made unto salvation. *The confessed faith is the secured salvation.*

There are many ways in which faith may be confirmed. In things of this world faith is declared by word and act, by doing and suffering, in life and death. It is not only with a form of speech that the Christian is to confess his faith, but also and chiefly *by a life of consecration.* If his faith be the key-note of his desires, words, business, associations, aims, and plans—of the whole conduct and course of his life—then his character and career will be one grand diapason, ringing with the praises of Jesus. And that consecration will react upon his experience, will strengthen his faith, increase his love, multiply his consolations, and constantly confirm his assurance of final victory and eternal life.

5. To strengthen the things which remain, repent thoroughly, renounce your lukewarm, half-hearted service, and *give yourself wholly to God.* It is a shame that you are not filled with his Spirit, and flaming with his love. Think what a being God is, what goodness he has shown to you, what relations you sustain to him and to the eternal world, and consecrate all your powers to his work.

"The charge against Sardis," says Trench, "is not a perverse holding of untruth, but *a heartless holding of the truth.*" And this is *the* sin of the modern Church. It holds the truth heartlessly, and consequently does not act consistently, nor treat eternal things with the earnestness or solemnity which they demand. Sin must be hated before God can be loved. Give yourself, then, wholly to the business of the Christian life; put your heart, your best affections, into the work of Christ; count it all joy to be numbered with his suffering saints, and choose death rather than recreancy to the truth; and you will gain strength from your very momentum, your courage will be your salvation, and eternal life will be your reward; for he who wins the victor's palm shall wear the triumphant crown. Keep your garments undefiled, unspotted from the world, and you will be of that happy number of whom Jesus has said, "They shall walk with me in white; for they are worthy." "Here," says a commentator, "are many promises in one: the promise of life, for only the *living* walk, the dead are still; of liberty, for the *free* walk, and not the fast bound." And yet, perhaps, the chief thought is that of an outbeaming purity, so resplendent that it amounts to a glorification. Surely, this is worthy of an earnest seeking. Rutherford observes that many who never had a sick night because of Christ, nor yet a pained soul for sin, are, nevertheless, expecting heaven. Thousands are thus slain by a prevailing security. Be in earnest for salvation. Strengthen the things which remain, *that are ready to die!* Lay hold on eternal life.

Christ's permanent abode in our hearts is precisely our grand necessity. If we need Christ at any time, we need him all the time. He is our salvation, and without him we are unsaved. Every moment we need the merit of his death, and every moment we may have the merit of his death. We do not inquire how far this is the actual experience of the Church. Christ, doubtless, has more faithful ones who live in him, and are wholly consecrated to his work, than we know. But that this experience might become more general than it is—might become universal—is, we judge, beyond all dispute with believers in the New Testament. How many are parched in desert wastes who, by taking a few steps in advance, might come into a beautiful land abounding with springs of living water! How many are exposed to the furious, and ofttimes successful, assaults of the powers of darkness, who might dwell in a munition of rocks in perfect peace and safety! How many have only occasional glimpses of the glory which gilds the mount of transfiguration, whose privilege it is to abide in that land where the sun never goes down, and where the voice of singing birds is always heard! The great thing required is *the entire surrender of the will to Christ.* Let the consecration of heart and life for doing and suffering be complete, and the great peace of God will reign in the soul. How powerful the motives which urge us to this full and irretrievable devotion of ourselves to Christ and his service! We have no self-wisdom or self-sufficiency. We have within us no unfailing springs of consolation. We have no strength, heroism, or inspiration of our own ; we must hang on Jesus for all these things. HE IS OUR LIFE. Think of that glorious promise of the Son of God: "If ye abide in me, and my words abide in you, ye shall ask what ye will, and it shall be done unto you." What a marvelous promise! What princely endowments, what high privileges, what power, dominion, and usefulness, it vouchsafes to us! To *us?* Nay, except we meet the conditions, this promise is as far above us as the stars in the heavens. We cannot reach it; we cannot attain unto it. This promise belongs only to the soul dwelling in the constant communion of Jesus' love, and walking in every pathway of holy obedience. But more than the wealth of the Indies, more than all worldly honors, more than all pleasures of sense or imagination, more than all splendors of kingly rule or historic renown, is that promise worth to the man who can truly claim it for his own. God help us to lay hold on it for time and eternity! I fully agree with a recent writer who says: "The great want of the Church is not better creeds, but a better experience; not a multiplication of religious agencies, but an increase of religious power; not a more complete apparatus for her work, but a more complete union with her Master."

For a better experience, for an increase of religious power, and for a fuller union with Jesus, we must strengthen the things which remain, that are ready to die!

To maintain the Christian life we must produce the fruits of holiness. The external and internal life must correspond. Our walk must not give the lie to our words. The servants of God are not only made free from sin, but they have their fruit unto holiness. The beautiful, consistent, and symmetrical character of Jesus is their model and their inspiration. "As he is so are we in this world." "He that saith he abideth in him ought himself also to walk even as he walked." These words describe a grand necessity of the Church. When Jesus was in the world, he appealed to his miraculous works as a potent proof of his Messiahship, and said, "Believe me for the very works' sake." When he went away into heaven, he left his disciples to be his representatives, to show forth to the world the beauty and excellence of his religion. This living epistle is read by unregenerate eyes with the keenest interest. The majority of men do not get their impressions of Christianity from the Bible or from the study of the life and character of the Son of God, but from what they have seen of Christianity in the conduct of those who have professed to be the followers of Jesus. A pious mother has made many a man a Christian, through the tender memory of her living consecration to the world's Redeemer. We are all of us powerfully affected by example, and examples of godliness constitute the great demand of the Church and the age. We have enough of theory, enough of profession, but not enough of practice. We have argued and contended enough on the subject of holiness, but we have not enough *lived* holiness. The world demands, and has a right to demand, *the fruits of holiness.* Are we saved from sin, from idle words, from evil tempers, from uncharitable judgments, from a worldly spirit, from selfish aims and ends? Do we in honor prefer one another, or are we all engaged in an ignoble scramble for the best places? Do we cheerfully maintain the institutions of the Gospel by our offerings and prayers? Do we visit the sick, relieve the needy, and uplift the down-trodden? Have we a tender solicitude for souls? Do we warn the ungodly, encourage the despondent, stir up the lukewarm, and cheer the hearts of all who are toiling in the Lord's vineyard? Are our sympathies enlisted for every work of charity, justice, and beneficence among men? Are we in full fellowship with Jesus in his longing and expectation that the earth may become his footstool, and be filled with his glory? Do men *know* that we are Christians, and thoroughly identified with Christ's cause, even while they oppose, deride, and persecute us? Do we carry our religion into all the relations of life, and in business, politics, society—on 'Change, at the ballot-box, and in the drawing-room—honor the name of God our Saviour? Is it evident to all that we are not self-seeking, grasping, covetous; but kind, considerate, generous, and consecrated in time, talent, and possession, to our blessed Lord? Especially, are we patient, forbearing, long-suffering? by good works putting to silence the ignorance of foolish men? Is it manifest that we are Christ's disciples because we have love one toward another? Are we of one heart and one soul in the Redeemer's work? Are we ready to suffer all things rather than hinder the Gospel of Christ? Is it the testimony of our conscience that in simplicity and godly sincerity, not with fleshly wisdom, but by the grace of God, we have had our conversation in the world? Finally, do we constantly seek those things which are above, where Christ sitteth at the right hand of God?

Let us examine and prove ourselves, and know that we are in the faith! Let us be credible and convincing witnesses for Jesus in daily life and conversation! Let us *show forth* to the world the excellency of this knowledge and experience of Christ!

"Wherefore also we pray always for you, that our God would count you worthy of this calling, and fulfill all the good pleasure of his goodness, and the work of faith with power: that the name of our Lord Jesus Christ may be glorified in you, and ye in him, according to the grace of our God and the Lord Jesus Christ."

6. We must learn to contemplate life as seen from

the gates of death, and from the stand-point of judgment and eternity.

Our vision of life changes according to the position we occupy in the contemplation. In youth, life is radiant with hope and promise. In mature years, the view is tempered to a sober hue, but we are still in the midst of the strife, with blood heated by the combat, and with indomitable purpose to succeed. The true view of life is the retrospective—the vision which rises before us as we gaze backward from the gates of death. It is only by looking through the eyes of age and experience that the young become wise, sagacious, and comprehensive. The steady gaze is the clear gaze. Second-sight, so called, is insight. It is only those who are wont to perceive that perceive distinctly. The prophetic strain, as the poetic fancy, is born of ripe experience.

Now, can any thing be more pitiable than a wicked old man? His life may have been, in a worldly way, a great success; but who envies him? He has had honors, pleasures, opulence, power, friendship, love; but what remains to him? His sweetest joys have vanished, as the bubbles on the stream; the lips he most loved have turned to dust; he has had his full of distinctions, and the flame of his ambition burns low, like the embers in the grate, changing to ashes; he has houses, and lands, and stocks, and bullion, and costly gems, but his palsied grasp is loosening its hold on them, in spite of himself, and he begins to feel that they will soon be his no more forever. In the future he has no prospect. The grave looks dreary to him, and he is going into the grave. The thought of eternity is like a death-knell, and every moment he is drawing nearer to eternity. From judgment he shrinks, in a shiver of apprehension, and yet he must soon stand before God in judgment. Poor old man! He tries to enjoy life; but he cannot forget that death waits for him with hearse and plumes, and that he must go away alone into that other world! What is before him? He has sent no treasures to that distant shore; he has aspired to no throne in that immortal kingdom; he has won no crown of imperishable worth; he has made no friendships in the household of God, and he has no desire or relish for the enjoyments of heaven. The past is gone; the present is more a burden than a rapture, and the future is dark, dreary, and dreadful. What sad and sickening words were those of Prince Talleyrand, when, after fourscore years of power, wealth, and worldly splendor, he declared that life yielded him "no other result than a great fatigue, physical and moral, and a profound sentiment of discouragement with regard to the future, and of disgust for the past!" Is such a man to be envied?

On the contrary, a good old man must be regarded as happy. He may have passed his days in poverty, and obscurity, and affliction; but he has secured life's chief treasure, a virtuous character—life's grandest inspiration, an immortal hope. His past is a pleasing retrospect, whatever may have been his trials; his present is full of noble consolations, whatever may be his sorrows or burdens; and his future is beautiful and glorious as the gates of heaven. He has not lived for himself, but for his Saviour and his fellow-men, and his life has not been in vain. Death has no terrors for him. The grave may be "deep and soundless," but beyond its cloudy gloom he beholds the brightness of an immortal day. The friends who vanished from his earthly vision await him on that other shore. The world knows his poverty, but it does not know his riches. He has a secure, indefeasible, eternal possession.

He has not gained distinctions among men; but he is a prince, and a glittering crown will adorn his fadeless brow. To leave this world is to bid farewell to pain, and tears, and trials, and to enter into his Father's presence, to rest in his Saviour's bosom, to find the loved and lost of other years, and to become a full inheritor of everlasting life.

Hear Paul's triumphant shout from the gates of death: "I am now ready to be offered, and the time of my departure is at hand. I have fought a good fight, I have finished my course, I have kept the faith. Henceforth there is laid up for me a crown of righteousness, which the Lord, the righteous judge, shall give me at that day: and not to me only, but unto all them also that love his appearing." How heroic a past! How sublime a present! How transporting a future! Grand old man! He is superior to opposition, persecutions, afflictions, the contempt of his countrymen, the treachery of false brethren, the care of all the Churches; superior to privations, perils by land and sea, stripes, imprisonment, "deaths oft," the bloody edicts of Nero, and the immediate prospect of martyrdom! He reviews his past, and exclaims exultingly, "I have fought a good fight." He considers his present, in which men behold only bonds, imprisonment, death, and contemplates his riches, dignities, and honors: "There is laid up for

ME A CROWN." He pierces the future, and dwells joyously on the hour of his coronation. He will be acknowledged, exalted, glorified. "The LORD," whom he has served, and for whom he has suffered, will place that crown on his brow. It will be his own crown—studded with many stars, won, through the grace of Christ, in Damascus, in Jerusalem, in Corinth, in Athens, in Rome, in many other cities, and in the "regions beyond." The LORD, the righteous Judge, will give it to him at that day. He will take it from the hand of JESUS himself, and he will wear it, in his heavenly kingdom, forever. No marvel that this prince of missionary bishops sends forth such a shout—a shout of victory over sin and Satan—a shout that seems to stun the very ear of death, to rend the far-off heavens, and to ring in triumphant peals through successive ages!

Recently, in the city of Philadelphia, a good old man, greatly honored in the Church, after a holy life of eminent usefulness, in which pen and tongue were consecrated to Christ, went suddenly to his rest. And men who knew and honored Albert Barnes—and their name is legion—will read, with eyes swimming with joyous tears, these memorable words, which constitute the closing paragraphs of the last volume of his great life-work:

"I cannot lay down my pen at the end of this long task without feeling that with me the work of life is nearly over. Yet I could close it at no better place than in finishing the exposition of this book; and the language with which the Book of Psalms itself closes seems to me to be eminently appropriate to all that I have experienced. All that is past—all in the prospect of what is to come—calls for a long a joyful, a triumphant HALLELUIA!"

Happy old man! Only CHRIST can make life and death so beautiful, so full of satisfaction, so exultant so glorious!

XXXI.

THE LAW OF CHRISTIAN CHARITY.

"For ye have the poor always with you; but me ye have not always."—MATT. xxvi, 11.

It was Ruskin, I think, who said that "fools were made that wise men might take care of them;" and it is certain that, in a majority of cases, poverty may be traced to folly, idleness, and crime. Nevertheless, when a poor wretch stands shivering and hungry at our door, we cannot repulse him because of his improvidence and dissoluteness, and leave him to perish. We must put bread into the mouths of the hungry, and clothing on the limbs of the naked, although we know that the objects of our charity have been reduced to their miserable condition by wastefulness, intemperance, and the worst forms of transgression. Unthriftiness is not, after all, an unpardonable sin, and the worst men cannot be allowed to starve. That men do not deserve charity is no reason for withholding it. A majority, perhaps, of those who crave assistance need the forbearance quite as much as the beneficence of their fellows.

It must be conceded, however, that pauperism is a dead-weight on society. It drains away the life-blood of the community, and renders nothing in return. It is a heavier tax than any which the State imposes, and it has no compensations. It is simply a burden to be borne, a nuisance to be suffered, and a wrong and outrage which has to be endured. The man who, by industry and enterprise, provides for his own household, perhaps not without hardship and difficulty, finds that he has also to provide for the household of his neighbor, who has spent his time in idleness and dissipation. The unexpected result annoys him, and he rails at paupers as thieves. How far is his complaint just? How much have society and Christianity a right to demand? and what is the remedy for these evils?

There is in the world a legitimate poverty. This should never be forgotten: "Ye have the poor always with you." The maimed, the infirm, the orphaned, the blasted by providential visitations—these will remain proper objects of Christian charity, awakening the most tender and touching manifestations of Christian kindness and love, till the Son of God shall again appear on the earth. It is not difficult to provide for these in any community. What grinds people is the necessity of taking care of those who are able to take care of themselves, and who ought to do it. It is the bastard poverty, which has no right to be in the world, that men loathe and reprobate. And the evil is one of gigantic proportions. More money is wrung out of society to meet this necessity, by voluntary and involuntary contributions, than would support all the Churches and Church missions on the face of the earth. And this poverty—the product of waste, idleness, intemperance, and crime—can never be removed by charity. We might as well attempt to fill up the ocean by casting pebbles into its depths. How, then, is this question to be met? What remedy or relief is within our reach?

1. In the first place, *The sources of pauperism must be dried up.* The chiefest of these is intemperance. The waste of this sinful indulgence is immense. The amount paid for the fiery stimulant, the loss of time, the impaired and ultimately ruined health, the property destroyed, and the criminal acts, with all their consequences, which follow, make up, in the aggregate, such an imposition on honest industry as, if levied by a government, would excite an insurrection in any country under the sun. But if men will license, sanction, and support the rum traffic, they must calculate to carry its loads and experience its horrors.

Idleness imposes heavy burdens on society. The idlers are the drones which the busy bees have to toil through sunshine and storm to support. Many of them ought to be stung to death, or driven ignominiously from the hive. Loafers, dead-beats, and such characters, should be put to work, and made to earn their own livelihood. Young men, and young women, too, should be taught trades, or made masters of some useful and respectable business. It is a very significant remark in a recent message of Governor Brown, of Missouri, that a large share of those who are within the walls of the penitentiary had, when they came there, no trades, and no certain means of self-support. Idleness, poverty and crime naturally resulted. Parents are greatly at fault in this matter. The rich and influential classes ought especially to set a salutary example in this regard, and to train their sons and daughters to habits of industry, and prepare them for any and every exigency of life. When Louis Philippe was King of the French, he was accustomed to astonish his gay court and the attending embassadors of other powers by declaring that he was the only monarch in Europe fit to reign, for he had blackened his own boots, and he could do it again. In like manner, a Chicago clergyman affirmed over the ruins of his Church and of the homes of his people, "I have made a good horse-shoe, and I have not forgotten my trade." There was in it a manliness and self-reliance which stirred the heart of the nation. The young should be taught that labor is honorable, that idleness is a disgrace, and that for a healthy man to live on the products of another man's muscle and brain is a species of robbery—a sin and a shame. Habits of economy and of small and regular savings for future needs should be encouraged. Savings-banks have kept thousands of young men from extravagance, dissipation, and crime. The Christian doctrine, that what is given as a genuine charity for Jesus' sake, will be abundantly rewarded, even in this world, ought also to be diligently inculcated.

The most useful Christian charities, in large cities especially, are those which take care of young children, prevent their growing up in idle and vicious habits, find them good homes in Christian families, and insure them a future of decency and respectability. Such institutions lighten every man's taxes, as well as honor humanity and beautify our Christian civilization.

2. *Men must be helped by helping them to help themselves.*

This is the way we are helped to win the crown

of life. We can work out our own salvation, because God worketh in us. We receive strength to stretch out the withered hand. We go to Siloam's pool and wash, and come seeing. And this law of salvation is also the law of Christian charity. We must help men to help themselves. They do not so much need to have bread put into their mouths as tools into their hands. Their great necessity is opportunity. We must give them a chance—a chance to work, to live cheap, to save something, to provide for anticipated sickness, infirmity, and age, and to maintain their self-respect, independence, and manhood.

One of the grandest charities in which a wealthy man could engage in this city, or in any other city, would be the erection of blocks of cheap houses, which could be sold to laborers and artisans at from two thousand to three thousand dollars each, on long time and low rates of interest, so that, by paying scarcely more than the usual rent, a home and freehold property might, after awhile, be acquired. Such a man would get his money all back, confer an inestimable favor on hundreds of households, make himself myriads of devoted friends, and greatly increase his treasure in the kingdom of heaven. In like manner, men who employ their capital in business enterprises so as to give employment to others act a more Christian part than those who invest it in unproductive real estate, or miserly hoard it in the mad folly of a covetous greed. How plain, in view of all these things, is the Christian doctrine of our common brotherhood! We belong to one houshold; and to improve the condition of any one is to increase the prosperity of the whole family.

3. *The highest style of charity is charity to the souls of men.* What else does our Saviour mean when he affirms: "Ye have the poor always with you; but me ye have not always?" Consider the circumstances. Jesus was in Bethany at the house of Simon, and "they made him a supper." And while he sat at meat Mary took a pound of ointment of spikenard, very costly, and broke the alabaster box, and anointed the head and feet of Jesus with the precious unguent, and wiped his feet with the hairs of her head, and the room was filled with the fragrant odor. The quantity of ointment used has been thought much too large; but, as Olshausen argues, the whole act must be regarded as a kind of extravagance of love. Mary gave all she had without hesitating or economizing. Her gratitude and enthusiastic devotion sought the fullest expression. But this act of lavish love was sharply criticised. Some, at least, of the disciples of Jesus had indignation, and inquired, "To what purpose is this waste?" This ointment, they said, might have been sold for much, and given to the poor. "John informs us," says Whedon, "that the utterer of this benevolent *talk* was Judas; not because he cared for the poor, but because he was a covetous thief at heart, being carrier of the money-bag. Mary meant it for a token of love to him, the Redeemer of the world. There are thousands who think that money given for the Gospel had better be bestowed in mere temporal supplies; forgetting that it is much better to bestow upon men those *principles* which will make them wise, good, and industrious, than to give them supplies which will leave them as wicked and thriftless as ever.

Could the faith that Mary showed in the Redeemer inspire all the world, the poor would be easily taken care of." Judas made the calculation, and found that the ointment was worth three hundred pence, or about forty-five dollars ; "thrice the price," adds Whedon sharply, "for which Judas sold his Lord."

But our Saviour defends the uncalculating love of this devoted woman. "She hath wrought a good work upon me ; she did it for my burial ; ye have always the poor with you, but me ye have not always." Your charity toward the poor, in other words, will lack neither occasions nor objects for its exercise ; but this woman has performed a work of piety, prompted by overflowing love, which is worthy of commendation, and which shall secure her undying remembrance in my Church. "It is supposed by some that Mary had either been informed by our Lord of his approaching death, or that she had some prophetic presentiment of it. It may be remarked that, for the sake of propriety, our Lord was regularly accompanied by twelve male disciples ; but the Gospels take care to assure us that those who believed and loved him were not all *men;* but that *woman* in her place was not less true to his divine claims than man. Of this fact Mary is the most striking instance ; and the meek, silent, and sudden manner in which she comes from her retirement, perhaps from her place of prayer, where the sad future of our Lord may have been intimated to her, in to this feast, and performs this act of sorrowful affection, is a special exemplification. It may well be thought possible that our Lord communicated to her a clearer knowledge of his approaching death than to his disciples ; or it may be that to her, as to a divine love, was imparted the spiritual presentiment of the truth. And yet, finally, it is very possible that she acted from the simple impulse of love; and that our Lord himself, giving it a higher meaning, elevated the act into a prediction of his approaching burial."

This much, at least, is plain, that Jesus recognizes and honors an act of love and piety, and has embalmed it in fragrant memories for all ages, even though the claims of humanity, the temporal necessities of men, were urged as a reason why it should not have been performed. The Gospel of Christ is not a mere gospel of humanity—of reliefs and temporalties; it is devout, spiritual, and benevolent in the broadest and most extended applications. It considers all the interests of men, and especially the highest. It brings blessings of incalculable value to men, considered only in their temporal relations; but its divinest charity is for their souls—its grandest beneficence that which secures their immortality. In his note on the parallel place in John, Whedon says: "Covetousness and irreverence are here covered under the cloak of benevolence. The poor are, indeed, as the Scriptures abundantly teach, a prominent object of Christian duty. Yet poverty is no merit, but is very often the due penalty of idleness and unthrift. The due expenditures of art and taste are right, as tending to civilize and elevate mankind; the wealth laid out in awakening the sentiment of worship is still more right, as contributing to spiritualize the heart of man." It is a significant remark of Bengel's, that "avarice makes the poor its pretext, and that sometimes seriously; for it hates even genuine munificence;" and an unknown author has observed that the good work which was to be done soon or never, was preferable to that of which the opportunities were continual.

We must, then, if we enter into the spirit of the life and teachings of Jesus, devote ourselves, first and chiefly, to the interests of men's souls, making even charity to their bodies, the relief of their temporal needs, means of transmitting to them some spiritual beneficence. Their instruction and sanctification as immortal beings is the grand object of which we must never lose sight. They will often require to be fed and clothed and sheltered; but their highest necessities are, the bread of life, robes of Gospel purity, and mansions of rest in the heavenly kingdom.

We have recently been taught by one of our most deservedly eminent and truly evangelical ministers, that "so far as the conversion of souls is concerned, the chief use of preaching is its effect on the young. The great mass of our unconverted adult population is doomed, self-doomed. It is no limitation of the power of grace to say that, unless the world is visited with unrevealed and tenfold energies of the Holy Ghost *the impenitent adult masses will perish.*"

But the Church *has no right* to despair of the conversion of any soul this side of perdition; in every means of grace the salvation of sinners—all classes of sinners—ought to be expected.

The Scriptures teach us that there is fearful power in unbelief to stay the mighty hand of a loving Lord. And, perhaps, the general expectation among Christians that adult sinners will live and die sinners is the chief cause of their continued impenitency Is not this phrase, "The adult masses are doomed," an excuse for inactivity and unbelief, which has grown up in a formal, worldly, unconsecrated, backslidden, and infidel Church? Of course, a Church with all the sinews of its faith thus cut asunder expects nothing, and achieves nothing. The missionary successes of the Baptist Church taught its foreign missionary board the sublime words: "Attempt great things for God; expect great things from God." But this despairing utterance in regard to the probable future of adult sinners is in quite another strain. Though not so intended by its author, whose warm heart glows for the salvation of every soul, it is a saying which is as cold as an iceberg, as cruel as the grave, and as terrible as hell. It is bad theology, for it practically terminates probation. It is contrary to experience, for the Gospel has always triumphed over adult sinners, such as Paul, Luther, Bunyan, Newton, and thousands of others. It is bad philosophy, for it throttles faith, quenches hope, and cuts the sinews of every exertion.

It is, however, objected that, "unless the world is visited with unrevealed and tenfold energies of the Holy Ghost, *the impenitent adult masses will perish.*" Those unrevealed energies of the Holy Spirit are precisely what we ought to expect; and they will be given tenfold, and, if need be, a thousandfold, in answer to the faith and prayer of a consecrated and believing Church. But it is urged that scarcely any impression is made "on the outlying masses of false religion, and irreligion and crime." Of course not; for scarcely any effort is made in the direction indicated. A Protestantism which builds fine churches, in fashionable localities, where select societies can be secured, and which does not believe that vulgar, drunken, abandoned sinners can do any thing else than be damned, need not marvel that its career is not crowned with missionary successes, and that its altars do not thunder with revival power. Ought such an evangelism, however, to call itself by the name of John Wesley?

"Have you ever known," it has been asked, "ten Romanists converted in all your life? or ten Jews?" Suffer me also to ask one question: "Have you ever known ten Protestants, I will venture to say ten Methodists, in all your life, to make an earnest, loving, persistent effort to bring a Romanist or a Jew to Jesus?" Are not those classes even more zealous and self-denying for their own faith than we are for ours? How can we expect the Holy Spirit to be given, with its unrevealed and multiplied energies, except *to attend our testimonies*, to follow our believing prayers, and to make our feeble efforts powerful for the world's conversion? And have we any right to look for the Holy Spirit, except according to the measure of our faith and confidence and earnest expectation?

We must remember that the mission of the Gospel is to the poor, the unfortunate, the imprisoned, the sin and sorrow-burdened masses of men. If God has kept a poor, abandoned wretch out of hell, it is on purpose that he might be saved. Methodism will lose its glory when it ceases to go to the hospital, the prison, and the most abandoned locality, and when it no longer expects the world's reprobates to become the elect and chosen of God, at its altars.

Every body must preach this Gospel. We depend too much on the pulpit, too much on the Sabbath-school, too little on ourselves—*on God's blessing on our own testimony and labors.* We read of one sick of the palsy who was brought to Christ, "borne of four." It often requires a number of earnest souls, uniting their faith and labors, to bring a sinner to Jesus. And "*their* faith" prevailed. It was a quintuple faith ; perhaps nothing less would have sufficed.

We must come up to this standard. At the battle of the Alma, we are told, when one of the English regiments was being beaten back by the forces of Russia, the ensign in front stood his ground as the troops retreated. The captain shouted to him to bring back the colors ; but the reply of the ensign was, "Bring up the men to the colors."

There they are! Jesus planted them! In the world, on the very ramparts of hell, they wave! "*In hoc signo vinces.*" Nothing will suffice, except personal, consecrated effort ; but that will produce great results in the unlikeliest directions. It may bring a cross and a martyr's doom, but it will insure a crown and a heavenly glory.

Revivals of religion are born of such labors ; and revivals of religion bring joy to God's people, and awaken new and glorious hopes in dark and despairing breasts. Nevertheless, "the revival system" is denounced by a Churchly authority as being productive of certain "pernicious effects," which are "manifest to thoughtful men." And the labors of evangelists are specially deprecated, who, though "burning with zeal," are "uncontrolled by any diocesan authority." The rise of Methodism was precisely in this way. It was a flood which could not be confined within any appointed bounds. The Gospel rule is, "Let him that heareth say, Come." When men's hearts burn within them, they will testify of the grace of God; and when earnest Christian testimonies are given, some will heed and be converted.

The "revival system" is simply an attempt to make the preaching of the word and the appointed means of grace *immediately effective* in the conversion of souls. It goes on the supposition that men are instructed in divine things, that they know their duty, and they have only to seek in order to find the grace of regeneration. They need, according to the revival theory, to have their convictions deepened, to be awakened from sin's sleep to a consciousness of danger, and to be induced to engage at once in earnest efforts for the soul's salvation. Now, if sin be always a peril, if repentance be always a duty, if holiness be always a privilege, if the need of preparation for death, judgment and eternity be always important, and if the Gospel invitation be always, "Come, for all things are now ready," why should not the Church act as if she expected sinners to come and be saved without delay, and resort to all appropriate means and appliances to lead them to decision, immediate effort, and positive commitment to the obligations of a Christian life? The "pernicious effects" of which complaint has been made are rather the abuses than the legitimate results of the revival system, and many of them may be successfully obviated. Some evils are, perhaps, incidental to the system and inseparable from it. If one travels by steam he encounters peculiar perils, but then he *gets along,* which is the chief object in traveling after all. Formalism, to be sure, will never engender fanaticism ; but formalism is death. A Church may be so orderly and respectable as to lose utterly its evangelical power. It will thus escape many excesses ; but what will remain worthy of preservation? A Church is to be estimated like a mill, not by the massiveness of its external structure, the magnificence of its machinery and the splendor of its furnishings, but by the quantity of flour it will produce. The practical question is, What grist does it grind ? Better that a stone should burst occasionally in the rapid movement, than that our corn should be pounded in a mortar. And better that the regularly trained miller should "fire up" to the full capacity of his machinery, than that his failure to supply the people with bread should cause the irruption of fiery zealots, who would, indeed, meet the demand, at least for a season, but at great risk of disaster and death. Would the "followers of the impetuous Dominic," for instance, have been able to obtain such influence, if the regular clergy had been characterized by zeal and self-denial, and had not been "tempted by comfortable establishments into indolence and luxury of living ?" Why does the parochial system ever "degenerate into mere congregationalism," except for the lack of that spirit of evangelism, that disposition to do revival-work, that quenchless desire to witness immediate results, that burning love for souls and for Christ's cause which sends a minister not only through his parish, but beyond his parish, calling sinners to repentance, and gathering trophies for his Master? The burning zeal will flame forth, in utter disregard of diocesan authority, if such authority be employed for its suppression. Through the Church, or over the Church, a genuine revival of religion will sweep on, with resistless power, to its glorious consummation. The desire for the salvation of souls is not to be suppressed, but directed. Not only may separation and schism be prevented, but the Church itself substantially profited and munificently enriched. Let no Church presume to reject a revival. A flood like that of the Nile may cause many inconveniences, but the permanent result is a fertility which could not otherwise have been realized. The true policy is to welcome revivals, but guard against their abuses, conform them to Church usages, and make them tributary to denominational growth. Many a waste place may be rendered by them beautiful and productive as the garden of God. The best way, moreover, to keep other people from doing our work is to do it ourselves, and to do it a little better than any body else can. The Lord sometimes sends storms and floods on the earth, and they accomplish salutary objects when they come; but they usually follow protracted drouth, or some opposite and violent extreme.

May God bless his whole Church with the light of his countenance, and with grace to discern and wisdom to improve his merciful visitations!

XXXII.

THE SANCTIFYING TRUTH.

"Sanctify them through thy truth; thy word is truth."—JOHN xvii, 17.

THESE are the words of Jesus. They are a part of that last public prayer which he made with his disciples, just before his betrayal and agony. He prays that they may be kept, that they may be united, that they may have his joy fulfilled in them, and that they may be sanctified through the truth. Thus will they be perfected, become successful evangelists to the world, and behold, ultimately, the glory of their risen Lord in the everlasting kingdom. We must confine our attention, this evening, to the matter and manner of their sanctification. In other words, our theme is,

The truth of God, contained in his word, the instrument of our sanctification.

There are two prevalent errors in relation to this subject which must, first of all, be considered.

1. It is an error to suppose that the word is the source of sanctifying power. Only the Holy Spirit sanctifies—that is, cleanses, purifies, makes holy. The truth, however forcibly presented, embodied in whatever venerable forms, expressed in liturgies and homilies however excellent, or preached with whatever measure of eloquence and power, will not save

a single soul. The convincing, awakening, and transforming energy essential to the great work of salvation is the immediate result of the Holy Spirit's action on the mind and heart of the sinner.

2. It is an error to suppose that the sanctifying power will come, except through the truth, and from an application of the word of God to the hearts and consciences of men. If sanctification be realized, it is through the truth. The word of God is the sword of the Spirit. And it is this word—this sharp, powerful, two-edged sword of the Spirit—which pierces "even to the dividing asunder of soul and spirit, and of the joints and marrow, and is a discerner of the thoughts and intents of the heart." The truth, then, must be maintained, preached, expressed in sacrament and psalm, and relied upon as the Spirit's chosen instrument for the world's conversion. First comes hearing, then believing, then deliverance, exaltation, and eternal life.

The source, the instrument, the process, and the results of salvation are all distinctly set forth in this remarkable passage: "In whom ye also trusted, after that ye heard the word of truth, the Gospel of your salvation; in whom also, after that ye believed, ye were sealed with that holy Spirit of promise, which is the earnest of our inheritance until the redemption of the purchased possession to the praise of his glory."

Both of these errors, therefore, are to be avoided. The one leads to formalism, the other excites fanaticism; the one prevents and the other corrupts revivals of religion; and both of them obstruct the progress and triumph of a pure and holy Christianity in the earth.

The sanctifying power of the truth is demonstrated by the fact that the growth of man, of society, and of great ideas of justice, humanity, and the progress of the race, have been in and through the Holy Scriptures. How many moral necessities are met by the word of God! A standard of right and wrong is furnished, the advantages of integrity and beneficence are shown, powerful incentives to right conduct are presented, the future is revealed, and the way to God is made plain. The condition in Bible lands, as compared with pagan, of women, children, the aged, the deaf, the blind, the insane, the idiotic, and of all dependent classes, is a standing and very forcible illustration of the sanctifying power of the truth of God. Degraded classes, moreover, are at once uplifted when the doctrines and teachings of Holy Scripture are applied to their moral consciousness by the office and work of the Holy Ghost. It also deserves remark that Christian men feel concern for such classes, and are moved to labors, outlays, and sacrifices in their behalf just as they discern them in their relations to God, to the great fact of redemption, and to a revealed future of rewards and punishments. The gigantic wrongs which have cruelly oppressed humanity in every age, such as spoliation, slavery, and wars of kingly ambition, melt away before the power of Gospel truth as the great icebergs are dissolved in tropic seas; and the vices which have tyrannized over men, and the superstitions which have bound them as with fetters of iron—such as intemperance and idolatry—fly before the light of inspiration as the darkness before the breaking of the day.

For the institutions we most cherish we are indebted to the Bible. The family, the Church, and civil government are divine ordinances, divinely revealed in the Holy Scriptures. For the sanctity of our homes; for the peace and assurance of our community-life, guarded by law and protected by public sentiment; for the hopes we cherish in regard to the future of our children; for the instruction, communion, and pastoral watch-care of a living Church; for the progress of the race and the triumphs of a Christian civilization, we must confess always our obligations to the Holy Oracles. Indeed, if we consider man as organic, that is, in society, how manifest it is that the truth of God, on the one hand, eliminates evils, and, on the other, promotes all economical and social virtues!

It is, moreover, the grand necessity of our national life. Four causes ruin States: the enervation and corruption begotten of wealth and luxury; the existence of gross vices, such as licentiousness and intemperance; the conflict of classes and races, as being white or black, native or foreign born, or as representing labor and capital; the prevalence of great wrongs, such as slavery, infanticide, idolatry, and unjust and aggressive wars. It requires no argument to show that Bible truth is the remedy for each and all of these, and is the constant conservator of a true national life.

It is objected, however, that all these evils exist, to a greater or less extent, in the most enlightened Christian States. True; but consider: 1. In paganism they predominate; in Christendom they are restricted, shamed, and in process of utter extermination. 2. In Paganism they are wrought into the very texture of society, government, and religion; in Christendom they exist not as a consequence, but in defiance, of Christian doctrines and institutions. 3. To a considerable extent, Christianity has caused their removal; and the general prevalence of Bible truth would sanctify wealth, purge away gross vices, harmonize antagonistic classes and interests, and utterly abolish the cruel wrongs and outrages which afflict and crush humanity.

Bible truth and Gospel experience constantly; tend to produce a pure state of society and a high order of man. They are calculated and adapted to lift men from the slough of selfishness. They make self-forgetfulness and genuine magnanimity of soul possible. They inspire grand and heroic self-sacrifices, and they bring men into those sublime altitudes where they are superior to personal pleasure, indulgence, or advantage, and where they act for the good of their fellows, the honor of truth, and the glory of God.

The teachings of the Bible meet our spiritual necessities. They reveal God, the fact of redemption, the way to pardon and purity, the source of help and strength, and the everlasting possession. These are original, radical needs of the human soul, which cannot be satisfied in any other direction. I remember a grand passage in one of Mitchell's astronomical lectures, in which he argues that "the analogies of nature, applied to the moral government of God, would crush all hope in the sinful soul;" that "there is no deviation, no modification, no yielding to the refractory or disobedient," and that the guilty can find no refuge "in the iron, the adamantine, laws of physical nature." He says: "Suppose it were possible to endow one of these flying worlds—the earth we inhabit—with a will and a rational soul; and the earth, now an independent, thinking, willing being, should rise in rebellion against the laws of God's control, and refuse longer to obey. The rebellious planet exclaims, Let the sun attract me never so much, I care not for his heat, his light, his life; I refuse to reciprocate the attraction; I have a power of will supreme; my destiny is my own! And thus the fatal decision is made. Slowly the rebel world wheels, at each revolution, farther and yet farther from the great center of life and light. In spiral circuit it separates farther and still farther from its wonted path, till, finally, cold and darkness and a coming death begin to assert their empire over the misguided world. With a start of horror, and a shudder which shakes it to the very center, it now wakes from its dream of independence, and exclaims, I will return! I will return! Alas! the return is impossible. The laws of nature are irrevocable. The sun may yet attract with living power the lost wanderer; but the bond is broken, the equilibrium is forever destroyed, and this rebel planet must become a wandering star, for which is reserved the blackness of darkness forever! Close forever, if you will, this strange Book, claiming to be God's revelation—blot out forever its lessons of God's creative power, God's superabounding providence, God's fatherhood and loving; guardianship to man his erring offspring, and then unseal the leaves of that mighty volume which the finger of God has written in the stars of heaven, and in these flashing letters of living light read only the dread sentence: 'The soul that sinneth, it shall surely die!'"

Such is the chill and darkness of deism! A world without a Redeemer! a soul without a Saviour! But he who clasps this Bible to his bosom may exclaim with rapture, Blessed be God for a vision higher than the heavens; for a revelation of the supernatural and eternal; for the cloudless sky of God's forbearing and restoring love, bright with rainbow hues of pledge and prophecy, lighted up with constellations of promise, surpassing far the sweet influences of the Pleiades, and blazing with a glory unknown to Arcturus and his sons; effulgent every-where with outbeaming manifestations of the divine mercy and forbearance; having, like our Southern hemisphere, for its chiefest glory the sign and semblance of the Cross, no longer planted on the earth, but glowing in the heavens, and radiant with apocalyptic vistas opening and reaching even to the throne of the eternal God!

There are some lessons to be derived from this subject, which deserve serious consideration:

1. Parents ought to read the Bible to their children. "The spiced embalming," it is said, "outlasts the mummy in his rocky tomb;" and the fragrance of family worship—of hearth-stone teachings of divine truth—will survive the lapse and changes of years. It will live in the memory, a source of admonition, instruction, and sanctifying power, long after the lips which uttered the precious message have ceased to speak and turned to ashes.

2. Readiness to receive the truth is essential no-

bility of soul. "These [in Berea] were more noble than those in Thessalonica, in that they received the word with all readiness of mind, and searched the Scriptures daily whether those things were so." These Bereans were intrinsically noble, for they were superior to prejudice, ready to be enlightened—to be rebuked even—and desirous to be led into all truth. "Readiness of mind," says Bengel, "and accurate scrutiny correspond;" and to this accurate scrutiny of her inspired oracles Christianity invites all opposers and infidels. She commends those who search the Scriptures daily to see whether the alleged facts of revelation are consistent, rational, and worthy of belief and trust. "Whoever would attain," says Locke, "to a true knowledge of the Christian religion, in the full and just extent of it, let him study the Holy Scriptures, especially the New Testament, wherein are contained the words of eternal life. It has God for its author, salvation for its end, and truth, without any mixture of error, for its matter."

La Capitale, an infidel paper of large circulation, printed at Rome, thus comments on Signor Ribetti's Wednesday lectures: "We do not at all agree with him that every thing in the Bible is genuine; but it must be confessed, there is no weapon so terrible as the Bible for fighting the Roman Catholic priesthood. In fact it [Romanism] lies crushed beneath these quotations. *This is not a Book; it is a millstone, grinding all the Lent preachers to powder."*

That is, the infidel sees that Romanism cannot resist Bible truth; but does not discern—strangely does not—that a Book which is more than a Book, even a divine millstone of judgment and wrath against sin and falsehood, will not only grind the Papacy to powder, but the whole superstructure of infidelity also. Not only the Church, but the world, is to be sanctified and saved by that revealed truth which is the word of God and the sword of the Spirit, and which was "written for our learning, that we through patience and comfort of the Scriptures might have hope."

There is in "English, Past and Present," a tribute to our English Bible which has been ascribed to John Henry Newman, a pervert to Romanism, but which Trench informs us, in a late edition of the work just mentioned, may be found in an Essay by the late Very Reverend Doctor Faber on "The Characteristics of the Lives of the Saints." In any case, it is Romish testimony to the value of those Scriptures which hallow our altars and adorn our homes. These are the words: "Who will not say that the uncommon beauty and marvelous English of the Protestant Bible is not one of the great strongholds of heresy in this country? It lives on the ear like a music that can never be forgotten; like the sound of church bells which the convert hardly knows how he can forego. Its felicities often seem to be almost things rather than mere words. It is part of the national mind, and the anchor of national seriousness. The memory of the dead passes into it. The potent traditions of childhood are stereotyped in its verses. The power of all the griefs and trials of man is hidden beneath its words. It is the representative of his best moments, and all that has been about him of soft, and gentle, and pure, and penitent, and good, speaks to him out of his English Bible. It is his sacred thing, which doubt has never dimmed, and controversy never soiled. In the length and breadth of the land, there is not a Protestant with one spark of religiousness about him whose spiritual biography is not in the Saxon Bible."

3. We ought to judge ourselves by the word—that word which will judge us in the last day. Wherein are we guilty? Let the Bible answer. What do we need in order to perfection of character, power of usefulness, and a good hope of eternal life? The Bible will show us. What are our privileges in the way of Christian attainment, the discernment of faith, and extent of influence? We may surely learn from the oracles of God. To what work of piety, beneficence, or evangelism, are we called? The Lord will instruct us from the word of inspiration. What are our possibilities of experience, growth, and Christian manhood? In whose teachings but those of Jesus can we find any thing like a satisfactory response? What is the measure of our just expectations for this world and for the world to come? The sure word of prophecy will guide our doubting feet until the day dawn and a cloudless and eternal splendor enraptures our vision. For all the needs, trials, and exigencies of life Bible truth will fully prepare us, if applied to our minds and hearts by the sanctifying power of the Holy Ghost.

4. The world is waiting and dying for the precious message of salvation. It is the imperative duty of those who have received this word of promise to give it to others who are in darkness and in the shadow of death; and the most beneficent results for individuals and communities, for time and eternity, will

follow. Give the world the Bible, and Paganism will disappear; the religion of Mohammed, which survives only because it enshrines a portion of the truth of God, will become wholly Christian or wholly false and contemptible; the ancient superstitions of Buddha will exhale as the mists of the morning, and the millions of China will turn from the philosophy of Confucius to the precepts of Jesus. Press on the public conscience the authority of God's word, and corruption in high places will be rebuked; the deadly miasms, born of the filth of great cities, will be purged away; intemperance will cease its work of wasting and death; desolated homes will be restored to Eden loveliness; Churches will become a living power, and thousands in the darkness of nature's night, and led captive by Satan at his chariot wheels, will be brought into the marvelous light of a Gospel day, and will be made to rejoice in the liberty of the sons of God.

XXXIII.

THE ETERNITY OF CHARACTER.

"He that is unjust, let him be unjust still: and he which is filthy, let him be filthy still: and he that is righteous, let him be righteous still: and he that is holy, let him be holy still."—Rev. xxii, 11.

"My Lord Cardinal," said Anne of Austria, to Richelieu, who exercised for a long time a cruel and despotic power, " God does not pay at the end of every week, but at the last *he pays.*" This is an assertion of the doctrine that God governs the world. He governs it in detail, that is, fully, comprehensively, absolutely. No human act escapes him. No thought or desire or secret purpose evades the glance of his searching eye. It is a necessity of the moral government of God, that every sin should be noticed in some way, either pardoned or punished.

And though this is not a world of retribution, and though injustice and oppression often seem to prosper and triumph, yet in the end *God pays.* And what is more, and more to the purpose of our text, he pays *in kind.* These Scriptures establish our point : " Say ye to the righteous, that it shall be well with him; for they shall eat the fruit of their doings. Woe unto the wicked! it shall be ill with him ; for the reward of his hands shall be given him." " His own iniquity shall take the wicked himself, and he shall be holden with the cords of his sins." "The backslider in heart shall be filled with his own ways"—the most terrible malediction which could be pronounced on him—"and a good man shall be satisfied from himself"—that is, with the consciousness of his own rectitude.

The Lord, moreover, says of such as have hated knowledge and despised reproof, and would none of his counsel, "Therefore shall they eat of the fruit of their own way, and be filled with their own devices; for the turning away of the simple shall slay them, and the prosperity of fools shall destroy them." "Evil men and seducers," in the very nature of things, "wax worse and worse, deceiving and being deceived."

Our characters constantly tend to fixedness. They harden by life's processes. The current of our natures grows stronger with advancing years. It becomes, finally, difficult, if not impossible, to change its course, except God's miraculous grace shall interpose. The Scriptures teach us this same truth: "Can the Ethiopian change his skin or the leopard his spots? then may ye also do good that are accustomed to do evil."

And yet this is a *remedial* dispensation. God interposes graciously and constantly in behalf of men. A miraculous mercy overflows from the divine heart to sinners. There are gentle interpositions which come like the dew, or the sunshine, or the summer rain; and there are mighty manifestations of God which shake us like tempests, or earthquakes, or volcanic eruptions. Our characters by these ministrations are transformed and revolutionized. Sometimes the transformation is gradual, like the breaking of the morning, the advance of spring, or the melting of icebergs in tropic seas. Sometimes it is sudden, as if men had been lifted at once to a higher plane of being, to move henceforth through a grander sphere. An earthquake in southern seas is said to have brought an island of diamonds to the surface; so by the convulsion of conversion the lessons of childhood, the virtues excited by the discipline of years, the inner graces of the Spirit, are brought to view, and men marvel at the miraculous change.

We see the same law working in society The supreme government of the world is on the side of the right. The Duke of Weimar said of the tyranny of the First Napoleon in Germany, "It is unjust, and therefore it cannot last." And, in the long run, the criticism is correct. Feudalism, despotism, slavery, aggressive wars, every species of wrong and outrage, disappear before the onward march of the Gospel. The general principle of the divine administration is expressed in these words : "He looketh upon men, and if any say, I have sinned and perverted that which was right, and it profited me not, he will deliver his soul from going into the pit, and his life shall see the light." The Word and Providence and Spirit of God are a trinity of mighty agencies to turn man back from destruction. The truth of God, morever, acts as a transforming leaven in society, and the end of Christ's reign is to set judgment in the earth.

But this text contemplates a period when these remedial agencies will cease; when probation will end; when retribution, unmixed with mercy, will begin. Then the Saviour will be no longer a Saviour. His atoning sacrifice will be no longer prevalent. His intercessions will close. He will no longer act as High Priest over the House of God. He will leave the mediatorial throne, and offer no more prayers for sinful man. Then the Holy Spirit will cease its gracious offices, and convince no more of sin, righteousness, and judgment. Then the Providence of God will no more mean, as always now, salvation. We shall then come to a fixed, unalterable, and eternal state. The unjust and filthy will remain unjust and filthy forever; the righteous and holy will remain righteous and holy forever. This will be the punishment—the reward; they will forever remain *what they are.*

It does not need the mist of darkness, the quenchless flame, the companionship of devils, to make a hell for a filthy and unjust soul. Like Milton's outcast archangel, such a soul might say, "Which way shall I fly? which way I fly is hell; myself am hell."

And, on the other hand, a soul conformed to rectitude, and possessed of holiness, has within itself a constant heaven, whether or not it has inherited, as yet, the cloudless land, the golden city, the robe, the palm, and the crown.

Think of remaining unjust, impure, hateful, envious, malicious, covetous, deceitful, proud, false, implacable, murderous toward every creature, and traitorous and rebellious toward God, *forever*—is not that hell? And to be just, pure, good, meek, gentle, loving, joyful, *forever*—to have, in a word, a great and noble character, in which all the fruits of the Spirit have come to perfection, and glow with immortal richness and beauty—is not that heaven?

1. We are taught by this subject, first, the fearful power and ruin of transgression. To-day, .your prompt decisive, strong "I will," and God's power-

ful grace, may enable you to turn from sinful indulgence and the pit of infamy, and to obtain a holy character and an immortal life; but to-morrow your power of choice will be weaker, your vision of moral excellence dimmer, your love of sinful indulgence greater, your slavery to wicked habits stronger, till, at length, bound securely to Satan's triumphal chariot wheels, you will be dragged irresistibly down to death and hell. Besides, you know not at what moment the resistless decree of the Almighty will close your probation, and fix your character and destiny forever.

2. The grandest aspiration of the soul is for holiness, and this should be our chief aim in life. Holiness is *wholeness*—that is, complete moral manhood. Can any thing more desirable be conceived? Dr. T. L. Cuyler defines holiness as "the habit of agreeing with God in all things." And all our troubles have come from our disagreeing with God. It is the highest wisdom to study to know the divine mind, and to conform therewith in heart and life. "Be ye holy," is the command of the Highest, "for I the Lord your God am holy." Thus he makes it possible for us to come into the same lofty and glorious plane of being in which he himself dwells. This is the creature's highest privilege, duty, and dignity. And full provision is made in the Gospel for the attainment of holiness, and for its retention as a living and abiding experience of the soul. Think of the unutterable bliss of being holy forever.

"Pursue," says Bishop Foster, "the upward destiny of a soul brightening under the smile of God forever; see its ever-increasing and unfolding beauty;

hear the ravishing melody of its triumphant song. A thousand ages are fled. Behold the augmented and ever-expanding glory, ascending, widening its circle, becoming more and more like God, and losing itself ever in his ineffable radiance. Such is the destiny of a soul washed in the blood of Jesus. Behold, on the other hand, a soul darkening under the frown of Jehovah. Ages fly away. Its darkness broods darker still; its sorrow gathers down in closer folds; *it is lost.* The lengthened periods of eternity roll by, but they bring no redemption; deep, dark, dismal gloom settles down around its sphere *forever.* Learn, by the contrast, the value of holiness. Its presence is life—its absence is eternal death. Could you pursue the contrast through eternity, could you have but a faint glimpse of the reality, you would no longer rest, but fly in trembling haste to a Saviour's wounds for shelter and for life."

O, bliss of the purified! O, mighty love of a Saviour! Are they not worthy of immortal song?

3. Finally, our great concern is with eternity. Wesley used to stir himself to activity and sacrifice with the battle-shout, "There is another world!" "Take this watch, my friend," said an English patriot, as he mounted the scaffold to die for liberty, "I have nothing to do with time henceforth; only with eternity." Soon this hour will strike for every one of us, and nothing will interest us for a moment but eternity, "Where will you spend your eternity?" was the title of an article which I somewhere read. It is a vastly important question. Put it in this shape: "What will be my character in eternity?" The answer to this will determine every thing else in respect to

your future. Christ's great question is, "What shall it profit a man if he gain the whole world and lose his own soul? Or what shall a man give in exchange for his soul?" And who will venture on an answer? Soon it will be said to every one of us, "He that is unjust, let him be unjust still; and he which is filthy, let him be filthy still; and he that is righteous, let him be righteous still; and he that is holy, let him be holy still." Beyond all changes of time comes the changeless, eternal state. Let us pray to God to bring us all, at last, to the heaven of the holy, where we may greet those who have gone before us, and dwell in a holy place, with a holy God, and "shout and wonder at his grace to all eternity."

XXXIV.

THE AMARANTHINE CROWN.

"And when the Chief Shepherd shall appear, ye shall receive a crown of glory that fadeth not away."—1 Pet. v, 4.

An attempt was recently made to assassinate King Amadeus of Spain. The diabolical outrage was not instigated, it is said, by personal enemies, but by political—by ambitious aspirants for the Spanish crown. And yet what is this crown for which men are willing to run such desperate risks? It is, at the best, only the insignia of position and power, with all the burden of care and responsibility which these bring. It is a diadem which has only the splendor of earth; it is a laurel wreath which must wither at the touch of the frosts of Time; it is an aureole which excites no special reverence, and has no fadeless attractions.

But the crown of which the apostle speaks is altogether of another character. Alford translates: "Ye shall receive the amaranthine crown of his glory." This crown, which the Chief Shepherd bestows, is one of unwithering and eternal splendor. Benson describes it as "a crown which shall bloom in immortal beauty and vigor, when all the transitory glories of this world are withered like a fading flower." And Clarke, striking through the metaphor to the foundation idea, affirms the promise to be, "an eternal nearness and intimacy with the ineffably glorious God."

Milton, describing the lofty ceremonial of celestial worship, says:

> "Lowly reverent
> Toward either throne they bow, and to the ground
> With solemn adoration down they cast
> Their crowns, inwove with *amarant* and gold;
> *Immortal amarant;* a flower which once
> In Paradise, *fast by the tree of life,*
> Began to bloom."

This amaranthine crown is elsewhere in the Scriptures represented as a crown of righteousness, a crown of life, and an incorruptible crown. We read also of the holy crown, the beautiful crown, the crown of the anointing oil, the royal crown, and the crown of pure gold. All these expressions indicate the exaltations, the privileges, the endowments, and the dignities which belong to Christian character and experience, and which are to compose the reward and glory of the saints in everlasting life.

The crown of pride and the corruptible crown describe, at once, both the splendor and the mockery of worldly hopes. The wicked exalteth himself, and glories in his possessions and distinctions; but his honors fall away from him, not as the stars from heaven, but as leaves from garlands of dead flowers.

There are hardly sadder words in the inspired record than these: "Then came Jesus forth, wearing the crown of thorns, and the purple robe." And yet in the vision of the apostle we see our blessed Lord, not only " made a little lower than the angels for the suffering of death," but also delivered, exalted, triumphant, and "crowned with glory and honor." The crown of thorns was probably not so much intended to inflict pain as to express contempt. It was, like the purple robe, an insult and mockery of his royal authority. Doubtless some flexible thorny shrub was used, which resembled the rich dark green of the triumphal ivy, and yet which was manifestly something else, thus giving pungency to the ironical purpose. It was part of the ignominy and shame to which Jesus was subjected when he offered himself a sacrifice for our redemption and immortality.

> "See, from his head, his hands, his feet,
> Sorrow and love flow mingled down:
> Did e'er such love and sorrow meet,
> Or thorns compose so rich a crown?"

But when heaven was opened to the far-reaching gaze of the Revelator, he saw One whose eyes were as a flame of fire, who had an incomprehensible nature, who "was clothed in a vesture dipped in blood, and his name is called, The Word of God." And concerning this exalted and glorious Being he makes this declaration: "On his head were many crowns." The Greek is *many diadems*, and it certainly indicates royal authority, absolute sovereignty, extended dominion, and many triumphs and possessions. Ptolemy Philometer wore *two* diadems, one for Europe and one for Asia. During the Middle Ages the Emperors of Germany received *three* crowns—that of Germany, which was of silver, and assumed at Aix-la-Chapelle; the crown of iron, which had formerly been peculiar to the Lombard kings, and was assumed at Pavia; and the imperial crown, which was received at Rome, and was surmounted by a miter, similar to that of the bishops, and indicated, perhaps, some measure of ecclesiastical authority. The Popes have for many centuries worn a triple crown, which is designed to signify their ecclesiastical, civil, and judicial supremacy. The three crowns of the papal tiara mark accessions of power at different periods. The first corona was added to the miter by Alexander III., in 1159; the second, by Boniface VIII., in 1203, and the third, by Urban V., in 1362. So on the victorious brow of the Son of God rest many crowns, evidences of his many conquests over sin, death, and hell, of his world-wide dominion, and of his supremacy over all powers and hierarchies on earth or in heaven. The crown of thorns and the scarlet robe were intended to caricature his royalty, and insult his authority; but the many diadems which he wears in glory indicate such position, power, and sovereignty as bewilder all human or angelic thought.

> "The Head that once was crown'd with thorns
>   Is crown'd with glory now;
> A royal diadem adorns
>   The mighty Victor's brow.
>
> "The highest place that heaven affords
>   Is to our Jesus given;
> The King of kings, the Lord of lords,
>   He reigns o'er earth and heaven."

And though the word for crown, and not the word for diadem, occurs in Rev. ii, 10: "Be thou faithful unto death, and I will give thee a crown of life;"

yet Trench argues, with great force, that not the garland of victory, but the diadem of royalty, is here promised to those who dare and endure the worst which evil men can inflict, even death itself; and that so our Lord associates his suffering saints with himself, gathering them to his bosom, and exalting them to an everlasting dominion.

Let us not faint, then, in our Christian endeavors. What self-denials, what labors, what persistent struggles, mark the course of worldly men! "They do it to obtain a corruptible crown; but we an incorruptible." Business success, rewards of ambition, pleasure, and power, are, at the best, insecure and perishable possessions. How poor in comparison with the good man's riches in glory! What a mere bauble the most resplendent of earthly diadems when contrasted with the crown of amaranth and gold which sparkles on the brow of glorified saints! The laurel and the ivy wreath will perish, and the royal fillet of diamonds and pearls will turn to dust; but

> "The starry crown
> That glitters through the skies,"

will never glitter less, but will shine, with the beauty of the morning star, forever. Heed, therefore, the admonition which Jesus himself has uttered, and "hold fast that which thou hast, that no man take thy crown." And "think it not strange concerning the fiery trial which is to try you, as though some strange thing happened unto you;" for "blessed is the man that endureth temptation;" and "when he is tried"— *tested, proved*—"he shall receive the crown of life"— the amaranthine crown of glory.

In Greenwood cemetery, on the headstone which marks the resting-place of a deceased maiden, are inscribed the beautiful words of the Song of Songs: "Until the day break, and the shadows flee away." There is something touching and tearful in the tenderness, the hope, and the promise which the words suggest. Beyond the night and darkness of the grave, the yearning heart, with prophetic instinct, looks and longs for the breaking of a cloudless day. And the thicker the darkness gathers around life's pathway, the more intense and constant the sighing of the soul for the splendors of that immortal morn, when all the shadows shall forever flee away.

Men live by hope. They bear the crushing burden of their sorrows, and their hearts do not break, because of their expectations of a better life. Out of this darkness, they say, we shall come into the light; the shadows will disperse, the heavens will glow, and, instead of sighing and tears, we shall obtain joy and gladness. And the hope itself illumines, the expectation brings realization, and what we covet we already, in some measure, possess.

There are those who say, "We would serve God for what religion affords us even in this present time, if it brought us no promise of a life beyond the grave." But this is a sort of impossible supposition, and, withal, a deceptive and fallacious statement; for what would Christian experience be without the hope of immortality? Take out of the Gospel the fact of the resurrection of Jesus, and the promise of our own resurrection which it involves, and what would remain? It would be like a light-house with no flame kindled on its summit. There would be no glad radiance for life's dark, troubled sea. The very marrow of the Gospel is in Christ's words, " He that believeth on ME hath everlasting life." Yes, he *hath* it. He has apprehended it. His hungry heart already feeds on the heavenly manna, and the living waters spring up in his soul. It is a conscious revelation of a reconciled God, and that is heaven. " We have also," says Saint Peter, " a more sure word of prophecy, whereunto ye do well that ye take heed, as unto a light that shineth in a dark place, until the day dawn, and the Day Star arise in your hearts." It is a memorable hour when the day dawns in the heart, and when " the bright and Morning Star " gleams out amid the shadows and dispels the gloom ; and Jesus is thus called not only because he brings light to our darkness, but also because he is the harbinger and herald of a bright, immortal day. After the Morning Star comes the sunburst of heavenly light and glory.

The whole Christian life is a journey from darkness to light. "The way of the wicked is as darkness ; they know not at what they stumble." And, what is worse, their foolish heart is so darkened, and so great is their ignorance, alienation, and blindness, that they will not come to the light lest their deeds should be reproved. " And this is the condemnation "—the occasion, the justification, and the consummation of it—" that light is come into the world, and men loved darkness rather than light, because their deeds were evil." Darkness is even personified by the apostle as *a power*, a terrible tyrant, from whom we need to be delivered, and from whose dreary domain we must be translated into the kingdom of

God's dear Son; because, as Christians, "we are the children of light, and the children of the day; we are not of the night nor of darkness."

Jesus is the true Lucifer—the true light-bringer, the awakener of hope and the source of inspiration. "I am," he exclaims, "the light of the world; he that followeth me shall not walk in darkness, but shall have the light of life." And thus is fulfilled the prophetic word of the Psalmist: "Light is sown for the righteous, and gladness for the upright in heart." The very object of the Gospel and of its dispensation in the world is to open the eyes which are blinded by transgression, and to turn the perverse and benighted from darkness to light, and to bring them from the power of Satan unto God. And Christians are made a chosen generation, a royal priesthood, a holy nation, a peculiar people, in order that they may show forth the praises of Him who has called them out of darkness into his marvelous light.

The heritage of the impenitent, who love darkness, shall be darkness: "They shall be driven from light into darkness, and chased out of the world." Those who have clung to the bondage of corruption shall be delivered "into chains of darkness," and, like the angels who kept not their first estate, "reserved in everlasting chains under darkness unto the judgment of the great day." To those who have been carried hither and thither by the tempests of appetite and passion, "the mist of darkness is reserved forever." Those who have rejected the offers of the Gospel, and resisted the rule and dominion of Jesus Christ, and hated and spurned the light and glory of his presence, shall gnaw their tongues for pain in a kingdom which is "full of darkness," where night reigns, and terror and death. The unspeakably awful doom of the ungodly is that they shall be filled with their own ways, and shall have the things which they have chosen. There is something inconceivably terrible in this giving up of the sinner, by divine judicial deprivation and visitation, to himself, to the darkness and death which he has blindly and madly chosen! And yet how manifestly just such retribution!

On the other hand, the pathway of the righteous is one which shineth increasingly, even to the fullness and splendor of a perfect day. He has enlarging light, and knowledge, and glory of the divine Presence, at every step of his progress in the King's highway of holiness, to the very gates of the New Jerusalem. It is true that "the darkness which is death" will fall, like a shadow, across his path; but it is also true that his Saviour, Jesus Christ, "hath abolished death"—overcome, counterworked death—"and hath brought life and immortality to light through the Gospel." Into this region, on which the shadow of death has fallen, the Christian must come, but a cheering light will radiate his path from the highest heaven. "O," exclaims Rutherford, addressing the trembling saint, "when Christ and you shall meet *about the utmost boundary of time and the entry into eternity*, you shall see heaven in his face at the first look, and salvation and glory sitting on his countenance and betwixt his eyes." The glory of God and the Lamb not only lightens the Celestial City, but also the steps of the saints as they journey thitherward.

Therefore, Christian, be of good cheer. "The night is far spent, the day is at hand." The night has been made beautiful and resplendent by the bright stars of faith and hope and promise, which have trooped up in our heavens; but how incomparably glorious must be the splendors of that immortal day! Your salvation is nearer than when you first believed. You have come some distance on your journey. Life's night will soon be passed, and the day of eternity will dawn. The last shadow will flee away, and the pure, undimmed light of heaven will be your portion forever.

Long may seem the way, and dark, and many and bitter the trials to be experienced, and fierce and terrible the conflicts with the prince of evil powers; but all will be forgotten, or remembered only to heighten present joy, if, at the last, you are enabled to exclaim, like the great apostle to the Gentiles : "I have fought a good fight, I have finished my course, I have kept the faith ; henceforth there is laid up for me "—for *me!*—" a crown of righteousness, which the Lord, the righteous Judge, shall give me "—*me!*—" at that day." And "in that day," in a higher sense than ever before, "shall the Lord of hosts be for a crown of glory, and for a diadem of beauty," to all who have put their trust in him, and taken him for their friend and portion. "What is to be refused," says Archbishop Leighton, "in the way to this crown? All labor is sweet for it. And what is there here to be desired to detain our hearts that we should not most willingly let go, to rest from our labors, and receive our crown? Was ever any king sad to think that the day of his coronation drew nigh? And then there will be no envy, no jealousies; all will be kings, each with his crown, each rejoicing in the glory of the others, and all in His who that day shall be all in all."

>And when, through grace, our course is run,
>The battle fought, the vict'ry won,
>Then crowns unfading we shall wear,
>The glory of thy kingdom share,
>With thee, our glorious Leader, there,
>   In endless day.
>
>Then, in thy presence, heavenly King,
>In loftier strains thy praise we'll sing,
>When with the blood-bought hosts we meet,
>Triumphant there, in bliss complete,
>And cast our crowns before thy feet
>   In endless day.

THE END.

www.ingramcontent.com/pod-product-compliance
Lightning Source LLC
Chambersburg PA
CBHW022111230426

43672CB00008B/1338